The Christian Lives by the Spirit

alba house DIVISION OF THE SOCIETY OF ST. PAUL
STATEN ISLAND, N.Y. 10314

The Christian Lives by the Spirit

By Ignace de la Potterie, S. J.
and Stanislaus Lyonnet, S. J.
Preface by Yves Congar, O. P.

Original Title: La vie selon l'Esprit, condition du Chrétien, published by Les Editions du Cerf, Paris, France.

Translated by John Morriss

Nihil obstat:
  Daniel V. Flynn, J.C.D.
  Censor librorum

Imprimatur:
  Joseph P. O'Brien, S.T.D.
  Vicar General, Archdiocese of New York
  August 8, 1970

The nihil obstat and imprimatur are official declarations that a book or pamphlet is free of doctrinal or moral error. No implication is contained therein that those who have granted the nihil obstat and imprimatur agree with the contents, opinions or statements expressed.

Library of Congress Catalog Card Number: 76-140283

SBN: 8189-0197-7

Copyright 1971 by the Society of St. Paul, 2187 Victory Blvd., Staten Island, New York, 10314.

Designed, printed and bound in the U.S.A. by the Pauline Fathers and Brothers of the Society of St. Paul, 2187 Victory Blvd., Staten Island, New York 10314 as part of their communications apostolate.

PREFACE

The following chapters, written by two different authors and under diverse circumstances, are marked by a profound coherence and logic.* From the first chapter to the last, the progression of ideas is continuous. Everything begins with the new birth of water and the Spirit (Jn 3, 5). Next, we have an unusually rich and new idea: the Christian is a man who lives in the faith under the permanent influence of the Holy Spirit, who, after having aroused such faith in whoever listens to the word of truth, allows him to assimilate that word and converts carnal man into spiritual man. The sacramental action of baptism, then that of the Eucharist is seen as accompanied by an act of the Holy Spirit, which the New Testament compares to an anointing and which vivifies us with the word of the Lord. How relevant is this doctrine—true from all time—to a period when the renewal of the Christian life aims to be both sacramental and biblical, liturgical and catechetic! The Christian thus understands himself as a man of the word and a man of faith, a man born of baptism and a man bound to the Holy Spirit, the "Paraclete," whose activity is revealed to us in this book through a close study of passages from St. John.

Christian man is thus called both to love and to freedom. The passages from St. Paul are so emphatic in this connection that we are reluctant to believe they are meant for us, and fear that they may lead to illuminism and anarchy: the Christian is free of the law inas-

---

*Chapters 1, 2, 4, 8, 9, and the Appendix were written by Fr. De La Potterie. while the remaining chapters were written by Fr. Lyonnet.

much as it is law, that is, an external restraint in comparison to the demands of love placed in the heart by the Holy Spirit. St. John goes so far as to say that the Christian, as such, is *sinless* (I Jn 3, 6-9). It is obvious that one can abuse such passages and, as St. Paul says, make "carnal" use of them. It is in awareness of this danger, re-affirmed by developments in the secular order, that the pastors of the Church have so often avoided proposing a doctrine which is, how-ever, expressed in the New Testament and which St. Thomas Aquinas stated in its full force: "It is the Holy Spirit himself who is the New Testament, in bestowing on us his love, plenitude of the law" (*Commentary on Hebrews*, 8, 10).

It is in the highest degree of these two themes of freedom and impeccability that we see the truth and value of the law that dom-inates the entire life of the Christian, who is called to love under the regime of "the already and the-not-yet," which are paradoxically united. The Christian is an "eschatological" man, who is already living in eternal life, that of the heavenly Jerusalem, which is free and without stain (Gal 4, 26; Ap 21; Eph 5, 27): "Now we are the children of God," and as such free and without sin, but "it has not yet appeared what we shall be" (I Jn 3, 2). We still live in the flesh, and in this respect we are still sinners, subject to pedagogical in-struction, visible signs and aids, teaching and authority. The two regimes must harmonize with each other within the Church so that the vindication of the one does not lead to the exclusion or neglect of the other.

The Christian is a man committed to love, to that love in par-ticular which the Holy Spirit transfers, so to speak, from the heart of God to our own heart (Rom 5, 5). He is summoned to perfect that love, and, with St. Paul as our guide, we learn what that *vocation to perfection is.* One can ask whether the Christian, "ani-mated by the Spirit," is not henceforth so committed to heaven that he is, as it were, prevented from a genuine participation in the work of the world: "My earthly joy, where then are you?" Once again, St. Paul is our guide; he offers us perspectives that are both very humble and very sublime. This dual note of humility and sublimity characterizes the fundamental law of the apostolate of which St. Paul is both example and teacher: the man who experi-enced "the thorn in the flesh" is he who formulated and signed with his life the motto of every apostle: "It is when I am weak that I am strong"; "I can do everything in him who fortifies me."

These enormous horizons are opened up for us in this book by a careful study of various passages, done in an exact and incisive way. The reader becomes aware, if he had not already realized it, how difficult it is to understand clearly the most profound passages of Holy Scripture. The authors do not speak glibly. Each passage is studied in a technical way according to the language that is used, the kind of literary composition, the place it occupies in the thought of the inspired writers. But the two learned exegetes, who help us to understand the sacred writers, reveal themselves as men who know how to combine the requirements of their exacting study with the references to the conclusions of traditional theology and the concerns of pastoral teaching. If these two considerations sometimes appear beyond the reach of certain exegetes, they are both recognized in this book in a remarkable way. Tradition is examined in the light of the Holy Scripture; the pastoral consequences are envisioned with often astonishing clarity, for example, regarding the relationship between baptism and confirmation, or the temporal activity of the Christian.

In reading these penetrating chapters, we have personally experienced in a new and intense way the immense spiritual joy that comes from an intimate contact with Holy Scripture. What power! What expansion and exultation for the soul! As we proceeded through our reading, we recalled the words of the Byzantine mystique, St. Simeon the New Theologian, who once described his own experience (*Disc.* 91):

> You entrusted me to your servant and your disciple, commanding him to wash me of any stain. He led me by the hand, as one leads a blind man to a fountain, that is, to the Holy Scriptures and to your divine commandments. . . . From that day on, you returned more often; each time I found myself before the fountain, you took my head and bathed it in the water, allowing me to see the brilliance of your light. . . .

The renewal of ecclesiology must be, like every renewal in the Church, a development from fundamental tradition: it is in this way that one can overcome, in the necessary continuity of life, cer-

tain inadequacies in the current presentation of the mystery of the
Church. And yet it seems more and more clear that the ecclesiology
of the Apostles, that of the Fathers and that of the liturgy—our
prime sources—encompass a certain anthropology. For the Fathers,
the Church is not first of all a social structure of which the faithful
would be but subjects: it is the people of the baptized living in
communion with each other, through the Holy Spirit, and by
means of the sacraments and discipline of the christian life. The
Fathers speak of the Church in commenting upon the life of the
people of biblical history and in exposing the reality of the christian life on the basis of the psalms, parables, baptismal initiation,
and eucharistic celebration. The Church and baptized man bring
to reality the same mystery; in speaking of one, we speak of the
other.

It is after a restrictive process of juridification, of which the first
movement is situated in the effects of the Gregorian reform (at the
end of the eleventh century) and which reaches a high point after
the death of the great doctors of the thirteenth century, that ecclesiology, having become a separate area of concern, became almost
uniquely a treatise of public law or a "hierarchiology." The law is
indeed sacred, the hierarchy is sacred, but neither the one nor
the other should enjoy complete domination.

Profiting from a half century of studies, which His Holiness
Paul VI praised highly in *Ecclesiam suam* (August 6, 1964), the
Vatican Council transcended, and even criticized, such juridicism.
It put the People of God at the head of its ecclesiology, uttering
these words which could be inscribed at the beginning of the
present volume: "The heritage of this people are the dignity and
freedom of the sons of God, in whose hearts the Holy Spirit dwells
as in his temple. Its law is the new commandment to love as Christ
loved us" (see Jn 13, 34).° In more than one place, the Council
reaffirmed the role of the Holy Spirit. Often, however, it seemed
to us, and the Council itself sensed, that its main efforts called for
the working out of a Christian anthropology of which itself traced

---

° Dogmatic Constitution on the Church (*Lumen Gentium*), II, 9, in *The
Documents of Vatican II*, ed. Walter M. Abbott, S.J. (New York, Guild
Press, America Press, Association Press, 1966).

but a few, imperfect sketches: the chapters on the People of God
and on the laity in the Constitution on the Church contain invaluable elements, as does Schema XIII. But the text on the Apostolate
of the Laity, the Declaration on Religious Liberty, and the invita-
tions to dialogue in the Decree on the Missions and the Declaration
on Non-Christian Religions call for a formal development of the
idea of Christian man and the law of freedom founded on love
which the Holy Spirit diffuses in our hearts. During the Second
Session of the Council (October 1963), while the participants were
beginning to discuss the project of the Constitution on the Church,
we had the privilege of conversing with two Orthodox observers,
one Greek, the other of Russian origin. They said to us: "If we
were making in our own churches a conciliar declaration on the
Church, we would first write a chapter on the Holy Spirit, then
another on Christian anthropology. And undoubtedly we would
stop there: that would be enough." On the other hand, they criticized the Vatican II study project for failing to provide a theology
of the Holy Spirit and an anthropology.

Such criticism is in large part unmerited, for the Council went
a long way after October 1963. To the extent, however, that the
expression of St. Bernard still remains true—"The document is fin-
ished, but not the work to be done!"—and the recovery by ecclesiology of its inalienable anthropological thrust is still incomplete,
the book that we have the honor and joy of presenting here is
offered, however imperfect its contribution may be, for the consideration of those who will continue the effort already made but
still not completed. *Finis operis, sed non finis laboris!*

Yves Congar, O.P.

CONTENTS

I

"To Be Born Again of Water and the Spirit"- The Baptismal Text of John 3, 5[*]

The above verse of St. John is one of the most important texts in the New Testament concerning baptism.[1] Of all the passages from the Fourth Gospel, this is the one that appears most often among Church writers of the first few centuries.[2] At first glance, the text offers no difficulty, but in the past as well as in the present, it has been explained in many different ways; a detailed examination of the text, moreover, shows how difficult an interpretation is. The differences of opinion are especially noteworthy regarding the exact relationship that exists between "water" and "the Spirit." Before trying to interpret Jn 3, 5, let us first show the various ways in which this verse has been explained.[3]

BRIEF SUMMARY OF EXEGESIS

Most commentators maintain the text of the verse as it is read in all the editions, that is, without eliminating the word *udatos*. Some have thought that this mention of water refers to the baptism of John the Baptist: Jesus would have thus taught Nicodemus that

---

[*] Text unchanged (except for some minor corrections) of a study that appeared in *Sciences ecclésiastiques*, 14 (1962), 417-443.
1. Special studies on this passage: I.-M. Vosté, O.P., "De spirituali regeneratione ex aqua et Spiritu," in *Studia Joannea* (Rome, 1930), 101-138;

a man had to submit to this penitential rite, but had also to receive the Spirit promised by the prophets.[4] Others believe that the verse should be understood on two levels: for Nicodemus, the water can refer only to John's baptism; on the other hand, for the evangelist, it pertains to Christian baptism in general.[5]

H. Rongy, "Le dialogue avec Nicodème," in *Rev. eccl. de Liège*, 34 (1933), 227-235; 287-293; P. Van Imschoot, "De colloquio cum Nicodemo," in *Collat. Gandavenses*, 34 (1937), 181-186; J. Graf, "Nikodemus," in *Theol. Quartalschr.*, 132 (1952), 62-86; F.-M. Braun, O.P., "La vie d'en haut," in *Rev. des Sc. Phil. et Théol.*, 40 (1956), 3-24; F. Roustang, S.J., "L'entretien avec Nicodeme," in *N. R. Th.*, 78 (1956), 337-358; S. Mendner, "Nikodemus," in *Journ. of Bibl. Lit.*, 77 (1958), 293-323. One may also consult the leading studies on baptism or the sacraments in general in the Fourth Gospel: C. T. Craig, "Sacramental Interest in the Fourth Gospel," in *Journ. of Bibl. Lit.*, 58 (1939), 31-41; W. Michaelis, *Die Sakramente im Johannesevangelium* (Bern, 1946); F.-M. Braun, O.P., "Le baptême d'après le 4e Evangile," in *Rev. thom.*, 48 (1948), 347-393; W.-F. Flemington, *The New Testament Doctrine of Baptism* (London, 1948); H. Riesenfeld, "La signification sacramentaire du baptême johannique," in *Dieu Vivant*, n. 13 (1949), 29-37; M. Barth, *Die Taufe — ein Sakrament?* (Zurich, 1951), 434-453; O. Cullmann, *Les sacraments dans l'Evangile johannique* (Paris, 1951); H. Köster, "Geschichte und Kultus im Johannesevangelium und bei Ignatius von Antiochien," in *Zeitschr. für Theol. und Kirche*, 54 (1957), 56-69; S. Smalley, "Liturgy and Sacrament in the Fourth Gospel," in *Evang. Quart.*, 29 (1957), 159-170; P. Niewalda, *Sakramentssymbolik im Johannesevangelium?* (Limburg, 1958); R. Schnackenburg, "Die Sakramente im Johannesevangelium," in *Sacra Pagina, II* (Paris-Gembloux, 1958), 235-254; L. Villette, *Foi et Sacrement. I. Du Nouveau Testament à saint Augustin* (Paris, 1959), 82-90; R. E. O. White, *The Biblical Doctrine of Initiation* (London, 1960), 241-264; E. Lohse, "Wort und Sakrament im Johannesevangelium," in *New Test. Stud.*, 7 (1960/61), 110-125; J. Ysebaert, *Greek Baptismal Terminology* (Nijmegen, 1962); G. R. Beasley-Murray, *Baptism in the New Testament* (London, 1963).
See also the more general studies, such as: P. Windisch, "Die Sprüche vom Eingehen in das Reich Gottes," in *Zeitschr. für die neut. Wiss.*, 27 (1928), 163-192; O. Betz, "Geburt der Gemeinde durch den Lehrer," in *New Test. Stud.*, 3 (1956/57), 314-326; W. Grundmann, "Die NEPOI in der urchristlichen Paränese," *ibid.*, 5 (1958/59), 188-205.

2. Th. Calmes, *L'Evangile selon saint Jean* (Paris, 1904), 183, n. 2; W. Jetter, *Die Taufe beim jungen Luther* (*Beitr. zur hist. Theol.*, 18) (Tübingen, 1954), 45: "Fur die Tradition ist Jo 3, 5 massgebend."

But what relationship exists between the water and the Spirit? For a small number of modern commentators, the verse would indicate that the Spirit is *given* by the sacrament.[6] This interpretation is difficult to defend, for according to our passage the effect produced in the believer is not the gift of the Spirit, but the new birth; water and the Spirit are the two principles from which (*eks*) this unique effect comes. Therefore, to consider the gift of the Spirit as a result of the action of the water, is to modify the data of the text, since these two words are connected by a simple *kai*.[7]

Thus the majority of commentators are right in *coordinating* the action of baptism and that of the Spirit: to the water must be joined the action of the Spirit,[8] and both together produce the new birth.[9] Many authors, however, attempt to go further: they try to

3. Hereafter, in this study, the commentaries on the Fourth Gospel will be cited only by the name of the author.

4. Bengel, *Gnomon Novi Testamenti*, in h. 1; among moderns, Th. Zahn, M. C. Tenney.
5. Gardner, Westcott, Hoskyns; compare R. E. O. White, *The Biblical Doctrine of Initiation*, 253-255.

6. Dom Calmet, Lightfoot; see O. Cullmann, *Les Sacraments* . . . , 46: "the new element consists of the effusion of the Spirit": C. H. Dodd, *The Interpretation of the Fourth Gospel* (Cambridge, 1953), 309; E. Osty, *Le Nouveau Testament* (Paris, 1955), 206: "Allusion to Christian initiation, baptism, and effusion of the Spirit"; M.-E. Boismard, art. "Eau" in *Vocab. de théol. bibl.* (Paris, 1962), col. 240. For J. Huby, S.J., *Mystiques paulinienne et johannique* (Paris, 1946), 167; and A. Wikenhauser, *in h. l.*, the Spirit is both the agent of baptismal regeneration and its effect.
7. See what Barrett wrote, p. 75: "John, it should be noted, does not say that baptism confers the Spirit; he says that water and Spirit are both necessary to birth from above."
8. Belser.
9. Maldonat, Tillmann, Lagrange, F.-M. Braun (in his commentary), Westcott, MacGregor, Barrett; likewise, J. E. Carpenter, *The Johannine Writings* (London, 1927), 417; J. Schneider, *Der historische Jesus und der kerygmatische Christus*, ed. H. Ristow and K. Matthiae (Berlin, 1961), 542: "Nach Joh. 3, 5 bewirken Wasser und Geist die Wiedergeburt." See White, *op. cit.*, 255, n. 3, which cites a number of witnesses on this close

establish a closer and more organic connection between the causality of water and that of the Spirit. The Spirit, they say, act *in or through the water* of baptism; that is, the causality of th water is simply instrumental to the principal cause, the action of the Spirit. This explanation has certainly been the most common one over the centuries.[10] And yet, it is not above criticism: for in interpreting the verse in this way, one is adding something to the text; one is again introducing a note of subordination between two elements which, in John, remain simply coordinate (*eks udatos kài pneumatos*). We do not claim that such an explanation is unjustified; but to justify it, one must be able to show, in other passages, that such a relationship between the water and the Spirit is indeed part of the evangelist's thought. Such a demonstration has not been given.[11] Thus, it must be said that, until proven otherwise, this interpretation is not truly founded on a strictly exegetical basis.

The above explanations have this in common: they underline in one way or another the extent to which the action of the Spirit and that of the water of baptism are perfectly one, even to the point of constituting but one single action. Some people even refer to

union of water and the Spirit: "Water and Spirit are said to be 'coordinate, correlative, complementary' (Westcott), 'conjoined' (Humphries), 'coincident, in conjunction' (Denney), 'conjoined, co-operate, coordinated' (MacGregor), 'co-operative' (E. F. Scott), etc."

10. It may be found, with slight variations, in the commentaries or homilies of Chrysostom (*P.G.*, 59, 148), of Theodore of Mopsuestia (*C.S.C.O.*, 116, 47), Ammonius (*P.G.*, 85, 1408 D - 1409 A), Cyril of Alexandria (*P.G.*, 73, 244 D - 245 A), St. Basil, *De Spiritu Sancto*, 15, 35 (*P.G.*, 32, 129, 132), and in the third mystagogical catechesis of Cyril of Jerusalem (*P.G.*, 33, 429 A). Chrysostom uses a comparison that will appear again and again in the history of exegesis: the water is like the material womb from which we are born, but the Spirit is the active principle; see Cornelius a Lapide: "Concurrit aqua quasi mater, et Spiritus Sanctus tanquam pater." Without always using this image, many modern commentators follow the same explanation: Büchsel, Schick, Calmes, Durand, the Dutch translation of St. Willibrord; and the specialized works of A. H. Haller, "Der Begriff der Wiedergeburt nach der Schrift," in *Neue kirchl. Zeitschr.*, 11 (1900), 592-620 (see 614); I. M. Vosté, *Studia Joannea*, 129; E. K. Lee, *The Religious Thought of St. John* (London, 1950), 188-190; R. Schnackenburg, *Die Sakramente im Johannesevange-*

the fact that the two substantives, "water and Spirit," are governed by a single preposition.[12] Nevertheless, there does exist an exegetical tradition which, contrary to the preceding explanations, tends to dissociate the water and the Spirit. This tradition maintains firmly that the water designates Christian *baptism;* but it refers the expression "to be born of the Spirit" to *faith* or to the practice of the virtues. This tradition is a very old, going back to the middle of the second century. Its first witness is the *Shepherd of Hermas.* What it tells us about the conditions necessary for entrance into the kingdom is stated with a precision that is quite surprising, for such a distant period. The entire section of *Sim.* IX, 12-16, may be taken as a commentary on Jn 3, 5. Here we find cited at least eight times the words of this verse, *eiselthein eis tēn basileian tou theou,* in a context that is clearly baptismal. But it is, on the other hand, unusual that the first part of the verse ("Unless a man be born again of water and the Spirit") is not found anywhere: the author has replaced it with different imaginative expressions, which describe in

lium, 245; L. Villette, *Foi et Sacrament,* 89; J. Ysebaert, *Greek Baptismal Terminology,* 143.

11. Certain authors, e.g., Westcott, try to do so by drawing together the mention of water and the Spirit from what is said in Gen 1, 2 on the Spirit of God who hovers over the waters (LXX: *pneuma theou epephereto epano tou hydatos*). This correlation of the primordial waters and the water of baptism occurs frequently in the baptismal typology of the ancients; see, e.g., Clement of Alexandria, *Eclogae propheticae,* 7, 1 (*G.C.S.,* 137): "It is through water and the Spirit that regeneration (*anagennēsis*) takes place, just like all of creation (*genesis*)." But that analogy is very probably not yet implicit in Jn 3, 5: John's text offers no relationship with the account of creation. Furthermore, the relationship between *pneuma* and *hydōr* is very different in the two texts: in Genesis, the Spirit roams *over* the waters; in St. John, there is a simple juxtaposition of water and the Spirit. See F. Roustang, *N. R. Th.,* 1956, 343, n. 11: "One could rightly object that in the account of Genesis, spirit and water seem to oppose one another." Moreover, the theme of the new creation is more Pauline than Johannine.

12. For example, I.-M. Vosté, *Studia Ioannea,* 129: "... et quia sub una praepositione *ex* uniuntur 'aqua et Spiritus,' unum etiam formale constituunt, unam activitatem habent: aqua significat et efficit ablutionem a maculis, Spiritu anima gratia ornante"; likewise, Westcott and Tillmann.

another way what is required for entrance into the kingdom. For
Hermas, these conditions are *baptism* and a *life according to the
Spirit*, that is, the practice of the Christian virtues. But these conditions seem to correspond, in his writing, to the two terms of the
Johannine verse, *water* and *the Spirit*, and to provide us with an explanation: it is not enough to receive baptism, one must also "be
born of the Spirit," live and act according to the Spirit.[13]

Justin is another important witness, for Jn 3:5 is about the only
Johannine text to be found in his writings.[14] In *I Apol.* 61, he describes in detail Christian initiation in its two essential movements:
the catechumens must first *believe* in the truth of Christian teaching, promise to live according to this doctrine, and pray for the
remission of their sins; then they are *baptized* (61, 2-3), "for Christ
has said: 'Unless you are born again, you shall not enter into the
kingdom of heaven'" (61, 4, citing Jn 3, 5). Baptism is called
phōtismos, "because those who learn (*manthanontōn*) these things
are enlightened" (61, 12) by faith. Thus, we understand clearly
two passages from the *Dialogue with Tryphon;* in the first, he calls

13. For an excellent commentary on this whole section, see E. Massaux,
*Influence de l'Evangile de saint Matthieu sur la littérature chrétienne
avant saint Irénée* (Gembloux, 1950), 293-300. He writes, on p. 295:
"One wonders if Hermas does not find in the Johannine text two necessary
elements for entrance into the kingdom: the first would be baptism and
would correspond to *ex hydatos* of John; the second, equivalent to *ek
pneumatos,* would be what could be called: 'an act according to the
Spirit' "; and 299-300, in the conclusion: "In short, in *Sim.* IX, 12-16,
Hermas, who is under the literary influence of Jn 3, 5, very probably
understands this Johannine doctrine in a very personal way; he saw in
the first part of the Johannine verse two necessary conditions for entrance
into the kingdom: water and the Spirit. The first of these conditions is the
baptism which Hermas expresses with his formulas: to bear or receive
one's name, to bear or receive the seal; the second condition demands that
man adopt the habits of virgins, that he imitate their virtues, that he
acquire their spirits, that he bear their names, that he follow their commands. *That is all that Hermas could include in the expression ek pneumatos* [italics ours]) since, for him, there is a close relationship between
the Spirit and the virtues . . . , they are actually the condition for the
indwelling of the Spirit and thus Hermas can easily establish in his own
mind an identity between the presence of these virtues and that of the
Spirit: where virtues are, there is the Spirit."
14. E. Massaux, *op. cit.,* 508.

the race of Christians "that which has been regenerated [*anagennēthentos*] by him [Christ], by means of water, faith and wood (*di' hydatos kai pisteōs kai xylou*) which contained the mystery of the cross" (138, 2).[15] Somewhat before this, he had called this same Christian race "that which is born of faith and the Spirit" (*ton de ek pisteos kai pneumatos gegennēmenon*" (135, 6). These two texts lead us to say that, for Justin, faith and baptism are both necessary for regeneration; but it is above all faith that is linked with the action of the Spirit.[16]

Let us pass more quickly over the following authors. Irenaeus sees in the two nouns "water and Spirit" of Jn 3, 5, respectively, baptism and "the invocation of the Lord" that accompanies it.[17] Origen distinguishes between those Christians who are simply born "of water" and those who are born "of the Spirit": the latter are those who have received the spirit of adoption and are deeply filled with the spirit of the Gospel.[18] St. Augustine, in the anti-Donatist controversy, gives a similar interpretation: a man must be born not only of water, but also of the Spirit, which must be understood in terms of a true conversion, a renunciation of the world and of sin, a transformation which cannot be effected in one day and which is not linked to baptism alone.[19] But it is above

---

15. This passage is part of a typological explanation of the deluge. But the doctrine it contains is very close to that of Jn 3: "the wood that contains the mystery of the cross" recalls 3, 12-17; *di' hydatos* repeats *ex hydatos* of v. 5; and *dia pisteōs* is the theme of the whole third discourse (vv. 11-21); but since *ek pneumatos* of John's text is not cited, one may believe that Justin wanted to express the Spirit's action by the formula *dia . . . pisteōs* (coming immediately after *di' hydatos*), especially since in 135, 6 he explicitly joins the words: *ek pisteōs kai pneumatos gegennēmenou*.

16. But he also relates the Spirit to baptism (*hagiōi pneumati bebaptismenōi, Dial.,* 29, 1), very probably under the influence of the Gospel texts (Mk 1, 8; Jn 1, 33).

17. *Fragm.* 33 (ed. Harvey, II, 497-498): *dia tou hagiou hydatos kai tēs tou kuriou epiklēseos katharizometha . . . , hōs paidia neogona pneumatikōs anagennōmenoi kathōs kai ho kurios ephē. ean mē tis anagennēthēi di' hydatos kai pneumatos, ou mē eiseleusetai eis tēn basileian tōn ouranōn.*

18. *In Matth.,* c. 11 (commentary on Mt 23, 1-12; G.C.S., Origenes, XI, 23, 26-27).

19. *De baptismo contra Donatistas,* VI, 12, 19 (C.S.E.L., 51, 310-311): "Aut

all John Scotus Erigenus who went further in this direction. He has provided us with a remarkable interpretation of this verse, indeed, one whose influence was strongly felt during the Middle Ages. For him, "aqua" designates the visible sacrament, that is, baptism, while "spiritus" indicates the invisible understanding of what happens in baptism, the *faith* that is given to us by Christian *doctrine,* under the influence of the Spirit.[20] This rather new explanation will be taken up again in two works of the twelfth century, which later won a wide audience, the *Glossa ordinaria*[21] and the *Glossa interlinearis;*[22] it also seems to have influenced the commentary of St. Thomas on the Fourth Gospel.[23] A similar interpreta-

si non nascitur ex Spiritu nisi qui veraci conversione mutatur, omnes qui saeculo verbis et non factis renuntiant, non utique de Spiritu, sed ex aqua sola nascuntur . . . ; potest quis baptizari aqua, et non nasci de Spiritu . . . fieri potest in ipsa intus Ecclesia, ut non habeant unum Spiritum sancti per justitiam et immundi per avaritiam, et tamen habeant unum baptisma."

20. *In h. l.* (*P.L.,* 122, 316 B-C): "Ex *sacramento* visibili et *intellectu* invisibili. Ac si aperte dixisset: Nisi quis *symbolum baptismatis* acceperit visibiliter, et spiritum, idest, *intellectum ipsius symboli* non perceperit, non potest introire in regnum Dei." And he adds a second explanation, but it hardly differs from the preceding one: "Quoniam homo ex visibili corpore et invisibili anima constituitur, necessarium erat sacramentum visibile ad purificationem visibilis corporis, sicut necessaria erat *invisibilis fidei doctrina* ad sanctificationem invisibilis animae."

21. *P.L.,* 114, 336 C: "Necessarium est visibile *sacramentum aquae* ad ablutionem visibilis corporis, sicut est necessaria *doctrina invisibilis fidei* (et) ad sanctificationem animae invisibilis."

22. *Biblia Sacra cum Glossa ordinaria* . . . , t. V (Antwerp, 1617), 1057-1058: "*Nisi quis renatus fuerit:* Id est spiritualem intellectum symboli percipiat."

23. *Super evang. S. Ioannis lectura,* cap. III, lect. 1, 2 (ed. Marietti, [Rome, 1952], n. 432-434), where he explains "renasci ex Spiritu" in relation to the spiritual vision given by the Spirit: "Si ergo visio spiritualis non est nisi per Spiritum Sanctum, et Spiritus Sanctus infunditur nobis per lavacrum regenerationis spiritualis: ergo non possumus videre regnum Dei, nisi per lavacrum regenerationis." This last statement — that the Spirit is given by baptism — was not in J. S. Erigenus, nor in the texts that derived directly from him: in these authors, the actions of the water and that of the Spirit were coordinate rather than subordinate.

tion is found in Luther[24] and in the famous Lutheran theologian of the seventeenth century, Johan Gerhard.[25] In our day, it appears again in different commentators, both Protestant[26] and Catholic.[27] Finally, we should mention a group of interpreters who deny any reference to baptism in this verse. One must mention here

24. We possess a number of Luther's sermons on Jn 3, 5. The two more important ones, as far as our present subject is concerned, are those of 1526 and 1538 (Weimar edit., X, 1/2, 293-306, and XLVII, 1-28): the Spirit, he says, is given in baptism and also operates in baptism; and what he produces in us, is faith (XLVII, 13). But what is especially characteristic of Luther is the fact that he attributes regeneration both to *baptism* and to *faith* in the word of God: "Dieselbige neue geburt ist nu die Tauffe, da wir in Gottes namen und durch Gottes wort und das wasser getaufft werden" (15). "Also geschiecht die giestliche geburt durchs wort Gottes, durch die tuffe und den glauben" (19). Compare this passage with another sermon "Soll er [der Mensch] aus dem Geist geboren werden, so gehört nicht mehr dazu, denn Dass er sich lasse taufen mit Wasser und auf das Sausen, d. i. auf das Wort, merke und dasselbe mit Glauben annehme, so wird er zu dem Reich Gottes geboren, und sonst durch nirgend" (cited in A. H. Haller, "Der Begriff der Wiedergeburt nach der Schrift, in *Neue kirchl. Zeitschr.*, 1900, 60). Luther also insists on another point, namely, that true regeneration presupposes a development, progress, in the faith: "Dise gepurt ist angefanngen in der tauff" (X, 1/2, 300); "Wenn wir getaufft sind und glauben, . . . so wachsen wir von tage zu tage im glauben, auch in den fruchten und guten wercken des heiligen Geistes" (XLVII, 13).
25. *Ioannis Gerhardi . . . locorum theologicorum, tomus nonus* (ed I. F. Cotta [Tübingen, 1769], Loc. XXI, cap. S, 236a): "Nullum datur ordinarium medium regenerationis quam verbum et baptismi sacramentum"; compare this with what he had already said in the preceding chapter, on the relationship between baptism and faith: "Baptismus non est simpliciter aqua, sed est aqua verbo Dei conjuncta; jam vero verbum Dei est medium illud per quod Spiritus Sanctus fidem in cordibus hominum . . . accendit" (152a). Still, we must note that in contrast with Luther and the medieval texts cited above, this author does not relate faith directly to the action of the Spirit, in Jn 3, 5, but to baptism in which the Spirit is active. On this point, he follows the common opinion: the Spirit acts "per aquam" (150b), "per illud (= sacramentum) fidem operatur" (152b).
26. E. A. Abbott, *Johannine Vocabulary* (London, 1905), n. 1494: "This [the regeneration from above and with the Spirit] introduces the notion of 'believing.'" See in particular Strathmann, 70: "Die Hervorhebung des Geistes als des entscheidenden objektiven und nachher im zweiten Teil

the names of Calvin and Grotius who interpreted "water" as a simple metaphor to designate the purifying action of the Spirit, which takes place without any external rite.[28] The same explanation has also been given by B. Weiss and M. Barth.[29]

des Gesprächs die Hervorhebung des Glaubens als des entscheidenden subjektiven Faktors sind sas für die Aussagen unseres Abschnittes und die Denkweise des Johannes Charakteristische"; Strachan, 134: "The work of the Spirit that must accompany baptism would be thus apparent in the candidate's confession"; compare with S. Smalley, "Liturgy and Sacrament in the Fourth Gospel," in *Evang. Quart.*, 1957, 165; W. Grundmann, "Die *NĒPIOI* in der urchristlichen Paränese," in *New Test. Stud.*, 1958/59, 199, n. 1; E. Schweizer, art. *pneuma, Theol. Wört. z. N. T.* VI, 439: to be born of the Spirit means "das Geschenk der Erkenntnis . . . das im Ereignis des Glaubens Wirklichkeit wird."

27. Actually, we found it in only one author; but in a brilliant passage, he gives an explanation that is very close to that of St. Augustine, cited above; see Paul-Marie de la Croix, O.C.D., *L'Evangile de Jean et son témoignage spirituel* (Desclée de Brouwer, 1959), 280: "While 'to be born of water' is reduced in time to a specific act, requiring adhesion in faith, 'to be born of the Spirit' is a reality with a perpetual future and marked by a requirement of constant renewal. It is in relation to the Spirit that we must become real 'children of God,' through daily acts and deeds. In both cases, there is birth, but under two very different forms. While one is a precise fact, accomplished once and for all, the other is always *in fieri*, in the process of being accomplished. Thus is made clear the new dimension of the spiritual life of the child of God."

28. *Corpus Reformatorum*, 47, 56: "Spiritum et aquam pro eodem posuit"; H. Grotius, *Annotationes in Novum Testamentum*, I, (Halle, 1769), 969.
29. M. Barth, *Die Taufe — ein Sakrament?* 445: "Das Wort 'Geist' definiert in Joh. 3, 5 das Wort 'Wasser'. . . . Dasjenige Wasser, welches die Zeugung von oben bewirkt und anzeigt, ist der Heilige Geist — nur und allein der Heilige Geist. Es gibt nicht ein Wasser und einen Geist als zwei Ursachen (*causae*) oder Mittel (*media*) der Wiedergeburt. Wasser und Geist stehen weder ursächlich noch signifikativ unter — oder nebeneinander. Denn nur der Geist ist das rechte Wasser!" Against such an interpretation Westcott wrote (49): "Hence all interpretations which treat the term *water* as simply figurative and descriptive of the cleansing power of the Spirit are essentially defective as they are also opposed to all ancient tradition." Later on we will return to the argument that M. Barth offers in defense of his explanation in the Johannine use of words joined together: "water and Spirit," 'Spirit and truth," etc. This is a stylistic detail that is important for the exegesis; see note 76 below.

Many commentators make use of literary criticism, before passing on to the theological interpretation of this verse. Such commentators distinguish two periods of writing for the text, and therefore interpret it on two different levels. The words *hydatos kai* would thus not belong to the original text, but would have been added later on to make the verse agree with the doctrine and sacramental practice of the early Church.[30] This explanation, based on the distinction of literary composition, can be understood in two further ways. According to the most radical interpretation, the addition would have been made in the Church after the writing of the gospel;[31] but this assertion is completely arbitrary, for the omission of the words *hydatos kai* is not supported by any evidence in the textual tradition.[32] For others, on the contrary, these words are purely secondary in the sense that they do not go back to the conversation of Jesus himself with Nicodemus; they would have been added later on by the evangelist when he was actually writing his text.[33] Over the last few years, Catholic critics have tended more and more to adopt this point of view.[34]

30. E. von Dobschütz, "Zum Charakter des vierten Evangeliums," in *Zeitschr. für die neut. Wiss.*, 28 (1929), 166.
31. K. Lake (cited by E. von Dobschütz, 166, note) and the commentaries of J. Wellhausen, A. Merx, R. Bultmann ("eine Einfügung der kirchlichen Redaktion," 98, n. 2); likewise, E. Lohse, "Wort und Sakrament im Johannesevangelium," in *New Test. Stud.*, 1960/61, 116-125.
32. Tischendorf, Soden, and Merk do not cite any witness for this omission; according to Nestle (18th ed., 1957), it would be supported by a manuscript of the Vulgate (Harl. 1023), by Justin and Origen. As for the latter two, the facts are inexact, and for the Vulgate manuscript, the indications are at least fallacious: according to the Harleian code 1023 (ed. E. S. Buchanan [London, 1914], fol. 67), the scribe had first written "ex spiritu," but then he *himself* crossed it out to replace it with "ex aqua"; and his text continues: "et spiritu sancto." Thus it seems he omitted "ex aqua" by error. Under these conditions, he is hardly the one who should be cited in favor of the omissions.
33. H. H. Wendt; J. H. Bernard; W. F. Flemington, *The New Testament Doctrine of Baptism*, 85-87.
34. F.-M. Braun, "La vie d'en haut," in *Rev. des Sc. Ph. et Théol.*, 1956, 15: "On the other hand, nothing prevents us from supposing that it [the word *hydatos*] was inserted in Jesus' remarks by John himself" (see also 16; on the other hand, in his previous article, "Le baptême d'apres le 4e

Thus, for a verse that is so simple in appearance, the most varied interpretations have been given. Only one point seems to be established: in the present text, *hydatos* designates Christian baptism. But the whole problem is one of knowing what role belongs, respectively, to the water and to the Spirit in the new birth of the believer.[35]

To answer this question, it is necessary to trace the history of each of these two themes in the development of the evangelical tradition. We shall, therefore, begin our examination with a literary analysis of the dialogue, to see if we should conclude that *hydatos* belongs to a more recent writing of the verse. Supposing that this is so, as we think it is, we will have to interpret the verse at two successive moments of tradition: it will first be necessary to specify the meaning of the original formula, where it was simply a question of "being born of the Spirit"; then we will examine the verse in its subsequent stage, after the insertion of *hydatos,* and we will ask what the evangelist meant by this more complicated expression: "to be born again of water *and* the Spirit." Study of the origin of the text and careful examination of the structure of the pericope will show clearly to which of the abovementioned interpretations one should subscribe.

LITERARY ANALYSIS OF THE DISCOURSE

To interpret Jn 3, 5, correctly, we should place the verse in its context, and to understand the latter, we must study the structure and mode of composition of the whole dialogue. Most

---

Evangile," in *Rev. thom.,* 1948, 371, n. 1, the author did not yet make this supposition and even seemed to reject it).; X. Léon-Dufour, "Actualite du 4e Evangile," in *N. R. Th.,* 1954, 456 and n. 14; H. Van den Bussche, *Het vierde Evangelie. I. Het Boek der Tekens* (Tielt, 1959), 53, 235; A. Feuillet, "Les thèmes bibliques majeurs du discours sur le pain de vie," in *N. R. Th.,* 1960, 1055-1056, n. 132: "John certainly specified the original teaching of the Savior, beginning with the baptismal practice in the Church." See also in this regard the article of H. Rongy, "Le dialogue avec Nicodème," in *Rev. eccl. de Liège,* 1933, 233. J. Leal, S.J., also admitted the possibility of considering the word *aqua* as a later addition

often, critics look for a plan of the chapter based on the development of ideas, but it is clear that divisions of this kind are rather arbitrary.[36] Let us try to present a structure that is derived more from literary criteria.[37]

The two introductory verses of the dialogue are closely linked to the last three of the preceding chapter. The name of Jesus is not even given at the beginning of chapter 3: *pros auton* (v. 2), left indefinite, must be understood as a reference to *ho Iēsous* of 2, 24 (repeated in *autos* of 2, 25c). "There was a certain man" of v. 1 echoes the words "what was in man" immediately preceding; and "the signs that thou workest" of v. 2c is, as it were, a reference

of the evangelist; see "Evangelio de San Juan," in *La Sagrada Escritura. Nuevo Testamento, I. Evangelios* (B.A.C.) (Madrid, 1961), 863.

35. White, *The Biblical Doctrine of Initiation*, 255: "The difficulty lies, of course, in correlating the water with the Spirit in the experience of regeneration in baptism."

36. Several authors divide sections 3, 1-21 into two parts: *a*) the dialogue, properly speaking (1-15); *b*) the commentary of the evangelist (16-21); thus, Westcott, Bernard, Lagrange, Van den Bussche, Tillmann follows the same principle of division, but he places the break somewhat higher: 1-12; 13-21. Such a distinction is artificial: nothing indicates that there is a difference between the "dialogue" and the personal "reflections" of John; for the evangelist, the whole discourse is one and represents Jesus' thought as well as his own ecclesial experience.
Other authors construct a plan according to the order of ideas or themes. Here are two examples:
Hoskyns: introduction (2, 23 — 3, 2); Jesus himself, the visible and historical man (3, 3-6); the death of the Son of Man (11-15); judgment and salvation, faith and works (16-21).
Bultmann: introduction (2, 23-25); the coming of the revealer and the *chrisis* of the world (3, 1-21), to be divided into two parts: the mystery of the new birth (1-8); the mystery of the Son of Man and the judgment of the world (9-21).
In such divisions, it is not clear how the various parts relate to one another; given the fact that all Johannine themes are closely allied, a grouping by ideas will always seem somewhat subjective. It is better to focus on the literary forms of the discourse; thus, one has a better chance of respecting the actual expressions of the author's thought.

37. Some good indications in the article of F. Roustang, "L'entretien avec Nicodème," in *N. R. Th.*, 1956, 338-340; X. Léon-Dufour, "Le mystère du Pain de Vie (Jean 6)," in *R. Sc. Rel.*, 1958, 481-524 (see 497-498, and note 37).

to 2, 23: "the signs that he was working." One should, therefore, consider the entire section 2, 23–3, 2 as an organically related whole, serving as an introduction to the whole dialogue. The theme of the introduction is clear: it is the faith of the Jews (represented by Nicodemus), which is but an incomplete faith for it is based solely on the *sēmeia* that can be seen.

The section 3, 3-21 develops according to a plan that occurs frequently in St. John: the first revelation of Jesus (3, 3) is expressed in enigmatic terms; hence the incomprehension of Nicodemus (3, 4). The objection expressed by the latter becomes the point of departure for a new revelation, longer than the preceding one, which depends both on the first revelation of Jesus and on the question of his interlocutor (3, 5-8). Then we have a second difficulty of Nicodemus (3, 9); Jesus is surprised (3, 10).[38] This leads to the third and last revelatory statement, the longest and most important of the three (3, 11-21). The schema for the whole is as follows: (1) revelation–question, (2) revelation–question, (3) revelation. These, it seems, are the basic statements of the whole dialogue. This is all the more probable in that each statement is introduced by an identical formula: "Amen, amen, I say to thee."[39] These three revelations, accompanied by Nicodemus' lack of understanding, form, therefore, three literary units.

38. Fr. Roustang has noted very well (339) that the beginning of Jesus' third response (v. 10), before the third "amen, amen, I say to thee," "is addressed personally to Nicodemus, but is not part of the teaching." The words "thou art a teacher in Israel and dost not know these things?" does not belong to the third revelatory discourse. It is related to the idea of Nicodemus' lack of understanding: here Jesus is reproaching the Jewish teacher for his ignorance regarding the preceding revelation.

39. Vv. 3, 5, 11. See the remark of Fr. Roustang (339): "The 'amen, amen, I say to thee' is intended to open up small discourses." Still it is surprising to note that he himself proposes a structure based solely on the development of theological themes.

The division we proposed above seems also to be the one favored by Fr. Mollat in the *Bible de Jerusalem*: there, the three discourses of Jesus (vv. 3, 5-8, 11-21) appear typographically in verses, with larger margins than for the prose sections, while the introduction (vv. 1-2) and two objections of Nicodemus (vv. 4, 9-10) run the width of the page. Fr. Mollat himself has confirmed the fact that our division of the dialogue is in agreement with his own.

What are the techniques of composition used by the author?[40] We should say a word about this, for it will enable us to trace better the train of development, to indicate the theme of each subdivision, and to situate precisely v. 5 within the dialogue. We just mentioned the three *supporting props* marked off in the text by the triple formula: *amen amen lego soi.* They indicate the three major subdivisions.

We should also point out a very frequent and sometimes rather subtle use of *Semitic inclusion.* In the introduction, as we already saw, "the signs that he was working" is repeated in "working the signs that thou workest." Another inclusion is closely related to the preceding: *theōrountes* of 2, 23 points the way to *oidamen* in 3, 2. Of course, such a correspondence is a less apparent one, but we should appreciate the precise meaning of these two verbs. *Theōrein,* in the beginning of the Gospel, marks an inferior degree of corporeal vision, a very attentive and curious look, but one that is superficial and unknowing with regard to spiritual realities.[41] However, *oidamen* indicates here a knowledge based solely on the sight of miracles,[42] as the following words underline explicitly: *"for* no one can work these signs that thou workest."* The word *oidamen* is, therefore, a throwback *theōrountes.* Since the "seeing" of signs is still very human and external, the "knowledge" that comes from it is no less so; the term *oidamen,*

---

40. These Johannine processes of composition have been studied very carefully, with respect to another dialogue, by C. Charlier, "La présence dans l'absence (John 13, 31 – 14, 31)," in *Bible et vie chrét.,* n. 2 (May-July, 1953), 61-75.

41. See E. A. Abbott, *Johannine Vocabulary* (London, 1905), n. 1598: "*Theōrein,* at all events at the outset of the Gospel, is used of unintelligent, superficial, or at least inferior 'beholding.' People (II, 13) 'beholds' Christ's signs, but Jesus does not trust them"; see G. L. Phillips, "Faith and Vision in the Fourth Gospel," in *Studies in the Fourth Gospel,* ed. F. L. Cross (London, 1957), 93-96 (see 84-85).

42. The verb *oida,* in St. John, still keeps its classic meaning; it designates a form of knowledge based on a vision. But in the present example, the "seeing" that precedes being of an inferior quality – since it does not raise a person to the plenitude of faith – the "knowledge" stemming from it also has a pejorative connotation. See our article "Oida et ginōskō. Les deux modes de la connaissance dans le 4e Evangile," in *Bibl.,* 40 (1959), 709-725, especially 717-718 (and note 2).

on the lips of Nicodemus, has a note of rather obvious content-
ment and satisfaction.

This is what Jesus wants to correct. The first two statements
take as a point of departure this still-too-human *oidamen* of
Nicodemus, in order to bring out its inadequacy, and to invite
the "teacher in Israel" to a higher knowledge. The word *oidamen*
of v. 2, which was a throwback to *theōrountes* of 2, 23, at the
same time leads to a new development. It forms an antithesis to
the beginning of Jesus' third statement: against the *oidament* of
Nicodemus, Jesus offers his own *oidamen* (v. 11), which follows
ou ginōskeis ("thou dost not know," v. 10) in the remarks of his
interlocutor. Thus, the roles are now reversed. Similarly, the title
didaskalos, which Nicodemus gave to Jesus in v. 2 with a polite-
ness marked by a certain flattery, is returned by Jesus in v. 10, not
without a certain irony. The first two statements are a kind of
corrective of the introductory theme (the seeing of miracles and
the imperfect faith of the Jews).

In this context, we understand the value of the formula "to
see (*idein*) the kingdom of God" in v. 3. The verb *oraō*, which
signifies in St. John the "look of faith,"[43] is an improvement over
the *theōrountes* of 2, 23 and the *oidamen* of 3, 2.[44] This spiritual
"seeing" will become a major theme of the discourse and of the
narrative that completes it. This is what emerges from the great
inclusion which encloses the entire chapter "*to see* the kingdom
of God" (v. 3) and "shall not *see* life" (v. 36).

The throwbacks to vv. 2-3 in v. 10 show that the first two discourses are closely linked: in deed, they both treat the same
theme of the "new birth." Several inclusions, within vv. (2) 3-10
emphasize this twofold literary unity; one, in the first discourse:

---

43. See "La notion de témoignage dans S. Jean," in *Sacra Pagina* (II, Gembloux, 1959), 193-208 (see 197-199: "the witness who has 'seen' and
the object of his witness.")
44. This progressive sequence of the three verbs is even more apparent when
one notices the *assonance* of the last two (if they are pronounced as they
should be, following the practice of the period); the transcription will
make it more clear:
— remark of Nicodemus: ...*idamen hoti*...
— response of Jesus: ...*ou dinatè idin*...

"to be born again" (v. 3) and "to be born . . . to be born again" (v. 4); another, in the second: "unless a man be born . . . of the Spirit" (v. 5) and "everyone who is born of the Spirit" (v. 8). Still others, in both discourses: "Jesus answered and said to him" (v. 3) is repeated in v. 10; likewise, "we know that thou hast come a teacher from God" (v. 2) corresponds to "Thou art a teacher in Israel . . . (thou dost not know these things . . .), we know" (vv. 10-11). Finally, "to be born again" (v. 3) is repeated in "to be born again" (v. 7) or "born of the Spirit" (v. 8).

In the third statement (vv. 11-21), there also seems to be a correspondence between the first verse ("our witness you do not receive," v. 11) and the last two ("does not come to the light," v. 20; "comes to the light," v. 21). Finally, one is perhaps justified in seeing another major inclusion for the whole dialogue in a comparison of the following texts:

A	B	C
"*came* to Jesus at *night*" (v. 2)	and	"*comes* to the *light*" (v. 21)
"thou *hast come* a *teacher* from God" (*ibid.*)	and	"the *light* has *come* into the world" (v. 19)

The first of these two correspondences is antithetical (*night—light*); the second synonymous and progressive (*come* as teacher —*come* as light). This great inclusion brings out in a marvelous way the evocative and symbolic force of v. 2 ("at night"), so well explained by St. Augustine.[45]

It remains for us to mention a third literary process, the most important one of the whole chapter: it has been called progressive linking, that is, the use of connective words.[46] These words, which

---

45. See F. Roustang, *art. cit.*, 352-355.
46. Dom Charlier (*art. cit.*, 64) described the process in these terms: "This typically Semitic process is . . . by no means artificial, no matter what is said of it. The 'recalling of words' only seems to govern the thought, whereas it is rather the internal logic of the explanation that naturally produces the words. Their chain-like repetition is produced by the verbal force of a train of thought whose profound continuity is underscored by the words used. This verbal outburst is in no way systematic, as is seen

summon one another (we will intalicize and number them below), show clearly the basic unity of the whole discourse; it is according to the rhythm of this linking that the thought itself gradually develops.

On the basis of these different techniques of composition, we may observe the fundamental structure of the whole dialogue:

INTRODUCTION (2, 23-3,2): Imperfect faith of the Jews.

2, 23-25 *a*) (The Jews) "Now when he was at Jerusalem for the feast of the Passover, many *believed* [*episteusan,* 1] in his name, *seeing* [*theōrountes,* 2] *the signs that he was working* (3). But Jesus *did not trust himself* [*ouk episteuen,* 1] to them, in that he knew all men, and because he had no need that anyone should bear witness concerning *man* (4), for he himself knew what was in *man* (4)."

3, 1-2 *b*) (Nicodemus, one of the Jews) "Now there was a certain *man* (4) among the Pharisees, Nicodemus by name, a ruler of the Jews. This man came to Jesus at night, and said to him, 'Rabbi, we *know* [*oidamen, idamen,* 2] that thou hast come a teacher from God, for no one *can* [*dunatai,* 5] *work these signs that thou workest* (3) unless God be with him.'"

FIRST TWO DISCOURSES (3, 3-10): Conditions for faith and entrance into the Kingdom.

v. 3 *a*) (*First Revelation*)"Jesus answered and said to him, 'Amen, amen, I say to thee, unless a man *be born* (6) *again* (7), he *can*not (5) see [*idein, idin,* 2] *the kingdom of God* (8).'"

v. 4 *b*) (*Non-comprehension*) "Nicodemus said to him, 'How *can* (5) a man *be born* (6) when he is *old? Can* (5) he *enter* (9) *a second time* (7) into his mother's womb and be *born again* (6)?'"

vs. 5-8 *b*) (*Second Revelation*) "Jesus answered, 'Amen, amen, I

---

in the fact that in several places the verbal link is replaced by an image or situations or else simply understood and suggested by the general movement." We shall see an application of this in chapter 2.

say to thee, unless a man *be born* (6) of water and the *Spirit* (10), he *cannot* (5) *enter* (9) into the *kingdom of God* (8). That which *is born* (6) of the flesh is flesh; and that which *is born* (6) of the *Spirit* (10) *is spirit* (10). Do not wonder that I said to thee, 'You must *be born* (6) *again* (7).' The *wind* [*Spirit, pneuma,* 10] blows where it will, and thou hearest its sound but dost not know where it comes from or where it goes. So is everyone who *is born* (6) of the *Spirit* (10).

vs. 9-10 (*Non-comprehension*) "Nicodemus answered and said to him, 'How *can* (5) these things be? Answering him, Jesus said, 'Thou art a teacher in Israel and dost *not know* (2) these things?' "

THIRD DISCOURSE (3, 11-21): True faith and eternal life.

vs. 11-12 (*Third Revelation*) "Amen, amen, I say to thee, we *speak* (11) of what *we know* (12, 2), and we *bear witness* (11) to what we *have seen* (12); and our *witness* (11) you *do not receive* [= you *do not believe,* 13]. If I have *spoken* (11) of earthly things to you, and you *do not believe* (13), how *will you believe* (13) if I *speak* (11) to you of *heavenly things* (12)?

vs. 13-15 And no one has *ascended* (14) into *heaven* (12) except him who has descended from *heaven* (12); the *Son of Man* (15) who is in *heaven* (12). And as Moses *lifted up* (14) the serpent in the desert, even so must the *Son of Man* (15) *be lifted up* (14), that those who *believe* (13) in him may not perish, but *may have life everlasting* (16).

vs. 16-17 For *God* (17) so loved *the world* (18) that he *gave* (19) his *only-begotten Son* (15), that those who *believe* (13) in him may not perish, but *may have life everlasting* (16). For *God* (17) did not *send* (19) his *Son* (15) into *the world* (18) in order to *judge* (20) *the world* (18), but that the world (18) *might be saved* (16) through him.

vs. 18-19 He who *believes* (13) in him is not *judged* (20); but he who *does not believe* (13) is already *judged* (20; because he *does not believe* (13) in the name of the *only-begotten Son of God* (15). Now this is the *judgment* (20): *The light has come into the world* (11, 18), yet men *have*

loved the darkness rather than light [= *have not believed,*
13], for their *works* (21) were evil. For everyone who *does*
(21) evil hates *the light* and *does* not come to the light (11,
13), that his *deeds* (21) may not be exposed. But he who
does (21) the truth *comes to the light* (13, 11) that his *deeds*
(21) may be made manifest for they have been *performed*
(17) in God.' "

The above structure leads to several remarks.

At first sight, we notice an antithetical correspondence between the introduction and the third discourse. Both have as a
principal theme *the faith*: the still very imperfect faith of the
Jews in 2, 23-3, 2, the true Christian faith and its fruits of salvation in 3, 11-21. It cannot be a matter of chance if, throughout the
Fourth Gospel (excepting the prologue, 1, 12), the expression
pisteuein eis to onoma is found only in this one section, and just
at the beginning of the introduction (2, 23) and at the end of
the third discourse, where the verb *pisteuein* is mentioned for the
last time (3, 18c); the two formulas summon one another, with a
strong progression taking place from 2, 23 to 3, 18. The expression "to believe in one's name" does not mean only "to believe in
the person," as if the name were simply a Semitic way of designating the person. It means to adhere to the person, but at the same
time to recognize fully what his "name" expresses; it means to believe in the person precisely insofar as he is what his title expresses.[47] In 2, 23, the formula still remains vague and indefinite:
"many believed in his name" (the name is not specified); but the
following words of the verse show immediately by reason of
what quality of Jesus they believed: they believed in him as a
miracle-worker sent from God (see 3, 2: *apo theou*). This was
the "faith" characteristic of the Jews, which Jesus was to disavow
later on (4, 48).[48] At the end of the dialogue, on the contrary, the

47. See the excellent remarks of J. Dupont, in the article "Nom de Jésus,"
Suppl. au Dict. de la Bible, VI, col. 527-530; see also Westcott (commentary on Jn 8, 30: " 'to believe in his name,' that is, to believe in him
as characterized by the specific title implied (1, 12; 2, 23; 3, 18)."

48. One may perhaps be tempted to object to this interpretation on two grounds: *a*) the faith of the Jews is expressed here by *pisteuein eis* with the accusative, which is John's normal expression for the true faith; *b*) the *sèmeion* in the Fourth Gospel is preparatory to faith: how can one reproach the Jews for believing in Jesus because of his signs? Can such faith be described as "incomplete"?
We respond: *a*) Contrary to what some authors say (Blass-Debrunner, par. 187, 6; T. Camelot, O.P., "Credere Deo, credere Deum, credere in Deum. Pour l'histoire d'une formule traditionnelle," in *Rev. des Sc. Phil. et Théol.*, 1941-1942, 149-155), we believe that one should observe the fact that *pisteuein eis*, in St. John, is distinguished clearly from *pisteuein tini*. The first construction, unknown in secular Greek and in the LXX, is very characteristic of the Johannine style (38 times in Jn and I Jn, as against 8 times in the rest of the New Testament): it does not say only that a person holds as true what someone else declares (this is the meaning of the verb with the dative), but also indicates a true adherence to his person. Still, the nature of such adherence, and hence the quality of faith, are to be indicated ultimately by the context, that is, by the motive that inspires the attachment. Christian faith in Jesus is always designated by this formula *pisteuein eis* (e.g., Jn 12, 44, 46; 14, 1, 12; 17, 20; I Jn 5, 10, 13) and the verb is used generally in an absolute sense. For the initial faith of the Jews, we also find *pisteuein eis*, but here the motive of such faith is always indicated: it is the word of Jesus (8, 30), and everywhere else his *sēmeia* (2, 23; 7, 31; 11, 45; 12, 11, 37; see 6, 2, 14); such faith, based on signs, is disapproved of by Jesus (4, 48). But at the end of the public life, the evangelist writes this phrase, which is surprising after everything that precedes: "Now though he had worked so many signs in their presence, they did not believe in him" (12, 37), which seems to say exactly the opposite of the texts cited a moment ago. This leads us directly to the second point.
b) The *sēmeia* are certainly an effective means of preparation for the true faith, but on one condition: that is that a person should not stop at the material and external aspect of the sign, at the marvelous deed as such, but that the "sign" should reveal in Christ the "signified"; thanks to the signs, faith should extend to the very mystery of Jesus' person. The comparison of two texts of John shows this clearly: at Cana, the faith of the disciples was authentic, because the miracle revealed to them the *glory of Jesus* (2, 11). This is precisely what was lacking to the Jews who attached themselves to Jesus; they preferred *human glory* to the glory of God (12, 42-43). Only the faith that reveals, through signs, the *doxa* of Christ, is true faith. In the text of 2, 23, it is this still too human faith of the Jews that is involved. See on all this the judicious remarks of J.-P. Charlier, "La notion de signe (*sēmeion*) dans le 4e Evangile," in *Rev. des Sc. Phil. et Théol.*, 43 (1959), 434-448; the latter proved to be of great help to us.

faith required will be perfect faith: "to believe in the name of the *only-begotten Son of God*" (v. 18);[49] one must believe that Jesus is the only-begotten son of the Father, and adhere to him insofar as he is the Son and the representative of the Father. Before reaching this concluding formula, the third revelatory discourse had described in a powerful synthesis the essence of such Christian faith: Jesus bears witness to the things of heaven, he has been sent into the world to save the world, he is the Son of man "raised" from the earth and ascended into heaven, he is the Son of God. To win eternal life, a man must believe in him who is the One-sent-from-God, the Son of man and Son of God.

We can now appreciate better the great difference between the faith of the Jews and that of true Christians. It has been said that this dialogue "contains all the elements of a baptismal catechesis."[50] Perhaps one should say, on the basis of the comparison made between the introduction and the third revelatory discourse, that the whole dialogue is presented as a catechesis, but that the latter focuses above all on the real object and true dimensions of Christian *faith*.

Now let us examine more closely the intermediary section, which concerns us directly; that of the first two discourses, which are devoted to the theme of the new birth (v. 3-10). Here there is no mention of the verb "to believe."[51] This is not surprising, for

---

49. An analogous remark can be made for the whole Gospel: in the prologue (1, 12) is announced in a general way, for those who believe *eis to onoma autou,* the possibility of becoming children of God. But the whole Gospel is intended to reveal what that name is: it is that of "Christ" and "Son of God," with the qualities they express. Thus, the concluding verse (20, 31) is like the final statement and summary of all Johannine Christology: "But these [these signs] are written that you may believe that Jesus is the Christ, the *Son of God,* and that believing you may have life in his name" (see, in the first Epistle, the concluding verse 5, 13, which is completely similar). Between Jn 1, 12 and 20, 31, there is a kind of major inclusion, encompassing the whole gospel, just as there is between 2, 23 and 3, 18, for the dialogue with Nicodemus: this dialogue, therefore, offers us a small synthesis of the Fourth Gospel.

50. D. Mollat, *L'Evangile selon saint Jean* (Paris, 1953), 15.

51. The fact deserves to be mentioned: *pisteuein* is read in the introduction (see 2, 23, 24) and in the third discourse (3, 12-18: 7 times), but nowhere in the intermediary section: this is because the latter describes the

after mentioning the imperfect faith that is based solely on the seeing of miracles, Jesus here describes the *conditions* required so that a person might rise to the superior vision of faith and to the vision of the kingdom. For this, a new birth, a renewal of one's whole being, is necessary. The new birth, in vv. 3-8, is therefore presented as being absolutely indispensable for attaining to the life of true faith and for obtaining eternal life.

Let us try to situate precisely v. 5 in the movement of the whole dialogue. The expression "to be born of the water and the Spirit," which is an explanation of "to be born again" (v. 3), indicates the fundamental condition for "seeing" the kingdom, for "entering into" the kingdom.

But if we refer back to the structure of the discourse presented above, we will note that in contrast to the words "to be born" and "spirit" of v. 5 (connective words 6 and 10), the term "water" appears only this one time in the whole dialogue; one cannot then consider it as a connective word, for it does not constitute a link in the development. If one reads vv. 3-8 without the words *hydatos kai*, nothing changes, when the text is considered solely in terms of literary composition.[52] When the theme of v. 5 is taken up again and explained in vv. 6 and 8, there is no longer any mention of water;[53] only the formula "to be born of the Spirit" is discussed. In short, the two words *hydatos kai* are of secondary importance: they appear as something *extra*. But such an addition seems to have been made in a text whose structure was already fixed in its essential parts. The most obvious explanation is that in the older Johannine catechesis it was solely a question of rebirth in the Spirit: this was to reflect substantially what Jesus had previously said to Nicodemus. Later on, Christ himself was to promulgate the necessity of Christian baptism; and it is starting from this later teaching of the Master and the practice of the early

road one must travel over to pass from the incomplete faith of the Jews to the plenitude of Christian faith.

52. On the contrary, from the theological point of view, the difference is great, as we will show in the third part of this chapter.
53. The addition of *tou hydatos kai* in v. 8 in the Western text is evidently a harmonizing with v. 5.

Church that John, while composing his Gospel, would have brought together in this discourse the original theme of the birth *ek pneumatos,* and the subsequent theme, that of the new birth *ex hydatos.*

This becomes even more probable in comparing the other Gospels. Several commentators have emphasized the resemblance of our verse with the *logia* of the synoptics regarding the conditions required for entrance into the heavenly kingdom.[54] Contact with this older tradition seems certain, for the expression "kingdom of God" is a *hapax* in St. John, but it is current in the synoptics (kingdom of God, heavenly kingdom); the same is true of the verb "to enter (into the kingdom)." But in the different synoptic texts that speak of this entrance into the kingdom, there is no mention whatsoever of baptism: it is, therefore, probable that the original text of John did not speak of it either.

We grasp at once the importance of this observation: it does away with the difficult problem as to whether Jesus himself would have already spoken to Nicodemus about Christian baptism. Historically, this is very difficult to assert.[55] But Jesus was to teach later on that baptism is necessary for salvation. If the two teachings which are grouped together here really come from Jesus— although they were given under different circumstances—John, in bringing them together in this dialogue, remains perfectly

---

54. Hoskyns cites here Mk 1, 15 and Mt 12, 18: Bernard relates our verse to the text of Mk 10, 15; likewise, W. Grundmann, *Die Geschichte Jesu Christi,* 3rd ed., (Berlin, 1961), 196. For a more detailed comparison with the latter synoptic legion, see especially J. Jeremias, *Die Kindertaufe in den ersten vier Jahrhunderten* (Göttingen, 1958), 63-65; K. Aland, *Die Säuglingstaufe im Neuen Testament und in der alten Kirche* (Theol. Exist. heute, H. 86) (Munich, 1961), 67-71. From the Catholic side, the same relationship has been noted by W. Grossouw, "Het nieuwtestamentische mensontwerp," in *Theologische Week over de Mens* (Nijmegen, 1959), 76-88 (see 81-82).

55. H. Rongy (*art. cit.,* 233) had already expressed this difficulty: "Baptism is a positive institution: one can know it only if one knows the historical fact of its institution or if one sees it practiced. But at the time of the dialogue, Christian baptism is not yet a common thing: Jesus has not instituted it or even spoken of it. Here, he would be introducing a word, not on baptism itself, but on the effects of baptism. Such a word would present Nicodemus with an insoluble puzzle."

faithful to the doctrine and intentions of the Master, even if he has formulated this doctrine in the light of his own ecclesial experience.

Having seen the conclusions of our literary analysis, two questions remain to be solved. First, let us ask what was the meaning of the formula of Jn 3, 5 in its original tenor: "To be born of the Spirit." Next, we shall examine what the evangelist meant in indicating a more complex condition for entrance into the kingdom of God: "To be born of water *and* the Spirit."

INTERPRETATION OF VERSE 5

A) THE ORIGINAL TEXT: "UNLESS A MAN BE BORN AGAIN OF THE SPIRIT . . ."

Comparing this text with the *synoptic logion* of Mt 18, 3 (parallel with Mk 10, 15 and Lk 18, 17) is very instructive.[56] According to Matthew's text, Jesus said: "Amen I say to you, unless you turn and become like little children, you will not enter into the kingdom of heaven." In the two other synoptics, we read: "Amen I say to you, whoever does not accept the kingdom of God as a little child will not enter into it." One cannot ignore the extraordinary resemblance between this logion and the original text of Jn 3, 5. Should we explain this fact by saying that the Johannine verse and the synoptic logion go back to the one expression of Jesus?[57] Or should we say that John wanted to reinterpret here the text of Mark and Luke?[58] Both statements are gratuitous and cannot be proven. Let us instead confine ourselves to an objective comparison of texts: this is revealing, for even if the two logia, as is probable, were pronounced under different circumstances, Jesus would have indicated on two occasions con-

---

56. See in J. Jeremias, *op. cit.*, 64, a synoptic outline of the different texts.
57. K. Aland, *op. cit.*, 70: "Beide einander entgegengesetzte Aussagen [the text of Mk/Lk and that of Jn] haben gewiss eine gemeinsame Wurzel, ein Herrenwort"; see J. Jeremias, 63: who thinks that, in these different texts, "it is a question of one and the same word."
58. J. Jeremias, *ibid.*

ditions that were almost similar, if not identical, for entrance into the kingdom.

Already in the synoptics, we note important variations in the form of the logion. The text of Matthew is the earliest.[59] The condition necessary for entrance into the Kingdom is, in his text, "to turn and become like little children."[60] In Mark, as well as in Luke, this condition is expressed in a more advanced way: "to accept [*dechesthai*] the kingdom of God as a little child." This text is an important interpretation of the tradition by which "acceptance" of the evangelical message was the basic attitude required for entrance into Christianity.[61] This theme is dear to Mark, as can be seen in the way he expresses the first promulgation of the kingdom: "*Repent and believe in the gospel*" (1, 15).[62] Acceptance of the kingdom is done in faith: for Mark, the "turning" or "conversion" required for entrance into the kingdom is essentially the acceptance of the Good News, the act of faith.[63] In the text of 10, 15, Mark presents a completely similar condition

---

59. See J. Jeremias, *op. cit.*, 64, and n. 4; W. Grundmann, "Die *NÉPIOI* in der urchristlichen Paränese," in *New Test. Stud.*, 1958/59, 203-204, n. 5.

60. J. Jeremias (*ibid.*) interprets *straphéte kai genésthe* as a Semitic expression (Hebrew *šubh*, Aramaic, *tubh*, followed by another verb [here "to become"] to indicate that the action of this verb is done "again"); likewise, J. Joüon, *L'Evangile de N. S. J.-C.* (Paris, 1930), 112. But in this construction the verb *šubh* often retains its proper meaning; see F. Zorell, *Lexicon hebr. et aram. V. T.*, 826a.

61. Attention should be given to E. Lohmeyer, *Das Evangelium des Markus* (Göttingen, 1959), 204-205: this verse of Mark's reflects the vocabulary of the early community; see *dechesthai ton logon tou theou* (Acts 8, 14; 11, 1; 17, 11; see also Jas 1, 21; I Thess 1, 6; 2, 13). On this subject, see W. Grundmann, art. *Dechomai*, in *Theol. Wört. z. N. T.*, II, 53.

62. This added *kai pisteuete tôi euangeliôi* is found only in Mk.

63. See the excellent article of M.-F. Lacan, "Conversion et royaume dans les Evangiles synoptiques," in *Lum. et Vie*, April-May, 1960, n. 47, 25-47 (especially 27-35, on the nature of conversion in Mk); see 29: "He [Jesus] invites men to conversion and indicates the fundamental act for it, the one that will lead to all others, namely, the act of faith. To convert, is first of all to believe in the Good News that Jesus proclaims . . . . The start of the kingdom is the coming of Christ. *To accept the Kingdom is to accept Jesus, through faith*" (italics ours).

for access to the kingdom: the disposition that characterizes little children, the attitude of reception, an opening of the soul, readiness of the heart.[64]

But let us go back to Matthew's verse, which is closer to that of John. In the First Gospel, the condition necessary for entry into the kingdom is not only presented as a disposition of the soul; it is something more radical, more fundamental: a conversion, a "turning" (*straphēte*), which involves a genuine spiritual "becoming" (*genēsthe*).[65] The very use of the verb "to become" suggests that this change is not made on one occasion; Jesus asks us to transform ourselves gradually; he asks us to try to become little before God, like children.[66]

In the Fourth Gospel, the formula "to be born of the Spirit" is scarcely different. But the requirement of conversion is more radical than in Matthew, for the necessity of becoming a child is now placed at the very start of existence: *rebirth* is necessary for an entirely new life. And while the synoptics consider this transformation from the point of view of man, John emphasizes that such a change is possible only by an act from on high, the action of the Spirit. But it is still a question of the same reality, the conversion that springs from faith. "In St. John, conversion is the point of view that arises in faith and the act of repentance

---

64. M.-F. Lacan, *art. cit.*, 31 (citing Mk 10, 14-15): "Such is the fundamental disposition without which conversion is impossible, as well as access to the kingdom of God; one must be childlike, open . . . . Against this opening of the heart to the gift of God, there are obstacles denounced by Jesus." See W. Grossouw, *art. cit.*, 81 (which we translate from the Dutch): "It is clear what is meant by the expression 'to receive the kingdom of God like a child'; it means nothing else but openness to the gift of God, an attitude without reservation, humility also, which is proper to a child, and which is generally unnoticed. It is the attitude that Paul, with a quite different terminology, calls the faith that justifies the sinner."

65. W. Grossouw (*art. cit.*, 81) comments that "The first evangelist shows us what an immense spiritual and human revolution is demanded by this apparently insignificant legion."

66. M.-F. Lacan, *art. cit.*, 39: "Conversion is not an act that is made once and for all. For once a person becomes a child, he must remain so . . . . 'To become like children' is to recognize our weakness and thereby to open ourselves to grace . . . . It is understandable why conversion must be a never-ending process."

made with regard to 'him whom they have pierced' (3, 14f.; 19, 37)."[67]

The examination of the parallel passages in the synoptics leads us, therefore, to this conclusion: "To be born of the Spirit" is essentially to be born to a new life, which is a life of faith. This life of faith presupposes a new birth, a new way of being and acting. Only the Spirit can produce it in us.

It is remarkable that the *parallels* to St. John's expression lead us to the same result. It is also surprising that these texts, which are indeed so clear, are practically never cited by commentators with respect to Jn 3, 5.

The prologue of the Gospel contains the most explicit passage: Those who are born of God (*ek theou egennēthēsan*) are those who *believe* in the name of the Word, the true Light that came into this world (Jn 1, 13). In the First Epistle, the fact of "being born of God" (*pas ho genennēmenos ek tou theou*, 3, 9) is attributed to the action of the divine *seed* in us, that is, the word of God accepted in faith.[68] And, likewise, at the end of the Epistle: "Everyone who *believes* that Jesus is the Christ is born of God" (5, 1); "because all that is born of God overcomes the world; and this is the victory that overcomes the world, our *faith*" (5, 4). It is, therefore, quite clear: throughout his writings, John considers the new birth of the Christian as the direct and immediate effect of belief in Christ.[69] Of course, the original text of Jn 3, 5

---

67. D. Mollat, "Ils regarderont vers celui qu'ils ent transpercé. La conversion chez saint Jean," in *Lum. et Vie*, n. 47 (1960), 113.

68. See our article "L'impeccabilité du chrétien d'après 1 Jn 3, 6-9," in *L'Evangile de Jean. Etudes et problèmes* (Desclée de Brouwer, 1958), 161-177 (see Chap. 6 of the present volume); there we show that *sperma autou* can here designate only the word of God. Fr. Boismard confirmed this interpretation by a study of the baptismal foundation of this passage: *Quatre hymnes baptismales dans la première épître de Pierre* ("Lectio divina," 30), (Paris, 1961), 22.

69. As was shown by Fr. Paul-Marie de la Croix, *L'Evangile de Jean et son témoignage spirituel*, 309-310, to understand that doctrine, we must go back to the conditions for entrance into the first Covenant and must refer to the account of Abraham's vocation and his response to the divine call: "Nowhere are men aware at this point of the fecundity of faith

attributes the regeneration explicitly to the Spirit, and not to
faith; this is because the writer is here looking at this new
birth from the point of view of God and not man: the new birth
takes place through the action of the Spirit. The passage in I Jn
5, 1-6, which we just cited, shows, moreover, that for John there
is a very close relationship between faith and the Spirit: as we
explained elsewhere in detail,[70] the expression "it is the Spirit
that bears witness" of v. 6 means that it is the Spirit who makes
known the truth of Christ and thereby engenders faith. This is
a fundamental idea in St. John: the spirit is essentially the Spirit
of truth, the one who gives us a supernatural understanding of
the revelation brought by Jesus, and who enables us to enter into
the complete truth.

The doctrine of the original text of Jn 3, 5, therefore, is substantially the same as that of the synoptic logion, although it is expressed from another point of view and in different terms. We
can now understand the exact function of vv. 3 and 5 in the
complete structure of the whole dialogue. The latter, we said,
is a catechesis on the true dimensions of Christian faith. The
first two discourses of Jesus, on the birth "again . . . of the Spirit,"
indicate precisely what is required to enter into this new life:
it is the action of the Spirit, which alone can render us fit
(*dunatai*) to "see" the kingdom.[71]

---

and, first of all, of the fact that it is a 'birth.' " For by his faith in God
the patriarch was chosen to become father of the chosen people; his faith
in the promise led to the birth of that people who would be known as
"the people of the Promise." "Thus, before the phrase of the Prologue
in which, with the fulfillment of the Promise, the new Covenant is opened
up: '*To those who received him, who believe in his name, it was given
to become children of God . . . ,*' it is impossible not to invoke the first
Covenant concluded with Abraham, 'our father in the faith.' Impossible
also not to say that in both cases such generation and filiation are the
fruit of faith."

70. See "La notion de témoignage dans saint Jean," in *Sacra Pagina*, II
(Gembloux), 193-208 (see 202-206).
71. This theme of the new birth made possible by the Holy Spirit is found
elsewhere in the New Testament. In this regard, Fr. Boismard (*Quatre
hynmes baptismales . . .*, 22) observes that there are two series of texts:
in the tradition represented by I Pet 1, 22-23; 3, 23; Jas 1, 17-18; Jn 1,

B) THE PRESENT TEXT: "UNLESS A MAN BE BORN AGAIN OF WATER AND THE SPIRIT . . ."

The necessity of Christian baptism having been announced by Jesus and become a current practice of the Church, we can understand why John added something to the original text to indicate in a more complete way the conditions necessary for entrance into the kingdom. All the more so, since this passage is part of a larger whole, where the subject of baptism is brought up several times (1, 25-33; 3, 22, 23, 26; 4, 1, 2). But we will see that the interpretation just given for the old formula "to be born of the Spirit" is hardly modified; however, the insertion of the words *hydatos kai* does mean that the two fundamental conditions of Christian initiation are now indicated in the text: faith *and* baptism.

That faith and baptism are the two basic requirements for entrance into Christianity is a common teaching throughout the New Testament. It will be enough to recall here a few essential texts. It is in the synoptics that we find the most important indications: thus we have good reason to believe that this teaching comes substantially from Jesus himself. But it is important to note that it was proclaimed only at the very end of his life, during his appearances after the resurrection. This shows that it would be anachronistic to refer the promulgation of this teaching back to the conversation with Nicodemus, at the beginning of the public life. It is only in the conclusion of Mark's gospel

12-13; I Jn 3, 9, the Word of God is the principle of regeneration; on the other hand, in Pauline theology (Rom 8, 15-16; Gal 4, 6; Tit 3, 5), the new birth is attributed to the Spirit. But must the two points of view be disassociated? Just as the Spirit acts in us by the word of God, it is he who arouses in us belief in the word and makes the word efficacious. In our view, a text like Jn 3, 5, with the Johannine parallels cited above, makes possible a synthesis of the two lines of interpretation. One very interesting detail confirms our point of view: for the passage of I Pet 1, 22, one of the fundamental texts for the first theme (that of regeneration by the word), an important fraction of the manuscript tradition has added the words *dia pneumatos* after *tēs alētheias*: "having purified your souls by obeying *the truth* under the action of *the Spirit*"; here, the two lines of interpretation clearly conjoin.

that Jesus orders his apostles: "Go into the whole world and preach the gospel to every creature. He who *believes* and is *baptized* shall be saved, but he who does not believe shall be condemned" (Mk 16, 15-16; see Mt 28, 19).

The same teaching appears in the Acts: it is only after belief in the preaching of the Gospel that the neophytes receive baptism. Thus, for example, at Samaria: "But when they believed Philip as he preached the kingdom of God and the name of Jesus Christ, they were baptized, both men and women" (Ac 8, 12).[72] St. Paul is no less explicit: "And in him you too, when you had heard the word of truth, the good news of your salvation, and believed in it, were sealed with the Holy Spirit of the promise . . ." [= the seal of baptism] (Eph 1, 13). "Now it is God . . .who has anointed us with faith, who has also stamped us with his seal" [in baptism] (II Cor 1, 21-22).[73]

Elsewhere in his writings, John himself also emphasizes the close relationship between faith and baptism with regard to salvation. In recounting the incident of the lance on Calvary, the evangelist attaches special importance to the fact that water and blood came forth from Jesus' side (19, 34-36): for him, they symbolize the salutary efficaciousness of Christ's sacrifice, an efficaciousness which becomes operative in the Church, in the two great sacraments of baptism and the Eucharist. But to complete the ecclesial and sacramental meaning of this account, John adds a verse (v. 37) and a scriptural citation (Zech 12, 10), to emphasize what is expected from whoever is to receive the rewards of salvation: he must *look with faith* upon the one crucified. The same connection between faith and baptism is found most likely in the famous passage of the three witnesses (I Jn 5, 6-8). The triple witness, that of the Spirit, water, and blood, is situated in the context of the conditions required for entry into the Church: the witness of the Spirit indicates the anointing by faith, the water designates baptism, and the blood the Eucharist.[74] Thus, for

72. See Acts 8, 36-37 (Vulgate); 16, 14-15, 30-33; 18, 8; 19, 4-5.
73. On this interpretation of *echrisen* as the anointing of faith, see "L'onction du chrétien par la foi," in *Bibl.*, 40 (1959), 12-69 (for II Cor 1, 21-22, 14-30). See also pp. 82ff. in the present volume.
74. See *art. cit.*, in *Sacra Pagina*, II, 202-207. This interpretation was fully

John as well as for the other authors of the New Testament, the
role of faith in the reception of the sacraments is of the highest
importance; and the infusion of this faith is essentially attributed
by him to the action of the Spirit.

If we recall these different parallels, the interpretation of Jn
3, 5 no longer presents any difficulty: "Amen, amen, I say to thee,
unless a man be born again, he cannot see the kingdom of God."
We have here the same teaching as in Jn 19, 35 and I Jn 5, 6-8:
to enter into the kingdom, a new birth is required, and this is
effected in us by the baptism of *water* and by the *Spirit* who gives
us faith.

However, in contrast to what we said for the verse of the
three witnesses and the various New Testament passages cited
above, the mentioning of the Spirit (or elsewhere, faith) comes
after that of the water.[75] The reason for this, we believe, is simple:
here John no longer wishes, as in the other texts, to describe the
very moment of Christian initiation, where faith is a condition
of baptism. Rather, he wishes, as our analysis has shown, to give
a complete description of the Christian's life of faith; he wants
to show under what conditions a person passes from a very human and external faith, such as that of the Jews, to a life directed
by the Spirit. Even for a Christian, this is still a long way from
being achieved at the moment of his initial conversion and baptism. The evangelist is stressing the necessity for *progress in the*

accepted by Fr. Braun in his second edition of the epistles of John, in
the *Bible de Jérusalem* (234, n. b).

75. In the only Syrian version of Sinai, the inverse order is used: "of the
Spirit and water." What caused this inversion is perhaps the following:
in the liturgy of the Syrian Church, one of the most important rites was
a *prebaptismal* anointing, which was frequently related to the *Holy Spirit*.
Such an anointing was probably intended to symbolize the action of the
Spirit, who gives neophytes, before baptism, understanding of mysteries,
or the gift of faith; see *L'onction du chrétien par la foi*, 54-64 (see in
the present volume pp. 124ff.). In such a context we can understand
how the author of this version, in order to put the Gospel text in direct
agreement with the practices of his church, put the Spirit before the
water; but he thereby implied the, for himself, the Spirit's role was
precisely to stimulate faith — an exact exegesis of the text.

life of faith after one's conversion (see Mt 28, 19b-20). Thus, it is natural that he should have put *pneumatos* after *hydatos*, for after baptism it is the continuous action of the Spirit that will play the major role in the Christian's life. This is clear for another reason, the time difference for the verb *gennasthai* in vv. 3-8: it is not without reason that the verb is first used in the aorist in vv. 3 (repeated in v. 7), 4, 5; but in vv. 6 (*bis*) and 8, it is used only in the perfect: *to* (*ho*) *gegennēmenon* (*s*). Here, St. John no longer wishes to speak of the past moment of the new birth received in baptism, but to indicate the end of a development which a person should attain—complete conversion. He is describing a state to be reached, namely, the transformation, gradually achieved, from carnal man to spiritual man. Only the latter should be understood in the words of Jesus at the end of the second discourse: *ho gegennēmenos ek tou pneumatos* (v. 8); such a person is entirely docile to the movements of the Spirit, he is "born of the Spirit," he is himself spirit (v. 6).[76]

This doctrine is a profound one from both a theological and a spiritual viewpoint.[77] The importance of baptism is in no way

---

76. We should also recall a stylistic trait of John's which M. Barth has examined (*Die Taufe — ein Sakrament?* 443-445), namely, the use of coupled words ("Begriffspaare"): according to the author, the *kai* that unites the two words in this construction is an explanatory *kai*; thus, we should read Jn 3, 5: "water, that is, the Spirit." But Barth exaggerates the importance of the explanatory *kai* in St. John: in most of the examples he cites, the meaning of *kai* is different (e.g., 3, 11; 4, 23; 5, 24; 6, 69; 17, 3).

What is true, is that frequently in this construction the second term is the most important and carries the emphasis, for example, 4, 48: *sēmeia kai terata* (only instance of *teras* in St. John, to characterize Jewish belief in miracles: attraction mainly by *prodigies*); 6, 45: *pas ho akousas para tou patros kai mathōn*. This is also true of 3, 5: *gennēthēi ex hydatos kai pneumatos*, for only the word *pneuma* will be repeated in the following three verses.

77. It is understandable why a spiritual writer like Fr. Libermann, whose thought is strongly influenced by the Fourth Gospel, should read this verse as an invitation to open ourselves to the action of the Spirit in our souls; see his *Commentaire de saint Jean* (Desclée de Brouwer, 1958), 133: "After our baptism, the Holy Spirit dwells within us in a dynamic, life-giving way; he is there to become the principle of all the movements of our soul, and thus becomes, as it were, the author of our soul. It is

minimized: baptism of water remains the fundamental condition for entering into the kingdom of God. But the evangelist does not confine himself to this: to the necessity of the sacrament, he adds that of a renewal in faith—*a man must not only be born of water, he must be born of the Spirit too.* For as often happens in his Gospel,[78] St. John is emphasizing the necessity of a deepening of the life of faith, of the new life directed by the Spirit. This theme appears once more in the concluding verses of the chapter, where they are actually a summation of the whole dialogue: "For he whom God has sent speaks the *words* of God, for *not by measure does God give the Spirit*. . . . He who *believes* in the Son has everlasting life; he who is unbelieving towards the Son *shall not see life* . . ." (v. 34, 36).[79]

> up to us to be influenced and motivated by him and to follow more or less his holy impulses, according to the grace that is in us and the good dispositions that we have. The more the Holy Spirit becomes the principle of the movements of our soul, the more influence he has on its feelings and tendencies, the more he is heeded, the more perfect is his life in us, and the more holy we are."

78. See also Jn 8, 30-32; 14, 10-12; 15, 26; 16, 4, 13-15; 20, 29.
79. Is it not significant that according to this text (see also 6, 63) the action of the *Spirit* is identified with the communication of God's *words* by Jesus? The Spirit's work consists in instilling these words in believers' hearts and thereby arousing faith: the object of such faith is the truth brought by Jesus.

CONCLUSION

We now understand that one cannot ignore the critical problem raised by certain critics. Between the dialogue of Jesus with Nicodemus and the writing of the Gospel text appear the final preaching of Jesus, the sacramental practice of the early Church, and the teaching of the Apostle John. Together with several modern critics, one must admit that the verse of Jn 3, 5 very probably reflects this long Christian tradition; it is difficult to consider the word *hydatos* as part of the original expression.

The present text evidently refers to baptism. But opinion differs as to the relationship that exists between "water" and "the Spirit." There has been a rather strong tendency in the history of exegesis to subordinate the second term (*pneumatos*) to the first (*hydatos*), that is, to refer all the activity of the Spirit to that which he exerts in the sacrament of baptism.[80] The text of the evangelist does not support this interpretation. For it is certain that John is talking above all of a prolonged action of the Spirit,

---

80. One of the most typical examples of an almost exclusively ritualistic interpretation of our text is in *Pseudo-Clementine*. When Jn 3, 5 is cited, the word "spirit" is simply omitted; the emphasis falls only on "the water" of baptism: "Quid confert aquae baptismus ad Dei cultum? Prime quidem, quia quod Deo placuit impletur; secundo, quia regenerate ex aquis et Deo renate, fragilitas prioris nativitatis . . . amputatur, et ita demum pervenire poteris ad salutem, aliter vere impossibile est. Sic enim . . . verus Propheta testatus est dicens: *Amen, dico vobis, nisi quis denuo renatus fuerit ex aqua, non intrabit in regnum coelorum.* Et ideo accelerate, est enim in aquis istis misericordiae vis quaedam, quae ex initio ferebatur super aquas . . . Confugite ergo ad aquas istas, solae sunt enim quae possunt vim futuri ignis exstinguere; ad quas qui moratur accedere, constat in eo infidelitatis adhuc idolum permanere, et ab ipso prohiberi

both before baptism and throughout the whole span of the Christian's life. In his eyes, this action consists essentially of developing in us the life of faith: it is insofar as we respond to this action that we will be "born of the Spirit." *The life of the believer is a life according to the Spirit.*

Among the different interpretations given to this verse, we have already stated our own preference.

We must ally ourselves with the tradition represented by the *Shepherd of Hermas,* Justin, Irenaeus, Origen, Augustine, and the best representatives of medieval exegesis, who distinguished clearly a twofold supernatural causality: that of baptism, and that of the Spirit, exercised in the life of faith. Does this mean that, for John, faith and baptism are two parallel and independent realities? By no means. Their close relationship is suggested by the fact that they are always mentioned together each time John speaks of the sacrament of initiation. But the evangelist does not see this relationship as do later theologians: he does not describe faith directly as a gift received at baptism. For him, faith precedes (I Jn 5, 6), accompanies (Jn 19, 34-35), and follows (Jn 3, 5) the reception of Christian baptism, and it is to the description of this life of faith that he gives all his attention.

This interpretation is important in that it puts into clear focus the role of the believer in sacramental life. The new birth is not only the effect of a rite; in addition to the objective action of the sacrament, Jn 3, 5 underscores the subjective role of whoever receives it, the attitude of faith. The man who is called to become a child of God, must dispose himself toward this by faith; only a continual development of the life of faith will make of him a real child of God (Jn 1, 12), a man "taught by God" (Jn 6, 45), a man "born of the Spirit." And if anyone should object that this emphasis on the role of the believer diminishes God's role in the work of sanctification—since a man's willingness to receive is after all an attitude stemming from himself—the words *ek pneumatos* of Jn 3, 5 remind us that the attitude of faith is essentially, at all times, a gift of the Spirit.

---

ad aquas quae salutem conferunt, properare" (*Recogn.,* VI, 9, *P.G.,* 1, 1352); see the parallel text of *Homelies* (*Hom.,* XI, 24-26; ed. Resch, 166-167).

II

"Sin Is Iniquity" (I Jn 3, 4) *

The interpretation of this difficult, yet important verse of the First Epistle of St. John seems to have reached an impasse. Yet it must be overcome, for it is one of the key texts for the Johannine theology of sin. One of the more recent commentaries on the Epistle, that of R. Schnackenburg,[1] tried to move the interpretation in a new direction, which we think is a good one; but not have sufficiently explored it, he deemed it impracticable, and returned to the prevailing exegesis. Several authors, however, have declared the latter inadequate. We would like to take up the question once again, and try to support with new arguments the explanation once undertaken by Schnackenburg. We hope to show that this is the only one that corresponds not only to the

---

* This article first appeared in *Nouv. Rev. Théol.*, 78 (1956), 785-797. We have here added a few corrections and two more important modifications (see pp. 49 and 51ff., regarding the concrete identification of iniquity).

1. R. Schnackenburg, *Die Johannesbriefe* (Herders theologischer Kommentar zum N. T. XIII/3), (Freiburg, 1953), 164-165; 2nd ed., 1963, 185-187. What we say further on in the text is true only for the first edition; in the second, the author adopted the eschatological explanation of the verse, which we shall here present.

vocabulary of the New Testament period, but also to the context of the Epistle and the general thought of St. John regarding sin. First, let us put the verse in its context (3, 1-10):

1. Behold what manner of love the Father has bestowed upon us, that we should be called children of God; and such we are . . .
2. Beloved, now we are the children of God, and it has not yet appeared what we shall be. We know that, when he appears, we shall be like to him, for we shall see him just as he is.
3. And everyone who has this hope in him makes himself holy, just as he [Jesus] is holy.
4. Everyone who commits sin [*tēn hamartian*] commits iniquity [*tēn anomian*] also; and sin [*hē hamartia*] is iniquity [*hē anomia*].
5. And you know that he appeared to take our sins away, and sin is not in him.
6. No one who abides in him commits sin; and no one who sins has seen him, or has known him.
7. Dear children, let no one lead you astray. He does what is just even as he is just.
8. He who commits sin is of the devil, because the devil sins from the beginning. To this end the Son of God appeared, that he might destroy the works of the devil.
9. Whoever is born of God does not commit sin, because his seed abides in him and he cannot sin, because he is born of God.
10. In this the children of God and the children of the devil are made known. Whoever is not just is not of God. . . .

The interpretation of v. 4 depends on the meaning given to the word *anomia*. Almost all exegetes of recent times have translated it as: violation of the law, scorn for the law, or illegality.[2] Most

---

2. Thus the French translations or commentaries of Segond, Fillion, Crampon, Calmes, Loisy, Osty, Goguel-Monnier, Chaine, Bonsirven, the *Bible du*

also add that St. John has in mind here heretics of the Gnostic school, who considered themselves free from all law. This is, for example, the explanation of M. Goguel in the *Bible du Centenaire*: "A difficult text. Is not sin synonymous with violation of the law? It is possible that the author is thinking of those who took sin lightly and put sin outside the sphere of morality. To this tendency, he would oppose the rigor of divine law, such as the true disciples of Jesus conceive it, a law that does not tolerate sin."

But this explanation is beset by many problems. In the context, the question of law does not arise, and, as Brooke pointed out, if such were really the author's thought, he would have written exactly the opposite, namely: "the transgression of the law is sin," as St. Peter would one day say to the gnostics in *Pseudo-Clementine*: "Omne mandatum praeterire peccatum est."[3] Furthermore, one must ask what law St. John would have in mind. For the word *anomia* refers to *nomos*. But in the Johannine writings, the latter is applied exclusively to the Mosaic law. This is not the case here. Some exegetes (Brooke, Gutbrod) think it is a question here of

Centenaire, the *Bible de Jérusalem* (section on St. John, first edition), that of *Maredsous*, and two articles: one by P. Galtier, "Le chrétien impeccable" (*I Jean 3, 6 et 9*), in *Mél. de sc. relig.*, 4 (1947), 149; the other by M.-E. Boismard, "La connaissance de Dieu dans l'Alliance nouvelle d'après la première lettre de S. Jean," in *Rev. bibl.*, 56 (1949), 379, n. 1. Dutch authors use "schennis der wet" (*Canisiusuitgave*), "wetsverloochening" (Ned. Bijbeluitg.), "onwettigheid" (Poukens) or "wetsovertreding" (Keulers); Germans use "Gesetzwidrigkeit" or "Gesetzlosigkeit" (B. Weiss, Belser, Windisch, Meinertz-Vrede, Büchsel, Hauck, Kuss-Michl, and Schnackenburg in his first edition); the English use "lawlessness" (Lias, Westcott, Plummer, Brooke, Dodd, Ross the *Catholic Commentary*, and the *Westminster Version*) or "to break God's law" (*New English Bible*).

But among recent authors there is now a rather definite tendency to use some aspect of the meaning of "iniquity." Charue (followed by the *Bible du Card. Liénart*) accepted this translation, explaining it as "transgression of the divine will." The translation "iniquity," with its eschatological nuance, was accepted by F.-M. Braun in the second edition of the *Bible de Jérusalem*, in the new edition of Schnackenburg's commentary (1963), and in *Het Nieuwe Testament van O.H.J.C.* (Willibrordvertaling), (Bruges, 1961), 692: "de zonde *is* de boosheid."

3. *Recogn.*, VII, 37 (P.G., 1, 1369 D).

the Christian law of charity; this is highly unlikely since John always uses the word *entolē*, and in the present context nothing brings to mind that new law. Finally, most writers restrict themselves to saying that it is a question here of law in general, as an expression of the divine will. But such an identification of the will of God and law brings us to natural morality, an idea that seems little related to the biblical vocabulary.

What is presupposed in all these attempted explanations is that *anomia* must necessarily mean: transgression of the law, as the etymology indicates. But properly speaking, one should begin his study by examining the exact meaning the term had at the time, namely, in Judaism around the first century and in early Christianity. R. Schnackenburg did make some progress in this area, but there is need for further study.

MEANING OF THE WORD "INIQUITY" IN THE NEW TESTAMENT PERIOD

We can distinguish three stages in the semantic evolution of the word *anomia*. In the classical texts, it is the original meaning of "transgression of the law" that is common, for example, in the chorus of Euripides: "Illegality triumphs over the laws,"[4] or in the speech of Demosthenes: "Is it right to call that a law [*nomon*], or rather is it not a challenging of the laws (*anomian*)?"[5] From this, one passes easily to the meaning of anarchy, disorder, of which we also have evidence.[6] In almost all instances, the word is used in the singular.

The Greek Bible

The Greek Bible marks a new stage. With *anomia*, it translates about twenty different Hebrew words, most of which refer to sin in one way or another. But the direct connection with the word

---

4. Euripides, *Iphigenia in Aulis*, 1095: *anomia de nomon kratei.*
5. Demosthenes, *Against Timocratus*, 152.
6. For example, Plato, *Republic*, IX, 575 a.

law disappears. *Anomia* becomes practically synonymous with *hamartia;* these are the two main terms used by the Septuagint in speaking of sin.[7] These two terms are often found in the plural, to designate individual acts of sin;[8] but the reduction of a very varied Hebrew vocabulary to two Greek words does away with several different nuances. Nevertheless, we observe here the early appearance of one aspect of the term which will become more pronounced later on, namely, the satanic coloration of *anomia*. Indeed, on two occasions (II Sam 22, 5; Ps 17, 4), this term was chosen by the Alexandrine translators to express in Greek the Hebrew word *Belial*.

Judaism

But later Judaism and early Christianity above all deserve our attention. Here, the word *anomia* is used in two rather different contexts. First of all, the usage of the Septuagint continues in Hellenistic Judaism, that is, the term is a simple equivalent of *hamartia*.[9] The same is true of some of the early Christian writers.[10] Here also, there is no question of law. The New Testament also contains this usage, but it is remarkable that *anomia* is found in the plural only in the citations from the Old Testament (Rom 4, 7 = Ps 31, 1; Hebr 10, 17 = Jer 31, 34). In other instances, the term has for the authors of the New Testament a new resonance.

In fact, this new aspect is seen in many texts, Jewish as well as

---

7. Schnackenburg, *op. cit.*, 165, n. 1, cites as examples certain texts in which the two words are parallel: Ps 31, 1; 50, 4; 58, 4; 102, 10.
8. Kittel, *Theol. Wört.*, IV, 1078 (art. by Gutbrod). What we have just said shows already that it is hardly possible to explain satisfactorily the New Testament use of *anomia* (in particular, in I Jn 3, 4), beginning with the LXX, as A. Argyle tried to do in *Exp. Tim.*, 65 (November, 1953), 62-63. Since in the Greek Bible there is still practically no difference between the two words *hamartia* and *anomia*, it cannot be used to justify the explanation of the first term by the second in St. John's text.
9. For example, *Henoch* (Greek text, ed. Campbell-Bonner), 97, 6; 98, 1; *Ps. of Salomon*, 1, 8; 2, 3, 13; 9, 13; 15, 21 (in the plural, in all these texts); and 15, 9 where *hoi poiountes anomian* is the equivalent of *hamartōloi; Test. of Levi*, 2, 3; *Test. of Dan*, 3, 2.
10. I *Clem.*, 8, 3; 16, 5, 9; 18, 3, 5; 35, 5; 50, 6; 60, 1; *Shepherd of Hermas*, *Vis.*, II, 2, 2; *Mand.*, X, 3, 2; *Sim.*, 7, 2.

Christian. *Anomia,* which can be translated here at "iniquity," corresponds to the Hebrew *áwel* or *áwlah*. It is always used in the singular, for it no longer signifies individual sin but a collective state. It is essentially an eschatological term that designates the hostility and revolt of the forces of evil against the kingdom of God in the last days of the world; such hostility is characterized by its satanic aspect, by the control that is exercised by the devil.

One passage from the Testaments of the Twelve Patriarchs show this with utmost clarity. The patriarch Dan predicts to his sons the great defection at the end of the world:

> I know that in the last days you will move away from the Lord and will rage against Levi and oppose Judah. . . . I read in the book of Enoch the just that your prince is Satan. . . . [And he warns them]: Fear the Lord and beware of Satan and his spirits; . . . on the day when Israel will be converted, the dominion of the adversary will be over. But the angel of peace will fortify Israel in order that it may not fall in the last dangers [*eis telos kakon*]. But in the time of Israel's iniquity [*en kairōi tēs anomias tou Israēl*], the Lord will not abandon them but will transform them into a nation that does his will (*Test. of Dan*, 5, 4-6).[11]

The use of the word iniquity with this characteristic nuance is frequent in the new manuscripts of Qumran, especially in the *Manual of Discipline*. We must remember that the theology of the Dead Sea sect is clearly eschatological and dualistic. They are convinced they are living in the final days that will precede the Messianic era. They are the chosen community, the new Covenant, the party of God; they are in complete opposition to those outside, who are the children of darkness, the party of Belial.

This dualistic grouping is due to the action of the two spirits whom God has put at the head of humanity: "They are the spirits of truth and iniquity. In a fountain of light is the origin of truth, and in one of darkness is the origin of iniquity. In the hand of the Prince of Light is the control over all the sons of justice . . . ; and in the hand of the Angel of darkness is the complete control over

---

11. See also *Test. de Nepht.*, 4, 1.

the sons of iniquity" (I *QS,* III, 18-21).[12] "Until then [i.e., until the eschatological judgment] the spirits of truth and iniquity will struggle over the hearts of men" (*ibid.,* IV, 23). "[The world] is drawn to unholiness by the power of iniquity, up until the time of the last judgment" (*ibid.,* IV, 19-20). Note here how truth and iniquity are considered to be two opposite domains, where two different forces are at work. The text speaks indiscriminately of the empire of the Angel of darkness or the empire of iniquity. Iniquity is thus seen under its satanic aspect.[13]

What is the relationship of iniquity to personal sin? This point directly affects the interpretation of St. John's verse. The last text cited puts us on the right track: iniquity is considered to be a satanic power under whose influence impiety is committed. The following text reduces sin quite clearly to a diabolic influence: "All their revolts and their sins are brought about by the power of Belial" (I *QS,* I, 23-24). Iniquity, therefore, should not be identified simply with sins; it is the secret quality, the spirit, the tendency that inspires and provokes them. If individual sins are aroused by this diabolic power, they are at the same time the manifestation of it: "To the spirit of iniquity belong greed, injustice, impiety and lying, pride and the inflation of the heart, pretense and deceit, etc." (I *QS,* IV, 9). In itself, iniquity is basically an "abomination of the truth" (*ibid.,* IV, 17), but it is translated into various acts which show their evil origin quite clearly.

Truth and iniquity are the fundamental characteristics of two hostile groups. They indicate two ways of being, of belonging to two different worlds. The names by which their adherents are designated underscore this belongingness. The children of darkness are called: "children of iniquity" (I *QS,* III, 20; I *QH,* V, 8), "descendants of iniquity" (I *QMyst,* I, 1, 5), "men of iniquity"

---

12. Let us recall the abbreviations used to designate the Qumran manuscripts: *I QS* = Manual of Discipline; *I QH* = Hymns (ed. in *The Dead Sea Scrolls of the Hebrew University* [Jerusalem, 1955]); *I QSb* = Book of Benedictions; *I QMyst* = Book of Mysteries. The last two works were published in *Discoveries in the Judean Desert, I: Qumran Cave I* (Oxford, 1955).

13. See *I QH,* III, 12, 18, the symbolic trait of the woman who brings to life the forces of evil: she gives birth to the viper (12), but also iniquity (18).

(I *QS*, V, 2, 10; X, 20), "the generation of iniquity" (I *QSb*, III, 7). Most of these names allude to the "birth" of such men, to their origin, that is, to the control they experience from a being or principle, which is Belial, the Angel of darkness.

This division of men derive, therefore, from an identical division in the spiritual world, where the spirit of iniquity is opposed to the spirit of truth. In this sense, one may speak correctly of iniquity as a cosmic principle.[14]

The eschatological dualism of the sect is manifested in a concrete way in the total separation that exists between its members and those on the outside. This is one of the rules which the *Manual of Discipline* stresses very often: "Let them stay away from the men of iniquity" (I *QS*, V, 1-2); "Let not their wealth come in contact with that of the men of deceit, who have not purified their lives by freeing themselves from iniquity" (*ibid.*, IX, 8-9). The first attitude one should have in the eschatological age is contained in the following maxim: "Stay away from whoever has not turned away from all iniquity" (*ibid.*, IX, 20-22; see also X, 20).

The New Testament

If we examine the New Testament, we observe that the eschatological meaning of *anomia* appears most often. In the Gospels, only Matthew uses the term. As B. Rigaux notes correctly: "It is remarkable that it is always in a Messianic context."[15] Indeed, in the first two texts (Mt 7, 23; 13, 41) it is a question of the final judgment: those who commit iniquity will be thrown into the furnace of fire. The first of these two passages, a citation from Ps 6, 9, has in the Gospel context a strong eschatological coloration which it did not have in the Old Testament. The agents of *iniquity* are the false prophets (7, 15), whose appearance is one of the distinctive signs

14. J. Licht, "The Doctrine of the Thanksgiving Scroll," in *Isr. Explor. Journ.*, 6 (1956), 6.

15. B. Rigaux, *L'Antéchrist* (Gembloux, 1932), 255; the eschatological aspect of the word *anomia* was seen very clearly by G. Kittel, "Der Jakobusbrief und die Apostolischen Väter," in *Z.N.T.W.*, 43 (1950-51), 54-112 (see 74); see also W. Nauck, *Die Tradition und der Charakter des ersten Johannesbriefes* (Tübingen, 1957), 16, n. 1.

of the end of the world; they are also those who provoke scandal (13, 41) and who lead men astray. Another text mentions among the signs of the end of the world the fact that the charity of many will grow cold, because iniquity will arise once again (Mt 24, 12); here too, the workers of *iniquity* are identified with the false prophets who cause many to fall away (v. 11). In speaking to the Pharisees, Christ says that they are full of hypocrisy and iniquity (Mt 23, 28), but here too the point of view is eschatological: the hypocritical Pharisees are those who close off the kingdom of Heaven to men (23, 13); and the rest of the chapter evokes the great reality of the final punishment: "Serpents, brood of vipers, how are you to escape the judgment of hell?" (v. 33). The invective, "brood of vipers," too often explained in a simply psychological or moral way, has a clearly eschatological meaning; it designates those who belong to the serpent, the symbol of infernal powers.[16]

As to St. Paul, let us simply note that he calls the Antichrist "the man of iniquity" (II Thess 2, 3) and his secret hostility to the kingdom of God "the mystery of iniquity" (*ibid.*, v. 7).

One very interesting text is the beginning of the end of Mark in manuscript W. It can be used to summarize the main aspects of iniquity already indicated: "This age of iniquity and unbelief [*ho aiōn houtos tēs anomias kai tēs apïstias*] is under the domination of Satan, who prevents whoever is under the yoke of impious spirits from receiving the truth and power of God." Thus in most works of this period *anomia* is used to describe the state of hostility toward God at the end of the world.

Let us remember two items: first, the idea of the transgression of a law, common in classical times, is here completely absent from the term; we have seen no passage where the words iniquity and

---

16. Invective had already been used by John the Baptist (Mt 3, 7; Lk 3, 7), and by Christ himself on another occasion (Mt 12, 34), each time in a judgment context. Thus the exegesis is oriented in the wrong direction when one tries to explain the image by an allusion to the ruse of vipers or to their venom. The eschatological use of the symbol of the viper is found in the texts of Qumran: *Doc. de Damas*, VIII, 9-11; XIX, 22-23, and above all in the hymn we already spoke about (*I QH*, III, 1-18), which contrasts the mother of the male Infant and the mother of the Viper. See Kittle, *Theol. Wört.*, V, 678, 21-30.

law belong to the same context. What is in opposition to iniquity, is the plan, the will of God (see the first text of the *Testaments of the Twelve Patriarchs* cited above, p. 41f.). The word that ordinarily signifies the divine plan is not "the law," but "the truth." Secondly, in most texts iniquity appears under its satanic aspect: it is the domination of Satan that operates in the world, and to which all the children of iniquity are subject. Their individual acts of impiety are but a manifestation of a more profound state; they make clear the power of darkness that operates within them.[17]

"INIQUITY" IN THE FIRST EPISTLE OF JOHN

Let us now return to the verse of the First Epistle of St. John. One should not distinguish *a priori* the use of the word *anomia* from the simple meaning of *hamartia,* since this was the meaning it had in the Greek Bible and since it is found in a few authors of the first two centuries. But in the present context this meaning is impossible, unless one wishes St. John to engage in a pure tautology. The formula itself—*hē hamartia estin hē anomia*—presupposes a progression of thought; the second term should have a new meaning, which is not contained in the first. A similar nuance might well be present in the eschatological meaning of *anomia* described above. Obviously, we should not advance this meaning *a priori* and in an extrinsic way, but should analyze the phrase carefully to see if this meaning is the right one. Actually, we shall see that the eschatological nuance of the term is naturally called for by the context, and gives v. 4 an excellent meaning.

Eschatological Meaning of Anomia

As P. Galtier has noted very well,[18] section 2, 29-3, 10 form a unit, clearly circumscribed by an inclusion. The initial formula ex-

---

17. This inquiry can be pursued in early Christianity. There too the word iniquity is used regularly in the eschatological sense; see *Didache*, 16, 3, 4; *Ep. of Barnabas*, 4, 1; 14, 5; 15, 5-7; 18, 2.
18. P. Galtier, "Le chrétien impeccable," in *Mél. de sc. relig.*, 4 (1947), 143-144.

presses the theme in a positive way, and the final formula repeats it in a negative way: "Everyone who does what is just has been born of him" (2, 29); "Whoever is not just is not of God" (3, 10)

The theme expressed in these two verses is developed further in the intermediary verses. We can express it as follows: the children of God and the children of the devil, and the way in which they manifest their belonging to one group or the other. Let us note that the theme of filiation is but a repetition or variant of the general theme of the Epistle—communion with God (1, 3).

To grasp the development of thought in this passage, we should recall the literary structure used by St. John. P. Boismard has studied it in a remarkable essay[19] which shows the essential importance in the Epistle of an invisible spiritual reality, which is made manifest by an external sign, namely, the moral conduct of whoever calls himself a Christian. "Henceforth, the essential aim of the Epistle is not to present a teaching on the necessity of faith and franternal love for obtaining divine life, but to point out clearly who they are who truly possess within themselves divine life, communion with God."[20] In other words, the proper theme of the Epistle is not an exhortation of Christians to the practice of virtues or the avoidance of sin, but the announcement of a profound spiritual reality which they bear within them, and the visible manifestations of which the author makes clear.

This reality is *divine filiation*. It is briefly described in 3, 1-2 (and already in 2, 29): through a gift of divine love, we are the sons of God. However, this many-faceted life still remains hidden. It will become clear only in the next life, when we will be like unto Christ, the Son of God.

In an antithetical way, vv. 3-10 show the concrete attitudes dictated by this mysterious reality of the Christian life. St. John is fond of great contrasts: he opposes the children of God and the children of the devil, and describes their respective moral conduct. Such conduct serves to point out to which of the two groups men belong. Furthermore, for the group of God's children, a reference

19. M.-E. Boismard, "La Connaissance dans l'Alliance nouvelle d'après la première lettre de saint Jean," in *Rev. Bibl.* 56 (1949), 371-376.
20. *Ibid.*, 375.

to Christ is regularly added; for him also, as well as for the Christian and as an example for the latter, is mentioned either a state: "he is holy" (v. 3), "he is without sin" (v. 5), "he is just" (v. 7); or his salvific work: "to take away sins" (v. 5), "to destroy the works of the devil" (v. 8). Likewise, for the other group, is indicated the action of the devil: "he sins from the beginning" (v. 8). But for our own analysis, we may disregard the third term of the argument (the reference to Christ or the devil) and concentrate on the two aspects mentioned each time: the spiritual reality, and its external manifestation.

Here, first, is the series concerning the children of God. Each verse expresses both the internal spiritual reality and the moral conduct. We put in italics the words that describe the internal reality:

> And everyone who *has this hope in him* makes himself holy,
>   just as he also is holy (v. 3).
> No one who *abides in him* commits sin . . . (v. 6)
> He who does what is just *is just* (v. 7)
> Whoever *is born of God* does not commit sin . . . (v. 9).

All these phrases, expressed in either a positive or negative way, are basically equivalent. They consist each time of two parts; one describes the Christian's way of living: he does not sin, becomes holy, practices justice. The other indicates the profound reality that motivates and inspires such conduct: the Christian is he who is born of God, abides in him, possesses hope (in his likeness to Christ), and is just.

In contrast to the first group are mentioned, the children of the devil:

> Everyone who commits sin *commits iniquity also* (v. 4).
> And *no one* who sins *has seen him, or has known him* (v. 6).
> He who commits sin *is of the devil* (v. 8).
> Whoever is not just *is not of God* (v. 10).

Here too the correspondence in the four propositions is immediately evident, and even more distinct than in the preceding case. The second part of the proposition indicates each time the spiritual state of whoever commits sin or fails to practice justice. Four expressions are used to describe this mysterious reality: the sinner is not of God, has neither seen nor known him, is of the devil, and commits iniquity. From the parallelism of expressions "to know God" and "to abide in God," P. Boismard rightly concludes that in the Epistle knowledge of God must indicate more than a purely intellectual knowledge, and imply a participation in divine life, the possession of a divine principle.[21]

The same reasoning holds true for the marks that characterize the interior reality of the sinner. "Not having seen or known God" (v. 6b) is the same as "not being of God" (v. 10); "committing iniquity" must also be synonymous with "being of the devil" (v. 8) and the opposite of "being just" (v. 7). We can see, therefore, that the literary structure itself of the passage orients the interpretation of the word *iniquity* in v. 4 in a specific way. The term belongs to a series of expressions that describe the spiritual reality of the sinner, his situation, his interior state, and not so much the evil act he commits.

Unbelief and Iniquity

But about whom is John actually speaking? What is the specific *sin* (*hē hamartia*) which he describes as *iniquity*? For the whole passage clearly involves a polemical argument. According to many exegetes,[22] the author is thinking of heretics; on the contrary, R. Schnackenburg interprets the passage as directed against Christians who let themselves fall into sin. But it seems that this is only a false dilemma. The appellation "dear children" (v. 7) and the exhortation to abide in Christ (v. 6) show that John is talking directly to *believers;* but the sin he is warning against is the sin of *heretics.* He wants to prevent the faithful from being deceived

---

21. *Ibid.,* 381: "We just saw how all the expressions 'to be in communion with God,' 'to be born of God,' 'to remain in God and God in us,' finally 'to know God,' have in common the fact that they designate the same reality."

22. See the commentaries of Wendt, Chaine, Kohler; likewise, M. Goguel, *L'Eglise primitive* (Paris, 1947), 499: "Certainly he is thinking of a specific group of heretics when he expresses this axiom."

by the method that is characteristic of false teachers.

Several indications suggest such an interpretation. The passage 3, 3-10 is parallel to the section 1, 5-2, 2, where the exhortation addressed to the faithful regarding sin is made by the author because of a claim of false teachers, namely, that of believing themselves to be without sin. In 3, 4, 8 also, it is probably against heretical conduct that John warns believers. This is indicated explicitly in v. 7, where John exhorts them by saying: "Dear children, let no one lead you astray" (see Mk 13, 5). Leading men astray is one of the typical characteristics of the children of darkness in the eschatological dualism. We may recall that in St. Matthew the notion of iniquity and that of leading men astray often occur together, when it is a question of false prophets.

Another indication is even more important: contrary to what he will write in v. 9, where he will leave the word "sin" indefinite (*hamartian ou poiei*), in v. 4 and 8 John uses the more involved formula, with the article: *ho poiōn tēn hamartian* ("who commits *the* sin"), a construction that appears again only in Jn 8, 34 (see also Jn 1, 29). It is a matter, therefore, of a specific sin, one that is well known: in the dualistic and eschatological context of this passage, it can hardly be anything but the typical sin of the "Antichrists," who reject Christ, the Son of God (2, 22-23). It is the sin which the Fourth Gospel had described as *the* sin of the world: that of *not believing in Jesus* (Jn 16, 11; see also 1, 10-11; 8, 21, 24, 46; 15, 21-22). It is important, therefore, to distinguish this fundamental sin, this rejection of truth, from the different sins committed by Christians, and about which John speaks in 1, 5-2, 2. Later on, in 3, 4, he calls this fundamental sin *iniquity*.

In view of the above, the meaning of v. 3, 4 becomes quite clear. John wants to warn believers against the sin of the "children of the devil" (v. 10), to which even the faithful remain forever exposed. Whoever commits *the* sin, he says (i.e., the typical sin of heretics), commits not only a morally reprehensible act; he commits *iniquity*, thereby revealing that he is basically a son of the devil (v. 8), someone who is in direct opposition to Christ and God and who is under the control of Satan.

We thus return to the meaning of *iniquity* which was common in Jewish works of the time and in early Christianity. At first sight, however, there would seem to be a difference: has not the eschatological resonance of the term *anomia,* so clear in all those works, disappeared in the Epistle? It is enough to reread chapter 2 to be convinced of the contrary: "Dear children, it is the last hour" (2, 18); "And now, dear children, abide in him, so that when he appears we may have confidence, and may not shrink ashamed from him at his coming [*en tēi te parousiāi autou*]" (2, 28). The start of the following chapter (v. 2) offers us an eschatological view of the future life, and it is this view—that of Christian hope—which must guide our moral action.

V. 4, thus understood, fits perfectly into the context of the section 3, 1-10. It has an exact parallel in v. 8, a fact that has not been sufficiently noticed: "Everyone who commits sin commits *iniquity* also" (v. 4); "He who commits sin *is of the devil*" (v. 8).

Another parallelism is no less informative, that of vv. 5 and 8b, both of which describe the salvific work of Christ:

v. 5	v. 8
. . . He appeared to take our sins away	. . . The Son of God appeared, that he might destroy the works of the devil

Sins are considered here as works of the devil, "because the devil sins from the beginning" (v. 8). The relationship between sin and Satan's control is, therefore, stressed throughout sections 3, 1-10. The formula "sin is iniquity" is now quite clear. It is not a matter of a transgression of the law, since the idea of law is completely foreign to the context; nor should one think of the precept of charity or the systematic acceptance of sin, as P. Galtier did.[23] On the

---

23. *Art. cit.,* 149-151. The interpretation of the doctrine of the Christian's impeccability given by Fr. Galtier, is followed by Fr. Boismard (*art. cit.,* 379, note), but we cannot accept it. The sin in question here would be an unusually grave sin, moral indifferentism, which admits faults systematically and as a matter of principle. But this exegesis is based solely on the meaning given to *anomia*: "scorn for the law." We have already explained our thinking on the latter. Moreover, if this were the meaning, John would be misleading us: in our verse, *hē hamartia* is in the singular, with the article and without a complement, a usage which

contrary, John is thinking of *unbelief,* of rejection of the truth, just
like the author of the long ending in Mark, cited above (p. 000),
who brought together terms *anomia* and *apistia,* to explain the dis-
belief of the disciples after Easter, in a typically eschatological
context: "This age of *iniquity* and *unbelief.*" In branding this rejection of the truth as iniquity, St. John wants to stress all of its
eschatological importance: it is a rejection of the Messiah, of the
Son of God and his entire work of salvation. In explaining *hamartia*
by *anomia,* the author, therefore, is not guilty of tautology; rather,
he wishes to invite his fellow Christians to extend their moral point
of view to the theological and religious spheres, and to consider
the seriousness of non-belief and the refusal of light.

In short, it is not just any sin that St. John considers as "iniquity,"
but rather the attitude of the Antichrists, which for him is the sin
par excellence: the refusal to believe in Christ. But let us not think
that the sins of believers are in no way connected with this fundamental sin of heretics. Indeed, after talking of sin (v. 4: *tēn hamartian*), John passes at once to the *multiplicity of sins* (v. 5: *tas
hamartias*), although he returns later on to the great *reality of sin*
(v. 8a: *tēn hamartian*); on the other hand, we have seen that it is
the plural "sins" (v. 5) which is made parallel with "works of the
devil" (v. 8). Thus for St. John all sins more or less pertain to the
sin par excellence, i.e., not believing in Christ. Each sin, in different degrees, arises from a lessening of faith. Thus, in a certain
sense, all sin is a rejection of the great realities of salvation, a free
acceptance of Satan's domination, a sinking into darkness. He who
commits sin, is already living under Satan's perverse influence (I
Jn 5, 18-19) and becomes a child of the devil.[24]

is found elsewhere only in v. 8, a parallel to the present text, and in
Jn 8, 34; but in these two cases the diabolical nature of sin is quite
clear. Also in I Jn 3, 4 "the sin" must refer to this same reality. According
to the context, such sin is not the systematic acceptance of each and all
sin, "sin out of principle and scorn for law" (P. Galtier), but the Antichrists' sin of unbelief.

24. This conception may seem exaggerated, but it corresponds precisely with
St. John's point of view, which is a dualist one: the latter contrasts quite
clearly the children of light and the children of darkness, the children
of God and the children of the devil. We have already said how such a

THE JOHANNINE THEOLOGY OF SIN

In conclusion, we would like to offer a brief confirmation of the interpretation presented above. As we have explained it, the verse of I Jn 3, 4 brings together in a concise formula a concept of sin that is found in various places throughout the Gospel and Epistles of St. John.

In contrast to St. Paul or the synoptics, the author of the Fourth Gospel nowhere mentions a series of individual sins, such as steal-

dualist structure is characteristic of the apocalyptic literature.

In our view, the well-known verses of 3, 6-9 on the impeccability of the Christian should be interpreted in light of the above. They do not apply exclusively to the failures of those who sin deliberately, as Fr. Galtier thinks but to every serious sin. However, here St. John puts himself on the theological and mystical plane. He is reasoning from the divine realities that are in us, as is clearly understood by Severus of Antioch and St. Augustine, followed by Fr. Bonsirven, *Ep. de saint Jean,* 1954, 156-158: the Christian lives in a new spiritual milieu; he is subject to the perverse activity of Satan and to the work of God. If he is led by this divine action, he sins no more, and is even incapable of sin; as long as he lives as a son of God, that is, in harmony with the divine seed in him, he is assured of not sinning. The parallel with I Pet 1, 22-23, which Fr. Boismard calls our attention to (*R. B.,* 1956, 203-204), casts a new light on this passage. In I Pet, it is said that the incorruptible seed, by which we are born to a new life, is God's word; by obedience to the truth or to this word, the faithful sanctify their souls. In I Jn also, impeccability is explained as fidelity to an interior principle, obedience to the new law inscribed in the Christian's heart.

Fr. Galtier is thus wrong in seeing this explanation as tautological, as if it were reduced to this: when the Christian holds on to grace, he does not sin. Of course, on the logical and abstract plane, this would be a true tautology. But on the psychological and mystical planes of spiritual experience, these two propositions are no longer identical. We say to the Christian, not: "Do not sin, and you will remain in grace" (moral and ascetic point of view), but the reverse: "Remain close to God, follow the interior law within you, and you will sin no more" (mystical point of view). St. Paul gave a similar counsel: "Spiritu ambulate, et desideria carnis non perficietis" (Gal 5, 16; note the *fact* stated in the last verb). St. Ignatius of Antioch also speaks of impeccability for those who follow the law of the Spirit: "Carnales spiritualia exercere nequeunt, neque spirituales carnalia" (*Ad Eph.,* 8, 2); St. Augustine follows the same line of thought in his famous adage: "Ama, et quod vis fac." No doubt, a person can always forget to follow the Spirit's suggestions or to

ing, murder, adultery, etc. We might say that he rises to a higher level, from which he can encompass everything in one glance and reduce it all to one. His use of *hamartia* is striking in this regard. Out of 34 occasions (17 in the Gospel and 17 in the First Epistle), the term is used in the singular 25 times. Such usage is typical in the Fourth Gospel: the word "sin" is found in the plural in only three passages. In the first (8, 24), Jesus is talking to the Jews, but *hai hamartiai umon* only repeats in a more detailed way the singular *hē hamartia humōn* which precedes (8, 21). In 9, 34, which seems to be an exception, it is the Jews who are talking and it is their concept which is being expressed. Finally, the text of 20, 23 is no longer part of the public life, but is written from the viewpoint of the Church: the plural is used, as in several passages of the First Epistle, in a pastoral context. Thus we can say that the singular "sin" expresses the fundamental reality of sin, as the Fourth Gospel conceives it: man's negative response in his meeting with Christ. Also very characteristic of the Johannine vocabulary are the expressions "*to have* sin" (Jn 9, 41; 15, 22, 24; 19, 11; I Jn 1, 8), and the two others that describe sin as a permanent reality: "your sin remains" (Jn 9, 41), or as a state, "sin is not [*ouk estin*] in him" (I Jn 3, 5).

The beginning of this last text describes the work of Christ as "taking away sins." Here again, St. John uses the word in the plural, for in writing an epistle to a group of Christians, his point of view is pastoral. But when he considers Christ's work in a more theological way, he says through John the Baptist: "Behold, the lamb of God, who takes away *the sin* of the world" (Jn 1, 29), that is, who destroys the diabolic power of sin to which the world was subject. In the liturgy of the Mass, we read this text with the word sin in the plural, but St. John sees the world as a whole before

---

live in the state of love, and thereby will fall into sin. But it is legitimate, in the spiritual life, to ask Christians to rely above all on the realities of grace, to live always according to the Spirit, rather than following the inverse method of insisting first of all on moral effort to remain in the state of divine life.

On the above, see our study on "L'impeccabilite du chrétien d'après I Jn 3, 6-9," in *L'Evangile de Jean* (Desclée de Brouwer, 1958), 161-177 (see Chapter 6 in the present volume).

Christ, and the world has rejected Christ: that is its sin (Jn 6, 36; 15, 22). For the Fourth Gospel there is no other sin.

The acceptance or rejection of Christ is one of the major themes of Johannine thought, as is indicated in the very beginning of the prologue: "He was in the world . . . and the world knew him not. He came unto his own and his own received him not" (Jn 1, 10-11). By rejecting Christ, the world fell under the control of Satan, the prince of this world (Jn 12, 31; 14, 30; 16, 11; I Jn 5, 19); that is why, in a very real sense, he who commits sin becomes a slave (Jn 8, 34). Thus in the eyes of St. John sin is diabolic. This explains his tendency to relate the individual acts of the sinner to the great *reality of sin*, which is basically a refusal of light and truth,[25] an opting for darkness.

The verse of the First Epistle says nothing else but: "Everyone who commits sin commits iniquity also; and sin is iniquity." In teaching this to his fellow Christians, St. John wanted to show them the complete eschatological meaning of the sin of non-belief as a satanic power. At the same time, he was also inviting them to measure the tragic importance of this.

25. See P. Benoit, "Paulinisme et Johannisme," in *New Test. Stud.*, 9 (1962/63), 201.

III

The Paraclete[*]

The term "Paraclete,"[1] proper to St. John in the New Testament, is a word derived from the Greek,[2] but is rarely used in secular works. Ordinarily used in a juridical context, it designates any man who comes to the aid of someone, his assistant, his defender, or his advocate. Later Judaism borrowed the term from the Greek world, but gave it a more precise meaning: that of intercessor. Rabbinical texts use it exclusively to designate all those who

[*] This article (somewhat revised) first appeared in *Assemblées du Seigneur*, 47 (*Quatrième dimanche après Pâques*), Bruges, "Biblica," 1963, 37-55.
1. Much has been written on this subject. We recommend in particular: J. Huby, S.J., *Le Discours de Jésus après la Cène* (*Coll.* "Verbum Salutis"), new ed. (Paris, 1942); H. Van den Bussche, *La discours d'adieu de Jésus* (Coll. "Bible et vie chrét."), (Tournai-Paris, 1959); G.-M. Behler, O.P., *Les paroles d'adieux du Seigneur* (Coll. "Lectio divina," 27), (Paris, 1960). The following articles may also be consulted: M.-F. Berrouard, O.P., "Le Paraclet, Défenseur du Christ devant la conscience du croyant (Jn XVI, 8-11)," in *Rev. des scienc. philos. et théolog.*, 33 (1949), 361-389; J. Giblet, "Les promesses de l'Esprit et la Mission des Apôtres dans les Evangiles," in *Irénikon*, 30 (1957), 5-43; X. Léon-Dufour, S.J., art. "Paraclet," in *Vocab. de théol. biblique* (Paris, 1962), col. 742-743.
2. From *parakaleō*, to call to the side of.

intercede in favor of people before the tribunal of God: these would be, for example, the law (personified), angels, the good works of men, their merits, etc.

In his First Epistle, John applies the title "Paraclete" to the glorious Christ: "But if anyone sins, we have an advocate with the Father, Jesus Christ the just" (I Jn 2, 1).

How does Christ perform this role before the Father? The context explains: even in his glory, Jesus is before the Father as "a propitiation for our sins" (v. 2). This theme is developed at length in the visions of the Apocalypse, where we see "the slain Lamb" standing before God's throne (Apoc 5, 6, 9, 12; 13, 8). All the work of expiation achieved on earth becomes in heaven like a great prayer of intercession addressed to the Father. In this sense, Christ in his glory is truly an "advocate," an "intercessor."

However, the term "Paraclete" is applied everywhere else by St. John to the Holy Spirit, not to describe his role of intercession before God, but to characterize the role of assistance which he performs on earth among believers. All such texts belong to the discourses after the Last Supper, which are, as it were, the testament of Jesus before his return to the Father. After a formal promise that the Paraclete would come, Jesus indicates the three main aspects of his work: his function of teaching, the witness he bears to Jesus, and his role of accuser vis-à-vis the world.

THE OTHER PARACLETE

At the Last Supper, the disciples are troubled by the surprise announcement of Jesus' departure (Jn 14, 1). Up to that time, he had remained among them (16, 4; 14, 25), but now he tells them he will be with them for only a short while (13, 34). Soon they will no longer see him (16, 11), for he is going to the Father (16, 10). However, Jesus will soon return to his followers (14, 18), not only in paschal apparitions but in a completely spiritual, interior way: at that time, only his disciples willl be able to see him, in a vision of faith (14, 19). This will be the work of the Holy Spirit, who is called "another Advocate" (14, 16), for he will continue among the disciples the work begun by Jesus. In the great conflict that opposes Jesus and the world, the Spirit's task will be to defend the cause of Jesus among them and strengthen them in their faith.

It is in the disciples' interest that Christ should depart, for without this departure the Paraclete will not come to them (16, 7). The Father will give him to them at the request of Jesus and in his name (14, 16, 26); Christ himself, from the Father, will send him to them (15, 26). This Spirit who comes from the Father will remain with the disciples forever (14, 16), that is, until the end of time: throughout its earthly existence, the life of the Church will be characterized by the assistance given to it by the Spirit of truth.

The Paraclete and the World

Jesus announces a very clear principle: he will not manifest himself to the world (14, 22). The Paraclete will have to realize his spiritual presence among men, but this Paraclete "the world cannot receive, because it neither sees him nor knows him" (14, 17).

The expression "cannot," frequent in the Fourth Gospel, denotes a radical incapacity of the world with respect to the rewards of salvation. Left to themselves, men are incapable of coming to Christ (6, 44, 45), hearing his word (8, 43), and believing (12, 39).

The word *lambanein* used in St. John varies in meaning according to context: it has an active connotation and a passive one. When the verb pertains to Christ (1, 12; 5, 43; 13, 20), his witness (3, 11, 32, 33) or his words (12, 48; 17, 8), the emphasis is on the active participation of men, and the word should ordinarily be translated as "greet": the term is then almost synonymous with "believe" (see 1, 12). But when the verb is used pertaining to the Spirit, it has the more passive meaning of "receiving." For according to 7, 39, *to pneuma lambanein* and *pisteuein* are no longer synonymous: faith in Jesus is here a *condition* for "receiving the Spirit"; the latter, therefore, is a pure gift. The meaning of the verb is exactly the same in the text of the first promise: at the request of Jesus, the Father is willing to *give* the Paraclete (14, 16), but the world is incapable of *receiving* this gift of the Father. The reason for this incapacity will be explained at the end of the sentence by two different verbs: "because it neither *sees* him nor *knows* him."

Here Christ uses first a verb that describes the act of seeing. In St. John, this act has a very special importance, going from the simple physical seeing to interior vision, the contemplation of spiritual realities through faith. The verb *theōrein* used here means "to consider attentively," "to observe carefully," sometimes even "to contemplate"; it describes, above all, the attentive and searching look of someone who is observing, but it is never applied to a purely spiritual vision. If during his earthly life Jesus criticizes the world for not "seeing" the Spirit of truth, he means that the world fails to perceive him, to discern him, in his external manifestations. We must think here of the presence and action of the Spirit in the person, ministry and especially the word of Jesus himself (see 1, 32; 3, 34; 6, 63). Since the world has showed it was incapable of "perceiving" the Spirit at work during Jesus' life, it is also unable to "know" him.

For this reason, Jesus says, the world will remain incapable of "receiving" the Spirit of truth, whom the Father wishes to give to men; it does not have the disposition necessary for receiving this gift of the Father.

The Paraclete and the Disciples

The situation of the disciples is much different. It is to them that the Father will give the Paraclete (14, 16), and to them that Jesus will manifest himself (14, 21). If the disciples, in contrast to the world, can receive the Paraclete, it is because they are prepared for it: "But you shall know him, because he will dwell with you" (14, 17).

These words refer to the present state of the disciples immediately before Jesus' departure. During the public ministry, the Spirit was already present in the person and work of Jesus. In Christ, who dwelt "with" the disciples (v. 25), the Spirit was already acting; thus he too was "with" them (v. 25). The latter, despite their intellectual simplicity, had attached themselves to Jesus, and believed and knew that he was the Holy One of God (6, 64).

The promise, properly so-called, for the future is expressed in two different phrases. First, Jesus tells the disciples: The Father will give you the Paraclete "to dwell *with you* forever" (v. 16); and at the end of v. 17: "and he will be *in you*."

We should note carefully the use of prepositions in this first

promise. Until now, the Spirit was present only *near* the disciples
(*par 'humin*) in the person of Jesus. Later on, he will be *with them*
(*meth 'humōn*), and will also be *in them* (*en humin*). These three
prepositions mark a nice progression, for they describe very well
the more and more interior character of the Paraclete's action.

He will be "with them."[3] This formula does not indicate simply
a familiar presence of the Spirit close to the disciples, similar to that
of Jesus "close to" his followers during the course of his earthly life.
We must see here rather the idea of aid, assistance. Thus the text
contains already a discrete allusion to the future difficulties the
disciples will experience and the opposition over which they will
have to triumph. This is why, as of now, the Spirit receives the title
of Paraclete, "Defender."

He will also be "in them." A new kind of presence and action
of the Spirit is here promised by Jesus to the disciples: hence-
forward, he will act within their hearts. It is this full outpouring of
the Paraclete, this profound action of the Spirit following the
glorification of Jesus, which must be understood in connection
with the text of 7, 39, concerning the Spirit who would be received
by all those who believed in Jesus.

This first promise of the Spirit still does not tell us very explicitly what his action will consist of, but it does indicate two
main characteristics. First, it will involve a role of assistance: the
Paraclete will help the disciples to triumph in the great conflict that
will take place between them and the world. On the other hand,
his action will be essentially interior, and he will act as Spirit of
truth: his role will be to strengthen the disciples in their belief
in Jesus. These two functions will be explained in greater detail
in the following four promises.

THE TEACHING OF THE PARACLETE

Of the four other promises regarding the Paraclete, two pertain
to his role as teacher: the second and the fifth (14, 26; 16, 13-15).

---

3. The last part of v. 17 (*kai en humin estai*), with its verb in the future,
must be detached from what immediately precedes; in other words, the

For St. John, the role of the Spirit of truth consists above all in teaching: "These things I have spoken to you while yet dwelling with you. But the Advocate, the Holy Spirit, whom the Father will send in my name, he will teach you all things, and bring to your mind whatever I have said to you" (14, 25-26).

Jesus makes a distinction here between his own teaching and the future teaching of the Paraclete (*"But* the Advocate . . .") in order to suggest that the Spirit's action will be different from his own. He distinguishes two stages or, if you will, two great periods in the economy of revelation, the first constituted by his own word, the second by the teaching of the Spirit. Not that the revelation coming from Christ is incomplete or partial: Christ who is the Truth in person (14, 6), the Word of God incarnate (1, 14), can bring only the complete and definitive revelation. But the action of the Spirit is indispensable, although it is of another nature. This will be explained in the following remarks.

The Spirit's Teaching and That of Jesus

The Father will send the Holy Spirit "in the name of Jesus." Jesus himself was on earth "in the name of his Father" (5, 43), in close communion with the Father; thus he was among men to make known the Father's name, to reveal the Father (see 17, 6). Now we understand better what Jesus means when he says that the Paraclete will be sent "in his name." This does not mean simply that the Father will send him at his request or in his place, or as a representative of the Son, or to continue the Son's work. The name expresses what is most profound in the person of Christ, his position as Son: the Son, precisely as Son, will have an active part in the sending of the Spirit. This is why, in his farewell discourses, there are two complementary formulas: the Father will send the Spirit in the name of Jesus (14, 26): the Son himself will send the Spirit from the Father (15, 26). The formula "in my name" thus indicates the perfect communion between Father and Son

words "he will be in you" no longer depend on *hoti*: instead, they open up a new perspective and direct one's attention toward the time of the Church.

in the sending of the Spirit. The Father, undoubtedly, is the origin of this mission: the Son will send the Spirit "from the Father." But the Son also is a principle in this sending: it is "in the name of the Son" that the Father will send the Spirit. Father and Son are both principle of this mission of the Paraclete. Henceforth, if the Spirit is sent in Christ's name, his mission will be to reveal Christ, to make known his true name, that of *Son of God,* which expresses the mystery of his person. The Paraclete must arouse faith in Jesus as the Son of God.

The second half of the above-cited verse describes the Paraclete "in his office as teacher of doctrine" (Lagrange). This activity is described by two different verbs: "He will *teach* you all things, and *bring to your mind* whatever I have said to you" (14, 26). Certain authors see here two distinct roles; in other words, "whatever I have said to you" would only be the object of the second verb: in this case, when the Spirit "teaches" us, he would teach us something other than when he "brings to our mind" the words of Jesus. But such an interpretation runs contrary to the construction and movement of the sentence. It would also lead to a dangerous theological conclusion: that of postulating that the teaching of the Paraclete is independent from that of Jesus. This involves the temptation of introducing into the Church new revelations coming from the Spirit. (Recall, for example, the Montanism in the early Church and the spiritualist movement of Joachim de Flore in the Middle Ages.) As Fr. de Lubac comments: "There are two equally harmful ways of separating Christ from his Spirit: by dreaming a reign of the Spirit that would lead beyond Christ and by imagining a Christ who would always lead us just this side of the Spirit."[4] The Paraclete will not bring the disciples a new gospel: the life and teaching of Jesus contain all that we need know about the establishment of God's kingdom and the winning of our salvation. The role of the Spirit is essentially subordinate to the revelation brought by Christ.

"To teach," in St. John, is practically a verb of revelation. The Father taught the Son what the latter communicated to the world

---

4. H. de Lubac, S.J., *Exégèse médiévale* (Coll. "Théologie," 42), 2d part, t. 1, (Paris, 1961), 558.

(8, 28). But generally it is Jesus himself who is presented as the one who teaches (Jn 6, 59; 7, 14, 28, 35; 8, 20). Still, this teaching of Christ must not remain external to the believer: St. John stresses the necessity of making it interior, by accepting it with an ever more intense faith. This is the meaning of such typically Johannine expressions as "to abide in the doctrine of Christ" (II Jn 9), "to abide in his word" (Jn 8, 31; see also 15, 7-8). This is exactly where the action of the Spirit is—he too "teaches." He teaches what Jesus taught, but causes it to enter into men's hearts. There is, therefore, a perfect continuity in revelation: coming from the Father, it is communicated to us by the Son, but it attains its fullness when it enters into the most intimate part of our being through the action of the Spirit.

The precise nature of the Paraclete's teaching is also specified by another verb: he "will bring to mind" all that Jesus said. This theme of "recalling" or of "remembering" is strongly emphasized in the Fourth Gospel. More than once John notes that after Jesus' departure the disciples "remembered" a word or an act of the Master, that is, after the resurrection they grasped its true meaning and significance (2, 17, 22; 12, 16). This too involves the Holy Spirit: in "recalling" all that Jesus said, he will not only remind the disciples of a teaching they might have forgotten; his true task will be to *make them understand* internally the words of Jesus, to make them grasp such words in the light of faith, to make them perceive all the possibilities and importance of such words for the life of the Church.

Thus, through the secret action of the Paraclete, the message of Jesus ceases to be external and far-removed; the Holy Spirit internalizes it in us, helping us to grasp it spiritually and discover in it a word of life.[5] This word of Jesus, assimilated in faith through the Spirit, is what John will call in his First Epistle "the anointing" that remains in us (I Jn 2, 27);[6] the teaching of Jesus, present in

---

5. The translation "suggeret" of the Vulgate, although less exact, expresses well the method of the Holy Spirit's teaching, "by interior suggestion rather than by explicit word" (Lagrange); but such interior suggestions are given to us by the Paraclete by means of Jesus' words.

6. See our study, "L'onction du chrétien per la foi," in *Biblica*, 40 (1959), 12-69, esp. 30-47 (in the present volume, pp. 000ff.).

the believer, gives him the intimate sense of the truth (vv. 20-21), and enlightens him about many things: henceforth the Christian is "born of the Spirit" (3, 8). Having reached this level of spiritual maturity, he no longer has to be taught (I Jn 2, 27): all he need do is to abide in Jesus and let himself be taught by God (see Jn 6, 45).

The Fullness of Truth

In the fifth and last promise, Jesus takes up again the same doctrine and develops it a bit further:

> Many things yet I have to say to you, but you cannot bear them now. But when he, the Spirit of truth, has come, he will teach you all the truth. For he will not speak on his own authority, but whatever he will hear he will speak, and the things that are to come he will declare to you. He will glorify me, because he will receive of what is mine and declare it to you. All things that the Father has are mine. That is why I have said that he will receive of what is mine, and will declare it to you (16, 12-15).

Here again Jesus indicates what the role of the Holy Spirit will be in regard to his own words. At first sight, he seems to be contradicting himself: in 15, 15, he had said that all he had learned from the Father he had made known to his disciples; here, on the contrary, he declares that many things still remain to be said. But this time we are talking of a complement to revelation reserved to the Spirit. The latter will not propose new doctrine, but will provide a deeper understanding of the mystery of Jesus—his life, his actions, his words. The stress given to the adverb *now* at the end of v. 12 ("you cannot bear them *now*") offers a contrast between the present moment, that of Jesus' earthly life, and the time to come, the period after the resurrection and the coming of the Spirit (see also 13, 7; 16, 30-31). The "many things" which the disciples still lack are not points of doctrine which must be added by Jesus, but the full understanding of his person and message.

Like a knowledgeable guide, the Spirit of truth must "lead"[7] the disciples toward the whole truth. This verb is richer in meaning than the simple verb *docebit* (he will teach) of the Vulgate. The metaphor seems to have been taken directly from Ps 24 (25), 5 (Greek text): "Lead me toward your truth and teach me." The psalmist was asking God for a more perfect understanding of his truth, his teachings, his law. According to John's text, the truth toward which the Holy Spirit must lead us is the truth of Jesus, that of his teaching, his work, his whole person. The Spirit must enable us to penetrate the heart[8] of this truth and discover its fullness.

The Revelation of the Paraclete

The second part of the last promise (16, 13b-14) offers us a new point of view: here Jesus stresses the ministerial aspect of the Spirit's work in relation to the Son and the Father as well as the real newness of the Spirit's teaching.

The same idea occurs three times: "he will not speak on his own authority, but whatever he will hear he will speak"; and twice: "he will receive of what is mine." These expressions are similar, for "what is of Christ's" is what the Spirit "will hear" from him. Thus the text underscores heavily this doctrinal point; the Spirit does not draw from himself, nor is he the origin of the revelation he will bring. Just as Christ had not spoken on his own authority (7, 17f.; 12, 49; 14, 10), just as he had said only what the Father had taught him (8, 28; 12, 50), what he had heard from the Father (8, 26, 38), so too the Spirit will not speak on his own authority but will only say what he will hear. From whom will he hear it? From the Son, certainly, from whom he will receive "what is mine"; but also from the Father since all that is the Father's is the Son's (see v. 15a). Thus revelation enables us to enter into the very heart of the Trinitarian mystery: "Revelation is perfectly one: springing from the Father and working through the Son, it is completed in the Spirit."[9]

---

7. Here John uses the verb *hodēgeō,* to lead along the way (*hodos*), to guide.

8. The preposition *eis* not only indicates direction, but also signifies that the movement ends within the place that one wishes to reach.

9. Note of D. Mollat's in the *Bible de Jérusalem.* See also the fine commentary

One other expression is repeated three times in this promise: *anangelei humin*. It is the most important element since in this way Jesus explains how the Spirit enables us to penetrate the essence of truth. Most often the expression is translated as in the Vulgate, "He will declare to you," as if the Spirit's action was simply a kerygmatic proclamation. But it is of a completely different order. The verb *anangellein* has here the exact nuance that is usually found in the apocalyptic literature, "to reveal, to disclose." It is found many times in the Greek text of Daniel, with the meaning of "unraveling or making known the meaning of a dream, a vision, a prophecy."[10] This is also the meaning of the verb in St. John. Thus the Samaritan woman confides to Jesus what she expects of the Messiah; "When he comes he will tell us all things" (4, 25). Likewise, in 16, 25, Jesus contrasts the teaching "in parables," such as he practiced, with the clear explanations which he will give later on through the Spirit: "The hour is coming when . . . I will speak to you plainly of the Father."[11]

It is this same verb *anangelein* which John uses in 16, 13-15, to characterize the future activity of the Paraclete. In the literary tradition from which it comes, this verb does not mean "to bring forth a completely new revelation," but rather "to offer an explanation of a previous revelation," which has heretofore been hidden and mysterious. This will be the precise role of the Spirit: he will interpret for the Church the revelation brought by Jesus, which previously had not been understood. At the same time, says the

of Fr. Durand: " 'He will not speak of himself' is understandable only as long as one thinks of the Paraclete as 'substitute' for Christ, the one who must restate the Gospel, not to alter it nor even to add anything really new to it, but to illuminate it and to make it fruitful . . . . This is how the ancients thought of the respective roles of the Word and the Spirit: the Word, image of the Father, reveals God; the Spirit, bond of love, opens man's spirit and heart to the mysteries of divine life," "Le discours de la Cène," in *Rech. de scienc. relig.*, 2 (1911), 343.

10. See Dan. (Greek translation of Theodotion), 2, 2, 4, 7, 9 bis, 11, 16, 24, 27; 5, 12, 15; 9, 23; 10, 21; 11, 2.

11. Here one should read *anangelō* rather than *apangelō*. The meaning of the expression has been very well rendered in certain manuscripts of the old Latin version: "Palam de Patre *manifestabo* vobis."

text, "the things that are to come he will declare to you"; not that
Christ is promising the disciples the gift of prophecy, but rather,
in the light of Jesus' work and words, the Spirit will pro. de the
disciples with an understanding of the eschatological orc r. the
new economy of salvation, that is, "the new order of things that
comes from the death and resurrection of Christ" ( ). Mollat).
As it has been said so well, "To give the Christian mea ng of history, to show in all things the evidence of the divine j an (Ac 20,
27) to shed on every event, in every era, the bright light of
revelation—this is the Spirit's mission among the disciples."[12]

THE PARACLETE, WITNESS OF JESUS

So far in our discussion our only concern was the Spirit's mission to teach. The two promises concerning the Paraclete which
we must now examine underline another aspect of his activity:
his role as witness. We thus enter here into the context of a trial.
Many observers feel—and we shall return to this point later on
—that the notion of a trial is an essential part of the way in which
John presents the life of Jesus. On the other hand, we should
recall what we said before about the juridical origin of the title
Paraclete. We now understand why John stressed so emphatically
the theme of the Spirit-as-Paraclete, Defender of Jesus.

Let us read the text of the third promise:

> But when the Advocate has come, whom I will send from
> the Father, the Spirit of truth who proceeds from the Father,
> he will bear witness concerning me. And you also bear
> witness, because from the beginning you are with me" (15.
> 26-27).

The Hatred of the World

To interpret this passage correctly, a careful examination of
its context is of great help. The section preceding (15, 18-25) and

12. H. Van ·den Bussche, *Le discours d'adieu de Jésus*, 126.

the section following (16, 1-4) both discuss the world's hatred and its persecutions. Such a context of hostility explains the role of witnessing that the Spirit of truth must fulfill.

Quite naturally, we think of the verses of the synoptic Gospels in which Jesus promised his disciples the help of the Spirit in future persecutions. Let us recall the missionary discourse of Mat-thew, in which is described the rough treatment the disciples will get before tribunals (10, 17-25), a similar passage in Luke (12, 11-12), and, above all, a passage from the great eschatological dis-course (Mt 24, 9-14). We find in these passages parallels to almost all the themes of Jn 15, 18-16, 4, namely: the hatred of the world (Jn 15, 18-19, 23-25; see Mt 20, 22; 24, 9); reference to the maxim, "No servant is greater than his master" (Jn 15, 20; see Mt 10, 24; Lk 6, 40); warning of persecutions (Jn 15, 20; see Mt 10, 23; Lk 21, 12), which will arise on account of Jesus (Jn 15, 21; see Mt 10, 22; 24, 9); warning against scandal (Jn 16, 1; see Mt 24, 10); the rough treatment in synagogues (Jn 16, 2; see Mt 10, 17; Mk 13, 9; Lk 12, 11; 21, 12); the witnessing of the disciples (Jn 15, 27; see Mt 10, 23; Lk 21, 13).

These passages from the synoptics stress the Holy Spirit's activ-ity among the disciples in the midst of such persecutions: when they will be haled before the tribunals of kings, it is he who will speak through or in them (Mk 13, 11; Mt 10, 20). Luke states that it is the Holy Spirit who will teach them what they should say (Lk 12, 12). But nowhere in the synoptics is the Spirit con-sidered as *a witness*. On the other hand, in the Fourth Gospel Jesus says explicitly: "He will bear witness concerning me."

This Spirit of truth whom Jesus will send "proceeds" from the Father. The verb being in the present (see "procedit" of the Vul-gate), in contrast to the future "I will send," a great many com-mentators, especially in the Greek tradition, translate: "He proceeds from the Father," meaning by this the eternal procession of the Holy Spirit within the Trinity. But recent exegetes recognize more and more that in virtue of the whole context we must see here rather the temporal mission of the Spirit.[13] Indeed, this interpola-

13. This was the interpretation of Marius Victorinus: "Spiritum veritatis, qui a Patre adveniet," *Adv. Arium*, I, 13 (ed. "Source chrét.," 216). In our

tion, intended to establish the witnessing of the Paraclete, is understood better in terms of the mission: the Spirit, sent by the Son
and "coming from the Father," with whom the Son abides, is
thereby fully qualified to be witness of the Son among men.

The Witness of the Paraclete

For some, this witness is the work of the Spirit in the preaching of the Gospel, or else in the miracles and charismatic works
of the apostles. Others, who are thinking more in terms of the context of hostility in which the promise is made, see here the indictment by which the Spirit will confound the iniquitous judges of
Jesus. The context of persecution is certainly a starting point for
finding out the true explanation. However, let us emphasize that
the Spirit's witness is directed, not to the world, but to the disciples
("the Advocate whom I will send *you*," v. 26); to them he will be
sent precisely on account of the persecutions they will have to undergo. Moreover, here the Spirit's witness is formally distinguished
from that of the disciples themselves (see v. 27): it cannot be part
of the external witness which the persecuted disciples are called
to make before the tribunals. It is prior to that, and of a different
nature. Its true aim is not so much, as in the synoptics, to inspire
directly the defense or witness of the disciples, but to preserve
them from scandal, at the hour when their faith will be put sternly
to the test. We must, therefore, stress above all the interior aspect
of the Paraclete's witness: his role will be to enlighten the apostles
in the midst of adversity and to strengthen them in their faith.
At the moment when they are tempted to doubt, the Paraclete
will act secretly within them and bear witness to Jesus.[14]

own day, it is accepted by a good number of Catholics, by exegetes
(Wilkenhauser, Bouyer, Mollat, Van den Bussche), as well as by theologians (e.g., J. Isaac, O.P., *La révélation progressive des Personnes
divines* [Paris, 1960], 195-196).

14. Such is the interpretation of a number of modern commentators, e.g., M.-F.
Berrouard, O.P., *art. cit.*, 369-370, 373; J. Giblet, *art. cit.*, 30. Consider,
among the ancients, the beautiful commentary of Euthymius Zigabenus:
"But he will bear witness to me, by shining forth in your hearts, for a more

The Trial of Jesus

Why, in virtue of his illuminating action, is the Spirit considered a *witness* of Jesus? The answer is clear: the Spirit plays a decisive role in what has been called "the great trial" of Jesus' life. But doesn't a witness necessarily have a public character? We must remember that in St. John most of the great theological concepts have undergone a transformation. This is true of the themes of witness and of trial. The different witnesses about which the Fourth Gospel speaks do not have to testify before human tribunals regarding certain historical facts; they almost always bear witness to the very person of Jesus, the purpose of their witness being to have Jesus received, to induce men to believe in him. Here there is a remarkable interiorizing and spiritualizing of the idea of witness.

An analogy can be drawn regarding the notion of trial. According to the synoptics, Jesus declares that the disciples will be subject to actual trials: they will be delivered to the Sanhedrins and brought before governors and kings (Mt 10, 17-18; Mk 13, 9). In St. John, there is no longer any mention of such tribunals and their judges. The great trial the evangelist has in mind is of another order, namely, the great theological conflict which serves as a framework for Jesus' life and opposes him and the world, and finally ends in the condemnation of the world and the exaltation of Christ on the cross. Little does it matter to John what are in the reality of history the courts of justice that will condemn the disciples; these human tribunals disappear completely behind a unique, mysterious, faceless power—the world. This theme of the *world* underscores the full meaning of what is involved, namely, to be *for* or *against* Christ. This struggle goes beyond the opposition of the Jews against Jesus during his earthly life; it extends well beyond this, into the Church.

In this momentous religious trial in which Jesus and the world confront one another, the witness of the Paraclete will have its true meaning: before the world's hostility, Jesus' disciples will be

perfect assurance (*plērophorian*)," *In Joann.*, in h. 1. (*P.G.*, 129, 1420 A); and that of St. Augustine: "Utique quia ille perhibebit, etiam vos perhibebitis: ille in cordibus vestris, vos in vocibus vestris; ille inspirando, vos sonando," *In Joann.*, Tract. 93, 1 (*P.L.*, 35, 1864).

continually exposed to scandal, will experience doubt and discouragement, and will be tempted to give up the fight. At this very time the Spirit of truth, the Defender of Jesus, will intervene. Within the conscience of the disciples, he will bear witness to Jesus; he will strengthen them in their faith and provide them with the assurance that is properly Christian.

THE PARACLETE, ACCUSER OF THE WORLD

The fourth promise concerning the Paraclete is related to the third. Here too, the Paraclete will be seen in his office of witness, but from another, complementary point of view: he will be a witness for the prosecution against the sinful world.

At the announcement of Jesus' departure, the disciples are filled with sadness (16, 6). But Jesus reassures them in announcing the coming of the Paraclete:

> But I speak the truth to you; it is expedient for you that I depart. For if I do not go, the Advocate will not come to you; but if I go, I will send him to you. And when he has come he will convict the world[15] of sin, and of justice, and of judgment; of sin, because they do not believe in me; of justice, because I go to the Father, and you will see me no more; and of judgment, because the prince of this world has already been judged (16, 7-15).

The Paraclete and the Evil of the World

In this promise Jesus defines the future activity of the Paraclete in relation to the world. The term *elenchein* used here can have several meanings, and this is what makes the text somewhat obscure.

The various meanings of the verb are closely related to one another: 1) "to make an examination, an investigation"; 2) "to

---

15. For this way of rendering *elengxei* (instead of, "he will confound the world," which is the usual translation), see further on.

interrogate, question, put to the test"; 3) it can also indicate the result of the investigation: "to clarify a fact, expose it, unravel it"; 4) when it concerns people, the verb means: "to convince someone of error, furnish the proof of his guilt"; 5) let us finally mention the meanings derived from it: "to accuse, admonish, punish."

For Jn 16, 8, most commentators recognize the fourth meaning; the Paraclete will point out the world's wrongdoing. But this is rather ambiguous: it can mean either a simple objective presentation of arguments against the world, or an act of subjective persuasion within the mind of the accused: this would mean that under the persuasive action of the Paraclete sinners would finally recognize their sin and become converted. But if the verb is taken only in its objective sense, as the commentators usually do, a further question arises: before whom will the proof of the world's guilt be presented? Normally the *elengxis* is made in the presence of the guilty person. This would lead us to think that the Paraclete will establish the crimes of the world before the world itself, through the mouth of the apostles: by their intrepid witnessing, they will confound the world, so that the latter will have nothing to say in its own behalf. But is not the idea of the confounding of sinners a typically eschatological one? Is it not more appropriate in the context of the final judgment? In the daily life of the Church, in which Jesus' disciples are in continual contact with the world, such a powerful act on the part of the Paraclete does not seem appropriate; moreover, it scarcely corresponds to the facts.

In addition, the text in no way postulates such an interpretation. In itself, *elengxis* indicates only the objective exposition of proofs; only the context enables us to decide whether the guilty one is present or not, if the. demonstration of his crime is done publicly, and if it is addressed to him. In every hypothesis, this detail remains foreign to the meaning of the verb itself.

In the present case, nothing in the context leads us to think of a public indictment. The Paraclete will point out the world's iniquity, but he will do it within the personal conscience of the apostles.[16] For according to the introductory verse, it is to them

---

16. This is the interpretation of Fr. Berrouard, *art. cit.;* it has been adopted by a number of authors: D. Mollat, G.-M. Behler, *op. cit.*, 181-182, X. Léon-Dufour, *art. cit.*, col. 743, etc.

and for them that the Paraclete will come: "For if I do not go, the Advocate will not come *to you;* but if I go, I will send him *to you*" (v. 7). Likewise, in the following verses, it is a question only of Jesus' disciples: "...he will teach *you* all the truth" (v. 13). Finally, v. 10 also shows that it is only believers who are intended: "because...*you* will see me no more."[17]

Thus we see the meaning of the promise: in pointing out the guilt of the world, the Paraclete will act in a completely interior way, in the secret confines of the disciples' conscience. When their faith is put to the test, the Paraclete will give them the certitude that the world is sinful and that the truth is on Jesus' side. In this way, the promise made by Jesus will become for the apostles an extremely practical one:

> Rejected by the Jewish community because of their attach-
> ment to their Master, regarded as so impious that their being
> put to death will be considered as an act of worship to-
> ward God, the apostles, as loyal Jews, may well become
> scandalized. But it is at this very moment that they will
> receive the help of the Advocate, who will always be with
> and in them...for he will assure them beyond doubt that
> they are in the truth and that their faith is pleasing to God,
> by making quite clear the unjust claims of the cruel world.[18]

The action of the Paraclete will consist of strengthening the disciples' faith in these moments of crisis: positively, by drawing them ever closer to Jesus, and, negatively, by assuring them that it is the world that is in error. Thereafter, the disciples can overcome the scandal that haunts them and conquer the world: "And this is the victory that overcomes the world, our faith" (1 Jn 5, 4).

Here again, we note the reappearance of the Johannine concept of the great trial, already present in the third promise. Although on the historic level the disciples of Christ are condemned by human tribunals, on the level of faith and in the eyes of God it is they who judge the world and it is the world that is condemned:

17. And not "because *the world* will no longer see me"; this is what would
    be expected, if the proof were addressed to the world itself.
18. M.-F. Berrouard, *art. cit.,* 368.

Judgment is made on earth, but it is also made in the mind of those to whom the Spirit is sent. Before them is evoked the cause of Jesus, and, under the urging of the Paraclete, who offers them the real meaning of events, they rally to whoever has been condemned by the world and join the ranks of his followers. The world, in turn, pursues them; they become the guilty ones before its tribunals, while continuing to be, in their own minds, the judges of the world. Thus, it is as if two judgments are being made at the same time: the judgment of Christians before human tribunals constituted by the world, and the judgment of the world in the hearts of Christians, under the guidance of the Spirit.[19]

Sin, Justice, Judgment

According to v. 8, such a demonstration of the world's guilt by the Paraclete must involve three areas: "sin, justice, and judgment." During his earthly life, Jesus had been rejected by the Jews and was going to be condemned during the passion. The Paraclete will revise this process and will show the disciples that sin is on the side of the world, justice is on the side of Jesus, and the person who is really condemned in this religious confrontation is the Prince of this world. Each of the three aspects of the Paraclete's judgment of the world is repeated and explained in detail in the following verses: "Of sin, because they do not believe in me." As far as St. John is concerned, this is the essence of sin: the world has refused to believe in Jesus, the Messiah and Son of God.

"Of justice, because I go to the Father, and you will see me no more." This is not the justice of Christians, but that of Christ himself. The latter is often understood in terms of the personal sanctity of Jesus, his friendship with God, or else his own right in the conflict between him and the world. But the explanation given by Jesus in the following proposition suggests another interpretation: "justice" is to be taken in the sense of triumph, victory or glory, the

19. *Ibid.,* 373.

sense sometimes given to it in the Bible.[20] The justice of Jesus is his triumphant justice, which will burst forth after his glorification in heaven, when he will have returned to the Father. By assuring the disciples that Jesus is in a state of glory, the Paraclete will go a long way in showing them the tragic error of the world.

"Of judgment, because the prince of this world has already been judged." In the trial between Christ and the world, the historical dénouement will take place in the passion and death of Jesus: his exaltation on the cross and the refusal of the sinful world to believe in him constitute the condemnation of this world and its head, the devil. The illuminating action of the Holy Spirit will enable the apostles to discover, behind the events of Christ's death, the one who is the real instigator, the Prince of this world. The latter's activity will be denounced by the Spirit in the tribunal of the apostles' conscience.

> Truly acting as "Paraclete," that is, as Defender, as Advocate, the Holy Spirit has, so to speak, done over the trial of Jesus; as Spirit of truth, he has reestablished the complete truth in this awesome drama.[21]

20. See A. Descamps, *les justes et la justice dans les Evangiles et dans le christianisme primitif . . .* (Louvain, 1950), 90-93.
21. G.-M. Behler, *op. cit.*, 187.

CONCLUSION

When we look back over the five promises of the Paraclete, we cannot but be struck by their great unity: all in a certain fashion, are related to the life of faith of Jesus' disciples. The first promise (14, 16-17) underlines the fundamental opposition between the world and believers. The four others can be grouped in twos: the second (14, 26) and the fifth (16, 12-15) refer to the Spirit's role as teacher; the third (15, 26-27) and the fourth (16, 7-11), to his juridical action in the great trial in which Jesus and the world oppose one another. But according to each of these texts the special task of the Spirit will be to deepen the disciples' faith, by allowing them to understand from within the life and message of Jesus or by strengthening their uncertain faith against the attacks of the world.

Now we understand better why the Paraclete is given on several occasions the title of *Spirit of truth* (14, 17; 15, 26; 16, 13). The qualifier "of truth" characterizes the area in which the Spirit's action takes place. In the theology of John, his function is to *communicate the truth* to us, to teach it to us interiorly, to cause it to enter ever more deeply into the hearts of Christians. Thus, as a result of the hidden work of the Paraclete, the permanence and efficaciousness of Jesus' word is safeguarded within the Church for all time.

IV

Anointing of the Christian by Faith[*]

Chriso humas tōi pisteōs aleimmati
Clement of Alexandria, *Protrept.*, XII, 120, 5

Christian tradition, and in particular spiritual writers, often speak of an interior "anointing" of Christians. By this they mean an activity of the Holy Spirit that enlightens the soul, informs and guides it in the various circumstances of life. We should, therefore, understand what the doctrine of the Holy Spirit's anointing consists of. The very expression "anointing" was not created by spiritual theology; it was taken from St. John's First Epistle. We would now like to consider this idea of spiritual anointing in its New Testament context and the interpretation given it by tradition.

Only two passages in the New Testament speak of the anointing of the Christian, II Cor 1, 21 and I Jn 2, 20, 27,[1] a fact that makes

---

[*] This study appeared in *Biblica*, 40 (1959), 12-69. We here make certain additions (in particular, bibliographic items).

1. We will not talk of the anointing of the sick, which comes up in Jas 5, 14. There it is a question of a physical anointing with oil and the

explanation more difficult. We can approach the interpretation in different ways: by a detailed comparison of the two passages and by a historical survey of the various interpretations. But it is above all by a direct study of the verses, the vocabulary, the literary and doctrinal context, that we will grasp the true thought of the authors, Paul and John.

Gnostic Theme?

Before going on, let us consider for a moment the origin of the term "anointing." Since no real parallels to I Jn 2, 20 can be found in the Jewish world,[2] it has been said that the use of the word *chrisma* in this verse is taken from Gnostic terminology.[3] But when explanations of this type are offered, one fails to distinguish between two things: the origin of the materials used (terms, images, symbols, etc.) and the meaning they have in the system into which they are integrated. Thus the materials and vocabulary used by the Gnostics themselves can have the most diverse origins—pagan, Jewish, or Christian—but it is only their interpretation in this new doctrinal synthesis that gives them a properly Gnostic meaning.

A similar remark can be made for the authors of the New Testament. In the case that concerns us now, it is a fact that *chrisma* is used by several Gnostic authors subsequent to St. John. No doubt, the *spirit* in which the term is used is very different from the spirit of the First Epistle; but is it not possible that John borrowed the *word* from this milieu and christianized it?

Let us state immediately something that makes this completely improbable: all the Gnostic texts that can be cited as parallel to I Jn 2, 20, 27 belong to Christian Gnosticism.[4] In the hermetic

term used is *aleiphein*, and not *chriein* (or its derivative *chrisma*), as in texts we shall consider.

2. See Strack-Billerbeck, *Kommentar . . .*, III, 777.
3. R. Schnackenburg, *Die Johannesbriefe* (Freiburg, 2d ed., 1963), 152; Bultmann, *Theologie les Neuen Testaments* (Tübingen, 1948-1953), 435, n. 1.
4. R. Schnackenburg cites three texts: *alalo chrismati* (Hippol., *Ref.*, V, 7, 19; but see also 9, 22); *chrismati leuko* (Orig., *Contra Celsum*, VI,

Gnosticism, the words *chrisma* or *chriein* are nowhere to be found. Nor is the theme of anointing found in the Qumran writings published until now. Its presence among Christian Gnostics is explained very probably as a borrowing from the vocabulary of the Church; this is the opinion of some outstanding critics.[5] This is all the more likely since in many of these texts "anointing" is related formally to Gnostic "baptism."[6] From the viewpoint of terminology nothing allows us to say that it is St. John who made the borrowing.

On the other hand, the relationship made between *chrisma* and baptism by the Gnostics themselves is of great importance: it suggests that in the Christian texts on which they depend the theme of anointing was already linked to that of baptism. In fact, with the exception of Heb 1, 9 (which belongs to a series of biblical citations), all the passages in the New Testament containing the verb *chriein* refer to baptism, namely, three passages in Luke (Lk 4, 18; Ac 4, 27; 10, 38), which refer to the baptism of

27); *chrisma pneumatikon* (*Pistis Sophia*, ch. 86, 112, 128, 130). The first is part of a description of initiation among the Nassenes; the second, of a criticism of Christians by Celsus, but the description it gives refers rather to the practices of an unidentified Gnostic sect, similar to the Nassenes of Hippolytus (see F. J. Dölger, *Sphragis*, 89-94). As to the texts of the *Pistis Sophia*, they repeat Christian terminology (Jesus who reveals; baptism of fire and baptism of the Holy Spirit; the kingdom of the Father). Schnackenburg also refers to *Acta Thomae*, 27, 157, and *Odes de Sal.*, 36, 6. We can also add: *Apocryphe de Jean*, 30, 14-20 (*T.U.*, 60, 101), a passage from the *Evangile de Verite* (in the lacuna published in microfilm by P. Labib [Cairo, 1956]; now see M. Malinine, H.-C. Puech, W. Till, *Evangelium Veritatis* (*Supplementum*), f. 36, 1, 17-26 [Zurich-Stuttgart, 1961], 9), and two others, in the *Evangile selon Philippe*, n. 68 and 95; see H. M. Schenke, in *Th. L. Z.*, 84 (1959), col. 15 and 18f.; or the edition of R. McL. Wilson, *The Gospel of Philip* [New York, 1962, 130f. and 157f.]. All these new texts belong to Christian Gnosticism.

5. A. Benoit, *Le baptême chrétien au second siècle* (Paris, 1953), 203; this was also the opinion of Msgr. Duchesne (cited by Benoit, *loc. cit.*). The same opinion is found in F.-M. Sagnard (*La gnose valentinienne*, 423) and in J. Daniélou (*Théologie du Judéo-Christianisme*, 380).

6. See Schnackenburg, *op. cit.*, 108, n. 4, the texts of Hippolytus, Origen, the *Pistis Sophis*, the *Acta Thomae*, and the *Evangile selon Philippe*.

Christ,[7] and a passage in Paul (II Cor 1, 21), to that of *Christians.*
It is with the latter that we shall begin; we will then consider the
verses of St. John on the *chrisma* of the Christian; in the third part
of this essay, we will investigate tradition.

ST. PAUL (II COR 1, 21-22)

Because of a delay in his travels, Paul is obliged to defend
himself against a charge of fickleness made by some of the
Corinthians.[8] He demonstrates his reliability by appealing to the
fidelity of God as manifested in Christ (v. 18-20). It is this same
faithful God who gives Paul all his steadfastness: "Now it is God
who is warrant [*bebaiōn*] for us and for you in Christ, who has
anointed us [*chrisas hēmas*], who has also stamped us with his
seal [*ho kai sphragisamenos hēmas*] and has given us the Spirit as
a pledge in our hearts" (v. 21). In order to clarify the meaning of
chrisas in this verse, it is first necessary to study the two verbs
that surround it.

Strengthening in the Faith and
Stamping of the Seal

The verb *bebaioō* is normally used by Paul to indicate
strengthening a person in the Christian faith and in the teachings
of the Gospel (I Cor 1, 6-8; Col 2, 7; see Phil 1, 7: *en ... bebaiosei
tou evaggeliou*).[9] The text of Col 2, 6-7 is especially interesting,

---

7. In this regard, cf. our "L'onction du Christ. Etude de théologie biblique,"
   in *N. R. Th.*, 80 (1958), 225-252.

8. Regarding this text, see E. Dinkler, "Die Taufterminologie in 2 Kor. 1,
   21f.," in *Neotestamentica et patristica* (*Freundesgabe O. Cullmann*),
   (Leiden, 1962), 173-191; J. Ysebaert, *Greek Baptismal Terminology:
   Its Origins and Early Development* (Nijmegen, 1962), 263-266.

9. See in the LXX: *bebaiōson me en tois logois sou*, Ps 118, 28; for the
   Christian texts, see also: *tou kuriou ... ton logon bebaiountos*, Mk 16,
   20; *bebaian humōn pistin*, I Clem., 1, 2; *ton tēs pisteōs bebaion dromon,
   ibid.*, 6, 2; *spoudazete oun bebaiōthēnai en tois dogmasin tou kuriou kai
   tōn apostolōn*, Ignatius of Antioch, *Ad Magn.*, 13, 1; *hē bebaia tēs pisteōs
   humōn rhiza*, Polycarp, *Ad Phil.*, 1, 2.

and calls for a strengthening in the teaching received: *os oun parelabete ... bebaioumenoi en te pistei kathos edidaxthete.* In the text of II Cor 1, 21 also, the reference to preaching is quite clear: the strengthening of which v. 21 speaks (*bebaion emas sun umin eis xriston*) refers back to the preaching mentioned in v. 19 (*Iesous Xristos o en umin di' emon keruxtheis*). The divine act of strengthening affects Paul himself as well as the Corinthians (*bebaion amas sun umin*): the Apostle unites himself with his fellow Christians in order to emphasize their common strengthening in the same faith, the one that he preached (v. 19) and they received (v. 20).[10]

How is *shragisamenos* interpreted? Most commentators see here an allusion to baptism. The origin of the expression must be found in Judaism, where it is often question of the seal of circumcision.[11] These texts are subsequent to St. Paul, but the *sphragis* is already mentioned with regard to Jewish circumcision in Rom 4, 11 (see *Ep. Barn.* 9, 6) in the sense of sigillation—the technical meaning of the seal of circumcision is close. Elsewhere, Paul feels that the true circumcision is that of the Christians, that is, spiritual circumcision. "For we use the circumcision" (Phil 3, 3); he refers this "circumcision of Christ" explicitly to the moment of baptism, when Christians are buried with Christ and rise again with him (Col 2, 11-12).[12] Thus it is natural that the theme of the stamping of the seal, at first related to that of circumcision, underwent the same Christian transposition as the latter, and was also applied to baptism. We see it clearly in the Judaeo-Christian texts of the second century: *II Clementis* uses as equivalents the expressions *tērein tēn sphragida* (7, 6; 8, 6) and *tērein to baptisma* (6, 9);

10. The interpretation of E. Dinkler, (*art. cit.*), who thinks that the four participles in these verses (even *bebaiōn*) refer to baptism, seems impossible to us: it is voided by the difference in time (*bebaiōn* is in the present, the three others in the aorist) as well as by the semantic use of the four verbs elsewhere in the Pauline epistles.
11. See the rabbinical texts in F. J. Dölger, *Sphragis,* 53-54, and Strack-Billerbeck, *Kommentar,* III, 495, and IV, 32-33.
12. This is the notion of spiritual circumcision, which makes possible the passage of the *sphragis* — circumcision in the Pauline use of *sphragizeisthai* for baptism. This has been stressed by M. Verheijen, "Musterion, Sacramentum et la synagogue," in *R. S. R.,* 45 (1957), 321-337 (see 328).

and the *Shepherd of Hermas* has the important formula: *hē sphragis oun to hydōr estin* (*Sim* IX, 16, 4). At this point, the word *sphragis* had become a technical expression to indicate baptism. This usage appears again and again in various milieux. The conclusion of F. J. Dolger on this matter remains correct:

> It is certain that in the middle of the second century the word "sphragis," as a designation for baptism, already had a past behind it; otherwise it would not have broken out in such a simultaneous way in Asia Minor (Acts of Paul), in Lyons (Irenaeus), in Carthage (Tertullian), in Alexandria (Clement), in Corinth (II Clement), and in Rome (Hermas).[13]

But most often, only the regressive method is used here, that is, interpreting the verb *sphragisamenos* in St. Paul by starting with the clearest meaning *sphragis* had in the second century. This explains why some commentators refuse to pursue this exegesis. But there are solid arguments for it in St. Paul himself: several indications show that the stamping of the seal can only be understood in terms of baptism. In addition to II Cor 1, 21 two other Pauline texts have the verb *sphragizein* pertaining to the Holy Spirit: *en o* [= *Christo*] ... *pisteusantes esphragisthete to pneumati to agio os estin arrabon tes kleronomias emon, eis apolutrosin* (Eph 1, 13-14); *en o* [= *pneumati*] *esphragisthete eis emeran apolutroseos* (Eph 4, 30).

In these two passages from the Epistle to the Ephesians, as in the one addressed to the Church of Corinth, Paul is speaking to Christians. He uses *sphragizein* three times in the aorist, thereby indicating a definite moment in their past—when they were marked with the seal of the Spirit. This can only be the moment of Christian initiation. But opinions differ on the following point: Is the guarantee of the Spirit *baptismal grace* itself or rather the eschatological gift of the Spirit, already well attested to in the Acts (2, 1-11; 8, 17; 10, 44-47; 19, 6), and later called the sacrament of

13. F. J. Dölger, *op. cit.*, 80. This conclusion was repeated by A. Benoit, *Le baptême chrétien au second siècle*, 97.

confirmation? All the more so since in the Acts the purification of
baptism and the post-baptismal gift of the Spirit (by the imposition of hands) are frequently linked together to form the complete
initiation into Christianity.[14]

Seal of the Spirit Received in Baptism

By all indication, the seal of the Spirit is a gift received *in the
very act of baptism,* and not a post-baptismal gift. Three facts
serve to substantiate this:

a) According to Eph 1, 13, what precedes the impressing of the
Spirit's seal on Christians is marked by two verbs in the aorist participle: *akousantes ton logon tēs aletheias . . . kai pisteusantes.*[15] If

---

14. Ordinarily, as we have noted, the Pauline *sphragis* is viewed as a designation for baptism. A different interpretation is defended by Cornely
(*in h. 1*) and Prat, *Théolog. de S. Paul,* (7th ed., II, 163): *sphragis*
would apply only to the apostles and would designate charisms, which
are, as it were, the seal of the apostolic ministry. In the same vein, see
also R. Schnackenburg, *Das Heilsgeschehen bei der Taufe,* 85. Others
interpret it as confirmation, e.g., J. Coppens, *L'imposition des mains et
les rites connexes . . .* (Louvain, 1925), 271-275, and the commentaries
of Belser and Allo. But apart from the Pauline vocabulary, which we
shall consider shortly, the use of *sphragis* in the early Church constitutes
a strong argument against this interpretation. F. J. Dölger (*Sphragis,*
179-183) showed that this word was applied to confirmation only from
the third century on, in the Churches of the West; thus he too is led
to seeing in Paul's text a reference to baptism. See also A. Benoit, *op.
cit.,* 103-105, who writes: "It seems arbitrary to us to see confirmation
already in the Pauline *sphragis*" (105).

15. The two acts designated by *akousantes* and *pisteusantes* precede the
moment indicated by *esphragisthēte.* The aorist principle generally indicates the anteriority of the secondary action in relation to the main one.
There is, however, one exception (for narrative texts): when the participle and the main verb designate the *same* action, e.g., in Col 2, 11-12.
But this cannot be the case for Eph 1, 13 where the two participles
akousantes and *pisteusantes* are in the active voice and designate an act
of Christians, while *esphragisthēte,* in the passive, has God as the
logical subject of the act; these are, therefore, different acts. Thus, the
interpretation of M. Verheijen (*art. cit.,* 329) is inadmissible: according
to him, the imposition of the seal (= spiritual circumcision) would be
nothing else but faith, "but the faith that is present for the bath of renewal in the Holy Spirit." In other words, the imposition of the seal

the verb *esphragisthēte* designated a post-baptismal gift, we would expect to find in the words preceding it at least an allusion to the rite of baptism itself, the act *par excellence* by which one enters into the Christian life, and of which Paul speaks so frequently. But before *esphragisthēte* there are only two expressions describing the actions of those who wish to become Christians: They *have heard* the word of truth, the good news of salvation, and they *have believed* in it. This is the vocabulary of the kerygma, of the first announcing of the message to those who are not yet Christians.[16] The most important passage for grasping the nuances of those expressions is Rom 10, 14-18, which is constructed entirely on this relationship between preaching and faith. We cite only v. 17: *he pistis ex akoēs, he de akoē dia rēmatos Christou.* Faith is possible only among those who wish to *hear* the word of the Gospel (see v. 8: *ēkousan*) and are ready to obey it (*upekousan*, v. 16). This explains the two Pauline expressions: *akoe pisteos* (Gal 3, 5), the preaching oriented toward faith. For St. Paul, faith consists of obedience to the Gospel, as is clear in the equivalence that exists between the formulas *upakouein to euaggelio* and *pisteuein* in the same phrase of Rom 10, 16.

This reference to obedience or faith in the Gospel seems to have been a customary one in the early catechesis.[17] We find it again in the sending forth of the apostles in Mk 16, 15-16, in the famous chapter 6 of the Epistle to the Romans, which treats of baptism (see v. 17), and in I Peter whose baptismal character has been carefully noted by many within the past few years (1, 14; 1, 22, 23).

The verb *sphragizein*, therefore, belongs to a strictly baptismal

---

would precede baptism: *esphragisthēte* would thus be identified with *pisteusantes*. This is grammatically impossible, since the action of the latter verb is prior to that of the former.

16. The noun *akoē*, very close to *angelia* and *kerygma*, has become one of the technical terms used for the proclamation of the message. See Kittel, *Theol. Wört.*, I, 222 (also 220, 38-39).

17. See the study of E. G. Selwyn on the traditional formulas of catechesis, which are found again and again in the different epistles of the New Testament: *The First Epistle of St. Peter*, 365-466 (esp. 390).

context. The fact that the verb is mentioned immediately after the preaching of the Gospel and the act of faith, which precede the ablution, makes it practically certain that this impressing of the seal goes back to baptism itself.

b) The text of Eph 4, 30, where the verb *esphragisthete* appears once again, also belongs to the context of baptism. The whole section of Eph 4, 17-5, 20 develops the theme of the new life in Christ. Expressions of the baptismal catechesis abound here.[18] As in Eph 1, 13, the section begins (4, 20-21) by reference to the preaching that is heard and the teaching that is received: *umeis ou outos emathete ton Xriston ... auton ekousate* [*for the kerygma*] *... en auto edidaxthete* [*for the catechesis*]. Next are mentioned the obligations of the Christian, who has been recreated by God; he must lead a new life: *endusasthai ton kainon anthropon ton kata theon ktisthenta* (v. 24; see the baptismal section in Rom 6, 4: *en kainoteti zoes peripatesomen*). This new life implies a putting away of the old man: *apothesthai ... ton palaion anthropon*, v. 22; *dio apothemenoi to pseudos*, v. 25 (see also in a baptismal context: *apothemenoi oun pasan kakian ... os artigenneta brephe*, I Pet 2, 1-2; *apekuesen emas logo aletheias eis to einai emas aparxen tina ton auton ktismaton ... dio apothemenoi pasan ruparian kai perisseian kakias*) (Jas 1, 18, 21). Let us also note that at the end of the section vv. 5, 8-14 develop the theme of *light* in the Christian life. They close with a citation from an early Christian hymn: "*Awake, sleeper, and arise from among the dead, and Christ will enlighten thee*," which seems especially appropriate to the ceremony of baptism.[19] We should recall that the baptismal catechesis is often regarded in the New Testament as an *illumination* of Christians (Heb 6, 4; 10, 32).

We see then that the verse Eph 4, 30 fits into a typically baptismal context. Let us also note a very important detail, the relationship between the impressing of the seal and redemption: *esphragisthēte eis hemeran apolutrōseōs*. The same relationship was already seen in 1, 13: *esphragisthēte ... eis apolutrōsin*. Re-

18. See E. G. Selwyn, *op. cit.*, the outlines IV, V, VI (390-391, 394-395).
19. This is what J. Huby says (*Saint Paul. Les épîtres de la captivité*, 230), following M. Dibelius and F. J. Dölger.

demption is put in the perspective of the future (*eis*), as an eschatological reality still to be attained; but it is realized in the Christian life (1, 7: *echomen tēn apolutrōsin*) and consists principally in the remission of sins (*ibid.*: *tēn aphesin tōn paraptōmatō*., see Col 1, 14). But we know that in early Christianity the remission of sins was linked essentially to the act of baptism; on the other hand, the eschatological gift of the Holy Spirit, a participation in the gift of Pentecost (Ac 10, 45, 47; 11, 17), was considered as being distinct from this remission and subsequent to baptism. This is clear in Ac 2, 38: *baptisthētō hekastos humōn . . . eis aphesin tōn hamartiōn, humōn, kai lēmpsesthe tēn dōrean tou hagiou pneumatos* (that gift which the apostles just received; see Ac 1, 5, 8), and in 8; 17: *monon de bebaptismenoi hupērchon . . . tote epetithesan tas cheiras ep' autous* (see also 19, 5-6).[20] The redemption of Christians and the remission of sins make us think of baptism, and not the post-baptismal effusion of the Spirit.

Let us also note that in Eph 1, 13, the new Christians' object of faith is described at length: *ton logon tēs alētheias, to euangelion tes sōtērias humōn*. The formula *ton logon tēs alētheias* seemed adequate. Why add these few words on "the *good news* of salvation"? Because the whole context speaks of redemption (see v. 14: *eis apolutrōsin tēs peripoiēseōs*). But just as the latter is, so too is the theme of salvation linked .closely with baptism (*ho pisteusas esōsen hemas dia loutrou palingenesias*, Tit 3, 5); *kai baptistheis sōthēsetai* (Mk 16, 16); on the other hand, it is never mentioned in connection with the laying on of hands. Yet the words *to euangelion tēs sōtērias* pertain to the kerygma (*to . . . kerygma tēs sōtērias*, in the brief conclusion of Mark; see I Cor 1, 21); however, we know how often the kerygma speaks of baptism (see, for example, Mk 16, 15-16; Ac 16, 31-33).

The conclusion seems to impose itself: the relationship of cause and effect between the marking with the seal and redemption, on the one hand, and on the other, the context of *kerygma* and salvation, where the theme of the imposition of the seal is found, oblige

20. The grace of the two sacraments was clearly distinguished: baptism brought about the remission of sins (Acts 2, 38), while the postbaptismal gift of the Spirit, "the gift of Pentecost," was essentially oriented toward witness (Acts 1, 5).

us to see in the verb *sphragizein* a designation for baptism.

c) A final argument is provided by the same text of Eph 1, 13, namely, by the relationship between *akousantes ton logon tēs alētheias* and *pisteusantes* on the one hand, and *esphragisthēte* on the other. The act of faith in the word of truth is *anterior* to the impressing of the seal. The relationship between the verbs is important: "to hear the word" and "to believe" are conditions which must be met before a person can receive the seal of the Spirit. The latter is thus presented as *a seal on faith*. But is it not remarkable that this expression "seal on faith" (or its equivalent) appears in different texts, from the second century onward, to designate baptism?[21] In the *Extracts from Theology* (86, 2; G. C. S., Klemens, III, 133), Clement of Alexandria speaks of the believing soul (*pistē*) who has received the seal of truth (*to tēs alētheias labousa sphragisma*). In this text, baptism is considered a divine seal on the *truth* accepted in faith by the catechumen; this is what we saw in Eph 1, 13: *akousantes ton logon tēs alētheias ... esphragisthēte*. Other authors speak directly about the seal of *faith*: *hoi tēn sphragida tēs pisteōs athrauston diaphulaxantes* (Ps. Hipp., *De consum. saec.*, 42; G. C. S., Hipp., I, 2, 360); likewise, later on St. Basil: *esti gar to baptisma sphragis tēs pistoes* (*Adv. Ennom.*, III, 5; P. 6., 29, 665). In the West, Tertullian above all uses such formulas. In *De Poenit.*, 6, he uses terms that are almost identical with those of St. Basil: "Lavacrum illud obsignatio est fideli" (P. L., 1, 1349). The same idea appears again in *De corona*, 11: "Ablutione delictorum, quam fides impetrat obsignata in Patre et Filio et Spiritu Sancto" (*C.S.E.L.*, 20, 206, 19-20). The starting point for so strong a vocabulary is probably found in the Pauline expression of Eph 1, 13: *pisteusantes esphragisthēte*.[22] The belief of new Christians in the word of truth is marked by God with the seal of the Spirit.

Without doubt, in mentioning this impression of the seal (*sphragisamenos, esphragisthēte*) which Christians have received,

---

21. They have been studied together by F. J. Dölger, *Sphragis*, 99-104. We borrow these various texts from his study.
22. Note in Rom 4, 11 the connection that Paul makes between (the seal of) *circumcision* and Abraham's *faith*: *sphragida tēs dikaiosunēs tēs pisteōs*. For the relationship between *baptism* and *faith* (but without mention of the impressing of the seal), see Mk 16, 16: *ho pisteusas kai baptistheis*.

St. Paul is referring to the act of their baptism as a divine stamp of approval on their faith.[23] This conclusion is reached not only on the basis of later precisions in terminology in the texts of the first few centuries, but also by an analysis of the Pauline and New Testament vocabulary itself. Let us clarify one more point: Does the word *sphragizein* refer to the *exterior rite,* or does it designate only the *spiritual gift* conferred in baptism? While the various commentaries usually do not raise this question, it is an important one. In the Old Testament, circumcision was an external, permanent sign of a person's belonging to the Covenant. For St. Paul, that which corresponds to this in Christianity is a spiritual circumcision: the image of the "seal," transposed from circumcision to baptism, cannot pertain to the external, temporary act of the baptismal ablution as such, but only to the reality which, conferred at that moment, continues to exist, namely, the spiritual marking with the seal. This impressing of the seal (Eph 1, 13; 4, 30) is made with the help of the Spirit, and it is God himself who impresses it (II Cor 1, 22), and not the person who baptizes. The participles *sphragisamenos* and *dous,* connected by a single article, are closely allied: the second is an explanation of the first. This divine action, therefore, takes place *en tais kardiais hēmōn.* Nothing indicates that the mention of the impressing of the seal is a direct allusion to the external rite. Rather, it designates the spiritual gift conferred upon the baptized.[24]

---

23. Therein is resolved the question raised by various commentators on *sphragisamenos* in II Cor 1, 22: Does it concern all Christians or only the apostles? If the verb designates the baptismal seal, it can only be a question of Christians in general.

24. We look upon the interpretation of A. Benoit with certain reservations: "Paul is unfamiliar with a *sphragis* that would be an independent confirmation and separate from baptism. For him *sphragis* designates the whole of the baptismal act, with a more special emphasis on the gift of the Spirit" (*Le baptême chrétien au second siècle,* 107). It is true that the Pauline epistles do not mention the imposition of hands as a follow-up to baptism. But does one have the right to conclude that Paul is unfamiliar with it? In Acts 19, 5-6, it is said explicitly that Paul imposed his hands on the Johannites of Ephesus, immediately after their baptism. Thus it is dubious to say that for Paul there is but one gift of the Spirit (*op. cit.,* 104), but it is correct to say that in his epistles he mentions only baptismal grace; he designates it by *sphragizesthai*

Anointing by Faith

Having determined the immediate context of our discussion, we
can now attempt to explain the meaning of *chrisas* in the text of
II Cor 1, 21.

a) As to the *construction* of the phrase, there is general agreement that *theos* is the predicate, with *esti* understood. "Now it is
God who is warrant for us and for you in Christ, who *has anointed
us*, who has also stamped us with his seal and has given us the
Spirit as a pledge in our hearts." The four participles are grouped
in twos, each connected by a single article: (1) *ho bebaiōn kai
chrisas*; (2) *ho sphragisamenos kai dous*. We have already said
that the last two verbs designate the same reality, the spiritual gift
conferred in baptism. The added expression marked by *kai* that
precedes *sphragisamenos* distinguishes carefully the two groups;
it also seems to suggest that the mark of the seal takes place *after*
the reality indicated by *chrisas*: the God who has anointed us, has
also marked us with his seal. In other words, the anointing comes
before the impression of the seal; it *precedes baptism*.

b) What is St. Paul thinking of when he talks of an anointing
conferred by God before the baptismal ablution?[25] A comparison

in the three texts we have studied. Can it be said that *sphragis* designates
the initiation in general and implies a twofold communication of the
Spirit? Although it is not to be positively excluded, the indications we
have given show that Paul is thinking of the act of baptism itself; what
is involved in the imposition of hands and the postbaptismal gift, seems
here to be outside his range of vision.

25. The commentaries seem to be rather disoriented. In the Patristic tradition
and the Renaissance, there is a great divergence of opinion (for the
Middle Ages, see n. 28 below). Belser remarks that in the interpretation of
the two verses there has been over the centuries a divergence of views
and a lack of clarity (*Der zweite Korintherbrief*, 62). The situation is
not much better among modern-day commentators. For Heinrici, Cornely,
and Prat (*Théol. de S. Paul*, II, 163), who understand *hēmas* in terms
of the apostles alone, *chrisas* designates the spiritual anointing that prepares one for the apostolic ministry (this interpretation goes back to
Estius); but *hēmas* recalls *hēmas sun humin* and should thus refer to
all Christians (which is confirmed by the close relationship between
chrisas and *bebaiōn*: but as to the latter verb, the complement is certainly

with the passage in Eph 1, 13 tells us. It is surprising that commentators have not made use of this parallel. The two texts, however, are very similar: both mention the impression of the seal (II Cor: *theos ... sphragisamenos;* Eph: *humeis ... esphragisthēte*); both speak of the pledge of the Spirit with respect to salvation. The only difference—which in no way affects the theological content—is that in II Cor everything is seen from the viewpoint of God, while the text of the Epistle to the Ephesians considers the same reality from the viewpoint of Christians. What takes place before the impression of the seal in the two texts, therefore, probably designates the same reality, looked at from the two points of view. Let us put the two verses face to face:

Viewpoint of God	*Viewpoint of Christians*
(II Cor 1, 21-22)	(Eph 1, 13)
1. *Chrisas hēmas theos,*	1. *akousantes ton logon tēs alētheias ... kai pisteusantes*
2. *ho kai sphragisamenos*	2. *esphragisthēte*
3. *ton arrabōna ton pneumatos kai dous*	3. *toi pneumati ... hos estin arrabōn ...*

all believers). Belser and Allo interpret *chrisas* in terms of baptism, (as a rite, but what rite is meant?) and *sphragisamenos* in terms of confirmation; but that is impossible if, as we have shown, it is the latter verb that designates the baptismal gift. Moreover, the close connection between *bebaiōn* and *chrisas* then becomes very strange, since these verbs, so closely united, would designate two realities that are not of the same order, strengthening in the faith and the sacrament of baptism. E. Dinkler (*Die Taufterminologie in 2, Kor 21f.,* 180-182) and J. Ysebaert (*Greek Baptismal Terminology,* 291-294) have suggested that *chrisas* and *sphragisamenos* are two different designations of baptism; but such an interpretation is contrary to the fact that the signing with the seal is here presented as being added on to the anointing: thus they cannot be identified. A similar criticism must be raised against the explanation offered by Plummer, following Swete (*The Holy Spirit in the New Testament,* 385): the impressing of the seal, say these two authors, is a reference to baptism, and the anointing is purely spiritual. This is true.

The parallelism is immediately clear. If nos. 2 and 3 on both sides correspond so perfectly in the above diagram, there is good reason to believe no. 1 does also. This means that *chrisas* would correspond to *akousantes . . . kai pisteusantes,* the first verb indicating *divine* action, the other two *human* activity. The meaning of the divine anointing then becomes clear: it signifies *the action of God arousing faith in the heart of those who hear the word of truth.* Before receiving baptism, the catechumens received the evangelical message and were instructed in Christian doctrine in order to become true disciples of Christ (see Mt 28, 19); it is only then that the baptismal immersion was made in the name of God, an immersion whereby they were marked with the "seal" of the Spirit. Thus they became part of the "people of possession" (*peripoiēsis,* Eph 1, 13), and became members of the new Covenant. The "seal" of the Spirit is a sign of possession on God's part; it constitutes his response to the act of the catechumen who has "accepted" his word. In the old Covenant, there were two phases in the conclusion of the Covenant: the submission of the people of Israel to the conditions of the book of the Covenant, and the sprinkling of the people with the blood of victims, as a sign of the ratification of the Covenant on God's part (Ex 19, 7-8). Prior to that, Abraham's faith had also been "sealed" with a rite, circumcision, as a sign of the Covenant. The two moments are found again in the new Covenant: the faith of the catechumens and the divine seal.

But in this act of faith on the part of those who aspire to baptism, God is already at work. This is what Paul calls the *divine anointing;* it is a spiritual activity, on the same level as the impressing of the seal that will follow. But it is different in that it precedes baptism and is a preparation for it,[26] enabling the

---

But if one is not aware of the *anteriority* of the anointing in relation to the signing with the seal, it will be difficult to distinguish between them.

26. Some will wonder, no doubt, if it is so certain that the anointing is prior to the signing with the seal, as we have said; for the two verbs *chrisas* and *sphragisamenos,* having God as subject, could perhaps designate the same action, under two different metaphors. But the problem dis-

catechumen to adhere to the word of the Gospel. This "anointing" of God can be identified with the "drawing" of the Father, of which St. John speaks (Jn 6, 44); but Paul puts us in a more distinctly baptismal context.[27]

c) Does the interpretation we have made conform to the context? In particular, does it account for the close relationship between the two participles of v. 21, *bebaiōn . . . kai chrisas?* It seems so. In our opinion, it is only in the explanation we have offered that *chrisas* is in perfect continuity with everything around it. We said in the beginning that *bebaioō* signifies strengthening

appears if we compare these words with their parallel in Eph 1, 13, where *akousantes* and *pisteusantes* are certainly anterior to *esphragisthēte* (see above, n. 15). But *chrisas* is parallel with these two verbs of the kerygma. This confirms what was already suggested by the presence of *kai* before *sphragisamenos*: the anointing *precedes* the impressing of the baptismal seal.

27. This relationship to St. John is suggested to us by a medieval commentary, the anonymous commentary of the school of Abelard published by A. Landgraf, *Commentarius Cantabrigensis in epist. Pauli e schola Abaelardi*, 2 (in *Medieval Studies* [U. of Notre Dame, 1939], II, 2, 269-270). The explanation he gives is interesting, for it covers that of the whole Latin tradition. The latter interpreted almost unanimously "unxit" in terms of baptismal grace, by which we are anointed kings and priests (the clearest and most concise formula in this regard is that of the *Glossa interlinearis*: "Unxit nos in reges et sacerdotes per spiritum in baptismo.") For Abelard's disciple, the anointing of II Cor 1, 21 signifies the pleasant, interior attraction exerted on the Christian by the law of Christ, in contrast to the harshness of the old law: "Christus vero suavia praecepta afferens delibutus unguentis venit. Inde in Canticis dicitur: Curremus in odorem unguentorum tuorum, id est sequamur suavitatem praeceptorum tuorum non coacti, sed voluntate ducti. De quibus praeceptis dicit ipsa veritas: Iugum meum suave est et onus meum leve. Quae *suavitas praeceptorum nos Deo attraxit.* Et hoc est: qui 'nos unxit,' id est *qui per unguenta legis suae nos ad se traxit.*" The commentary does not say that in St. Paul the anointing is situated in a baptismal context. But the important point is that the anointing is no longer interpreted in terms of the grace of baptism, but, in Johannine style, of the interior attraction to the means whereby Christ draws us to himself by "his law" and his doctrine. This interpretation resembles very closely the one we have given. It shows the continuity between St. Paul and St. John, an idea we in turn will stress later on.

in the *faith*, in the Gospel which has been preached to Christians; but *chrisas*, which comes right after, recalls the role played by God in the origin of such faith. Thus we understand perfectly how closely related *bebaiōn* and *chrisas* are: both concern a unique divine action, which at first *arouses* in men's hearts an adhesion in faith, and later on strengthens Christians in their adhesion.[28] Paul had to prove his fidelity and the intensity of his word. He does so by appealing to the fidelity of God (v. 18), who communicates and transmits himself to all believers: the fidelity of God has been manifested in Christ, in whom there is no "yes and no." But it is this Christ whom Paul and his two companions, Silvanus and Timothy, preached at Corinth (v. 19); in saying a solemn "Amen" in their liturgical meetings (v. 20), the Corinthians indicate their complete agreement with God's word, and thus also with the preaching of the Apostle on Christ.[29] This is why Paul speaks in v. 21 of their common firmness in the same faith (*bebaiōn hēmas sun hēmin*): he was the herald, they the beneficiaries. How then could they accuse Paul of inconstancy, since his Gospel is theirs, the word of the trustworthy God? The purpose of vv. 21-22 is also clear: after having shown their common attachment to the same faith, Paul emphasizes that this faith in them is due solely to the work of God. He who strengthens them in the faith—Paul who preaches it, and the Corinthians who bear witness to it—is God, who by his anointing (*chrisas*) led them all to believe in his word. It is he also who then put the seal on his work by giving them the pledge of the Spirit at the moment of baptism.

The immediate context of II Cor 1, 21-22 enables us then to give the word *chrisas* a coherent exegesis. The difficulty involved in the interpretation of this expression arises from the fact that

---

28. Belser is right in emphasizing the time difference between *bebaiōn* et *chrisas*: the anointing (*chrisas*, in the aorist) refers to a more or less distant period when the Corinthians were brought to the faith; the verb *bebaiōn* (in the present) indicates that God is now making them persevere in this faith. Belser's mistake was to interpret the anointing as the baptismal *rite* itself.

29. See W. C. van Unnik, "Reisepläne und Amen-Sagen. Zusammenhang und Gedankenfolge in 2. Korinther 1, 15, 24," in *Studia paulina in honorem J. De Zwaan* (Haarlem, 1953), 215-234 (see 226).

the verb "to anoint" normally makes one think of a rite and the fact that parallel texts in this case are rare: nowhere else in the Pauline literature is the slightest reference made to an anointing of Christians. Here, however, Paul speaks of it as being a well-known fact, without supplying any commentary; he had already referred to it more than once in his catechesis. But how did he come to compare the divine action in the act of faith to an "anointing"? This is what we must now consider, before passing on to the text of St. John.

Anointing of the Christian and Anointing of Christ

With several other critics,[30] we believe that the probable basis for this Pauline expression is to be found in the texts of Luke on the anointing of Christ in baptism (Lk 4, 18; Ac 4, 27; 10, 38). First, let us remember that elsewhere in the New Testament, as well as in II Cor 1, 21, the verb *chriein* is always used in a figurative sense: in Heb 1, 9, it refers to the celestial anointing of Christ at the moment of his entrance into glory; and in three other passages, all from Luke, it pertains to the prophetic anointing of Jesus in the Jordan.[31] The verse of II Cor 1, 21 on the anointing of the Christian offers several interesting resemblances with these passages on the anointing of Christ at the beginning of his ministry. In both cases, it is a question of a spiritual anointing: in Paul's text, it is God who has anointed Christians; according to Ac 10, 38 also, it is God who anoints Christ, and this anointing is done with the Holy Spirit. In each case the context is a baptismal one. But

---

30. Heinrici, Lietzmann, Plummer, Cornely. Likewise, Prat (*Théologie de saint Paul*, 7 ed., II, 315, n. 3) and Schnackenburg (*Das Heilsgeschehen . . .* , 85). Prat cites texts of the New Testament with *chriein*, e.g., Acts 4, 27 and 10, 38, and adds that there is "probably an allusion here to one of these two texts." For this reason, Prat and others understand *chrisas* here as the "preparatory anointing for the apostolic mission." We shall shortly return to this question.

31. In the Old Testament, only the prophetic anointing is always to be taken in the figurative sense. See our article "L'onction du Christ," in *N. R. Th.*, 1958, 225-226; R. Koch, *Geist und Messias* (Vienna, 1950), 125. The text from which comes the expression in St. Luke is Is 61, 1.

early theology drew much of its inspiration from Christ's baptism to explain the baptism of Christians.[52] Thus it is quite understandable that one should speak of an *anointing* of the Christian with respect to his baptism; also, that this anointing does not designate an exterior rite; finally, that this anointing of Christians cannot be explained by any biblical or Jewish antecedent. It speaks of itself, if the model is the baptism of Jesus.

But the differences in the two uses of the word "anointing" should not be minimized. For Christ, the anointing with the Spirit took place *after* his baptism (Lk 3, 21: *Iēsou baptisthentos*); in the Christian initiation that Paul describes, it *precedes* the baptismal ablution. And above all, the anointing in the Jordan was essentially a *prophetic* anointing, preparing and inaugurating the mystery of Jesus, and oriented toward the proclaiming of the message (Lk 4, 18). For the Christian life, it is different: the baptized person undoubtedly also receives an apostolic mission to bear witness among men, but it is conferred on him—after baptism! —by the imposition of hands, as the Acts show us. On the other hand, the spiritual anointing, conferred before baptism, has as its object the origin and development of faith. Because they have not taken sufficient notice of these differences, several authors, relying too heavily on passages from Luke, have interpreted *chrisas* in II Cor 1, 21 in terms of the apostolic mission. But this would be foreign to those people who have not as yet been received into the Church!

Must we, therefore, abandon the idea of seeing in the baptismal anointing of Christ the antecedent and model of the anointing of the Christian? We think not. In addition to the points of similarity noted above, there is one more, which is of great importance: for Christ and for the Christian, the anointing is conferred essentially *in view of the word*. Christ is anointed by the Spirit to *proclaim* it, the Christian to *adhere to it by faith*. The solution of the problem of the slight change of meaning in the word "anointing" is no doubt of a theological order. It probably must be found in the essential differences that exist between the person and situation of Jesus and that of the Christian; the unity and richness of the

32. See *L'onction du Christ,* 247, n. 61.

mystery of Christ is refracted in different ways in the believer's
life.

This explains the change in perspective when we pass from
the passages of Luke (anointing of Christ) to that of Paul (anointing of the Christian). For Christ, the spiritual anointing was both
an *illumination* and a *stimulus*. But it could not be a matter of
faith. Only the idea of stimulus is emphasized in the passages:
baptism is shown as the inauguration of Jesus' ministry; as such,
it prefigures the gift of Pentecost, the baptism of the Spirit. But
for the Christian, the sending of someone on a mission must be
preceded by accession to the faith, personal adhesion to the word
of truth, and a deeper understanding of that word. The word
"anointing" has been chosen to designate this aspect. Its use, moreover, is not arbitrary: the anointing of Christ was also an illumination. It was part of the continuation of the prophetic anointing
of the Old Testament. But the experience of the prophets consisted
essentially of the "knowledge of God": [33] they too had first *received
communication* of God's word; it is only afterwards that they were
able to *transmit* it to the people. So too with the Christian life: the
light of faith precedes witness. And we shall see later on[34] that if,
in the Acts, the gift of the Spirit is normally granted after baptism,
it is not so for the pagans of the house of Cornelius: on them the
Spirit descends *before* the ablution, because they must first believe
before becoming witnesses. In short, the idea of the coming of
the Spirit upon Christ undergoes a certain disassociation when the
Christian is involved; thus, the baptism in the Jordan is both the
model of Christian baptism and that of the baptism of the Spirit
(confirmation). The mentioning of an anointing for the Christian
is derived from this baptism of Jesus; but it is used in the New
Testament only in regard to baptism of water, in particular, for
the grace of faith, which is also of a prophetic order, as is the
grace of witness. Later tradition will speak of a *post*-baptismal
anointing, with regard to this grace of witness which is the baptism
of the Spirit. Thus, the two anointings—that which precedes and

---

33. See E. Jacob, *Théologie de l'Ancien Testament* (Neuchatel, 1955), 193-
    198.
34. See further on, pp. 125-128 in the present volume.

that which follows the baptismal ablution—both stem in one way and another from the anointing of Christ in the Jordan.

Of course, in all this there is a good deal of speculation. Too little evidence is available to retrace with certainty the origin of the Pauline theme of the "anointing of the Christian." But the line of development which we have traced seems the most likely one. On the other hand, it is important to note that the relative uncertainty that remains regarding the origin and antecedents of the expression in no way affects the interpretation we have given for II Cor 1, 21. Thanks to parallels in the other Epistles and the study of the vocabulary of the verse itself, we can consider as certain that the divine anointing of which the Apostle speaks designates *the action of God in the origin of faith* among those who embrace Christianity. The text of John which we shall now study will fully confirm this exegesis. At the same time, it will supply us with a genuine theological appreciation of the Pauline concept.

ST. JOHN (I JN 2, 20, 27)

In the whole New Testament the noun *chrisma* appears in but one place, I Jn 2, 18-28, but here it occurs three times (vv. 20 and 27), each time with respect to Christians: "But you have *an anointing* from the Holy One and you know all things" (v. 20); "And as for you, let the *anointing* which you have received from him dwell in you, and you have no need that anyone teach you. But as *his anointing* teaches you concerning all things, and [this teaching] is true and is no lie, even as it [the anointing] has taught you, abide in him [Christ]" (v. 27).

We have retained for the moment the translation of the word *chrisma* as "anointing," along with the Vulgate and the Latin tradition. However, several authors say that, properly speaking, the term signifies not the act of anointing, but the ointment or oil with which one anoints. We shall return to this point, after trying to determine the meaning of *chrisma* in the context of the Epistle.

According to the most common interpretation, *chrisma* designates simply the anointing with the Holy Spirit.[35] But this explanation is too vague, for we can imagine different kinds of activity on the part of the Spirit. Some exegetes specify further that it is primarily an illuminating act, an interior teaching.[36] A rather different explanation has been put forth by Reitzenstein and Dodd[37]: *chrisma* designates Christian doctrine, of which v. 24 speaks, the word of God accepted in baptism. This opinion has been rejected firmly by a good number of interpreters. But we believe it contains an important element of truth, which should be integrated within the customary explanation. We were led to this conclusion almost in spite of ourselves, by a detailed examination of various texts.

The Vocabulary

As in the preceding section, the semantic study of the expres-

---

36. We will return in the third part of this article to the interpretation of the ancients. Among the moderns, let us cite a few authors. In a special article devoted to the verses in question, J. Michl wrote "Der Geist als Garant des rechten Glaubens," in *Vom wort des Lebens. Festschrift für Max Meinertz*, 1951, and also adopted this opinion. R. A. Knox describes the anointing as the "bestowal of the Holy Spirit after baptism." The phrase "after baptism" and the rest of the text show that the author is thinking of a sacramental rite, no doubt, that of confirmation. W. Nauck (*Die Tradition und der Charakter des ersten Johannesbriefes* [Tübingen, 1957], 94) interprets *chrisma* as the gift of the Spirit at the moment of baptism; likewise, A. M. Hunter, *Introducing New Testament Theology* (London, 1957), 134, n. 1. The older commentaries of Belser (1906), Camerlynck (1909), and Vrede (1924) saw in *chrisma* the sacrament of confirmation. Fortunately, almost all recent authors do not speak of an exterior rite. For it is clear that *chrisma* is to be understood metaphorically (see v. 27: *menei en humin, didaskei humas*), just as the anointing of Christ in baptism. See J. Michl, *art. cit.*, 143, n. 15.

36. Chare, 532: "the illuminating and sanctifying action of the Holy Spirit"; same formula in De Ambroggi, 220; Bonsirven, 146: "interior teaching of the Holy Spirit"; likewise, Schnackenburg, 161; J. Michl, *art. cit.*, 145.

37. R. Reitzenstein, *Die hellenistischen Mysterienreligionen*, 3d ed., 1927, 396-397; *Die Vorgeschichte der christlichen Taufe* (Leipzig, 1929), 184 and n. 1; C. H. Dodd, *The Johannine Epistles*, 62f. The latter remarks that the two interpretations (by the *Spirit* or by the *word*) are perhaps less different than would appear; there would be, above all, a difference of point of view. We shall arrive at an almost identical conclusion at the end of our study.

sions in which the word *chrisma* appears serves to clarify its meaning.

a) The anointing is a gift which Christians *have received* at a moment in the past (v. 27). The verb *lambanein* is used several times in St. John for spiritual goods: "And of his fullness we have all received" (Jn 1, 16); "Receive the Holy Spirit" (20, 22). But since the Johannine Gospel is a gospel of revelation, it is concerned in particular with the "receiving of Christ" (Jn 1, 12; 5, 43; 13, 20), who brings us the revelation of the Father. This involves above all accepting his message in faith: receiving his words (Jn 12, 48; 17, 8), or the commandment that comes from the Father (II Jn 4), but especially the witness of Christ (Jn 3, 11, 32, 33; see also 5, 34). In I Jn 2, 27, where the words *ap' autou* refer to Christ, the anointing *received from him* is probably also related to his word.

To what period does the aorist *elabete* refer? The parallel passages indicate that it refers to the beginning of faith among Christians. The Apostle speaks of this period on different occasions. But all of a sudden in these passages the formulas appear that are characteristic of the *kerygma*. In the context we are studying, we find in v. 24 a reference to the preaching made to Christians: *ho ap' archēs ēkousate*. The mention of the "beginning" belongs to the vocabulary of the *kerygma;* in the Epistle it occurs twice, not far from the present passage: *entolēn hēn eichete ap' archēs* (2, 7); *angelia hen ēkousate ap' archēs* (3, 11; see also II Jn 5, 6). What is said of the Antichrist refers also to this same moment in the past: *ēkousate hoti antichristos erchetai* (2, 18); likewise, in a more general way, to what is said of the word that is preached to Christians: *ho logos hon ēkousate* (2, 7).

We know that the vocabulary of *kerygma* is rare in St. John.[38] Thus it is all the more striking when he uses it regularly in these passages where he reminds Christians of the moment of their conversion.[39] We see here the familiar terms of *angelia, logos,* and espe-

---

38. He never uses, either in the Gospel or in the epistles, the characteristic vocabulary of the *kerygma*: *kerussein, katangellein, euangelion, euangelizesthai*. On the other hand, *angelia* appears twice in the epistle (1, 5; 3, 11) and nowhere else in the New Testament.
39. W. Nauck (*Die Tradition und der Charakter des ersten Johannesbriefes,*

cially *akouein* (compare the Pauline formula *akoē pisteōs*). This would seem to mean that in reminding believers of what they received at that moment, John has in mind not so much the act of their baptism as the Gospel which has been preached to them and which they have accepted. This clarifies the formula *chrisma ho elabete*, which belongs to the same context, especially if we recall what was said above about St. Paul: before being marked with the Spirit's seal in baptism, Christians have heard the word (*akousantes ton logon*: the same terms as in I Jn) and believed in it (Eph 1, 13). The divine anointing (*chrisas . . . theos*) was the act by which God had aroused this faith in them (II Cor 1, 21). But in St. John too, the theme of anointing (*chrisma*) is undoubtedly related to a context that speaks of the first announcing of the word and the reception of it by those who wished to enter into Christianity.

b) In addition to *elabete*, there is in v. 27 a second verb in the aorist referring to anointing: to *chrisma edidaxen humas*. This past teaching continues in the present life of the Christian, since in the beginning of the phrase these same words are found with the verb in the present: to . . . *chrisma didaskei humas*. If we put aside Jn 9, 34 (the incident of the man born blind), *didaskein* in St. John is always a verb of revelation: it pertains to the teaching which the Father gave to the Son and which the latter transmits to the world (Jn 8, 28). Most often it is used to describe the activity of Jesus himself who teaches (Jn 6, 59; 7, 14, 28; 35; 8, 20): it is applied once (Jn 14, 26) to the Holy Spirit who "will teach" (*didaxsei*) us everything that Jesus has said.

It is this last text—which talks of the future teaching that will be made in the Church after the departure of Jesus—that offers the most interesting parallel with I Jn 2, 27. Nevertheless, in this verse of the Gospel, the Spirit's teaching is not presented as the communication of an independent and new doctrine, but as a recol-

---

84-86) has shown that the frequent mention of *ap' archēs* reminds Christians of the beginning of their Christian life, and specifically, of their baptism. But he did not pay sufficient attention to the presence of the kerygmatic vocabulary in this context: however, that compels us to think less of the *baptismal rite*, properly speaking, than of the *announcing of the word*.

lection (*hupomnēsei*) of Jesus' words. In John's vocabulary, this "remembrance" is concerned not only with the material tenor of Jesus' words, but also with the true understanding of them, their profound meaning, which the Spirit can reveal. It is important to note this intimate connection between the work of the Spirit and the historical teaching of Christ, in order to understand our present verse exactly. This is the only place in the Epistle where we find the verb *didaskein,* but it occurs here three times. The teaching of men, says St. John, is not necessary for Christians, for they have the *chrisma* of Christ who informs them about everything. The fact that at the end of the verse the verb is in the aorist shows that here too the author is thinking of the past, of the moment when they learned to know Christian truth. But while *elabete* signified the first acceptance in faith of this word of truth, *edidaxen* and *didaskei* indicate that from that moment on Christ's word has become for believers a true source of instruction.

Thus, *chrisma* is not the external teaching of the Church as such: the *chrisma* of believers is even more or less opposed to such teaching (*ou chreian echete hina tis didaskēi humas alla . . . to chrisma didaskei humas*). It indicates the word that has been preached, but insofar as it has become for believers an *interior reality,* an object of faith. Let us recall that St. Paul used the verb *chriein* to designate the divine action that made possible acceptance in faith of the word of truth; the *chrisma* of St. John is the result of this action, the word received and accepted in faith under the influence of the Spirit. Therefore, if by the aorists *elabete* and *edidaxen* John is recalling past events, these are events which were already of a spiritual order. In the word of Christ that was taught to Christians in the beginning, the Holy Spirit was already at work, and it is its relationship with Jn 14, 26 that makes the present verse so interesting.[40]

If such is the case, we understand perfectly that there is a real continuity between past teaching (*kathōs edidaxen*) and present teaching (*hos didaskei*). Let us also note that the reference to the

---

40. A textual variant in 2, 27 shows that tradition has seen this passage as being closely related to Jn 14, 26: in S. bo Cypr, one reads, instead of *chrisma didaskei, pneuma didaskei,* repeated at this point in the Gospel.

past when Christians received the *chrisma* is indicated in only two brief instances (a relative *ho elabete;* and a comparative *kathōs edidaxen*), and that from the beginning of the phrase all our attention falls on the main verb that opens the long period: *to chrisma . . . menei en humin.* In other words, *chrisma* is considered above all in its reality as *present* word (*menei*) and insofar as it is *interiorized* (*en humin*).

All of this may seem overly subtle. But it was necessary to bring out these various details, for it is only in this way that we can understand how the teaching by *chrisma* refers to *the word of Christ* as well as to *the activity of the Spirit,* and how the teaching received in the beginning by believers is what continues into their present life.

c) The three uses of *chrisma* in the present passage are accompanied either by a possessive or by the point of origin from which the anointing comes: Christians possess the anointing that comes from the Holy One (v. 20: *echete apo tou hagiou*); they received it from him (v. 27: *elabete ap' autou*); it is from him (*ibid.*: *to auton chrisma*). In each of these texts, the author is talking very probably not of the Father but of Christ; the title "Holy One" evokes his prophetic ministry, when he communicated the words of eternal life (Jn 6, 68f.). It is of no small concern either that the preposition *apo* appears twice, and not *para.* As Westcott has remarked, *para* designates the immediate source, the giver from whom one receives directly, while *apo* is used for immediate source, the giver from whom one receives directly, while *apo* is used for the mediate and first source, from whom those who receive are normally separated by a certain distance or by intermediaries.[41]

41. Westcott, *The Epistles of St. John,* 79 (see also 15). It would be wrong to insist too much on these nuances, since Hellenism tends to confuse *apo* and *para.* But this is not true for St. John, who always distinguishes them very carefully. Thus (*ex erchesthai*) to designate the incarnation, is always constructed with *apo theou,* when the disciples are speaking (Jn 3, 2; 13, 2; 16, 30), but when Jesus speaks, the verb is used with *para* (Jn 16, 27; 17, 8): for Jesus is "close" to the Father, while the disciples are "distant," knowing him only through the revelation of Christ. Similarly we find *lambanein para* when someone receives something directly, without any intermediary (Jn 5, 41, 44: men receive men; Jn 10, 18 and Apoc 2, 28: Christ receives from the Father), but *lambanein*

Therefore, *chrisma ho elabete ap' autou* presupposes that some transmission has already taken place between Christ and Christians; this is entirely normal if it involves the teaching communicated by Christ and transmitted in the Church, where it is preserved as coming from Jesus (*echete ap' autou*).

The objection may be made that the gift of the Spirit also goes back to the moment of baptism and it too could be a part of our expression. This is very unlikely, for, when he talks of what is received in baptism, John mentions a teaching, and not the Spirit. As to an immediate communication of the Spirit through the glorious Christ during the course of the Christian life, it is done without intermediaries, and would presuppose therefore *para* rather than *apo*.[42]

d) The three examples studied up to now refer above all to a time past when Christians received *chrisma*. The expression *chrisma*

---

apo when there is a certain distance or separation (I Jn 3, 22: men receive from God; III Jn 7: Christians in regard to pagans). Some may think that II Jn 4 is an exception: *entolēn elabomen para tou patros,* while in I Jn 4, 21 we read: *tautēn tēn entolēn echomen ap' autou,* but if we look closely, the rule is in force here also: in I Jn 4, 21, where the verb is in the *present,* the commandment is considered as a present norm in the Church, and so, for the author and his fellow-Christians, the origin of this commandment is already distant. On the contrary, in II Jn 4, John speaks of the *past*: he is present mentally at that moment when Jesus gave the great commandment; the disciples received the great precept from the Father, in the person of Jesus. Finally, let us note that *akouein apo* is never found in the Fourth Gospel: "to hear," by its nature, presupposes proximity between the person who talks and the one who listens; thus we always see *akouein para* (Jn 1, 40; 6, 45; 7, 51; 8, 26, 38, 40; 15, 15). In the Epistle, however, *akouein apo* appears once (I Jn 1, 5): *hē angelia hēn akēkoamen ap' autou kai anangellomen humin;* but here the verb "to hear" is in the present perfect: in the context of the Epistle, what is most important is the possession, *here and now,* of the message and its proclamation in the Church; the fact of having heard, already belongs to a rather distant *past,* whence the use of *apo.*

42. In St. John, there is no example of a spiritual gift received from Jesus and expressed with *lambanein*; but Acts 20, 24 shows that *para* would be normal: *tēn diakonian hēn elabomen para tou kuriou Iēsou.* See *ek* in Jn 1, 16: *ek tou plēromatos autou hēmeis pantes elabomen,* although here the nuance is different.

echete, which concerns the present, must be examined more closely; indeed, it confirms the interpretation we have given. *Echein* is, of course, a part of the mystical vocabulary of John, and would thus appear to favor the interpretation of *chrisma* as relating to the activity of the Holy Spirit. John uses this verb to mark the intimate union of the Christian with God: the believer "has God" (II Jn 9), "has the Father" (I Jn 2, 23; II Jn 9), "has the Son" (I Jn 5, 12; II Jn 9). But other formulas lack this resonance, namely, those where *echein* has as its object the words "law" or "commandment"; in the latter case, we are in a juridical or legal context. Schlatter has remarked that this is a rabbinical expression.[43] In fact, it is the Jews who say in Jn 19, 7: *hēmeis nomon echomen.* The expression (on the part of Jesus) is also found in Jn 14, 21: *ho echon tas entolas mou kai tērōn autas;* it means simply "to have the commandments," having received them from Jesus. It is natural in such a context to recall *from whom* these commandments come (in our case it is Christ): *tautēn tēn entolēn echomen ap' autou* (I Jn 4, 21), or at what moment they were received: *tēn entolēn echomen* [or *echete*] *ap' archēs* (I Jn 2, 7; II Jn 5). It is precisely to this literary context that the verse of I Jn 2, 20 is related: *chrisma echete apo tou hagiou* (see in this regard Jn 19, 7 and I Jn 4, 21, which we have just cited). Let us add that outside this passage John nowhere else uses the expression *echein apo*—here, in I Jn 4, 21, he uses it in regard to the *commandment* that comes from Christ. The expression "to have the *chrisma* coming from the Holy One" must, therefore, be interpreted in relation to this commandment, to the word of God which the Church received from Jesus.

e) Let us consider now the words of v. 27: *to chrisma . . . menei en humin.* Here we see the great advance made by St. John over Judaism: the word must be interiorized through faith. Here the role of the Holy Spirit enters in. The failure of the Jews was that they did not allow the word to penetrate within them where it would remain (Jn 5, 38); to remain in the word of Jesus, is to become one of his disciples (Jn 8, 31). The verb *menein* is very characteristic of the Johannine vocabulary.[44] To describe the union

---

43. A. Schlatter, *Der Evangelist Johannes*, 300-301.
44. See G. M. Pecorara, "De verbo 'manere' apud Johannem," in *Div. Thom.*

of Christians with *God* or *Christ, menein* is always in some way linked to a condition, for example: "He who eats my flesh, and drinks my blood, abides in me and I in him" (Jn 6, 57); "God is love, and he who abides in love abides in God, and God in him" (I Jn 4, 16). But the absolute or unconditional use of the verb is found once in the Gospel, for the *Spirit* of truth (Jn 14, 17), and four times in the Epistle, always in relation to *the word* of God or the teaching of Christ. The texts are as follows:

1) "*The word of God* 'abides' in you, and you have conquered the evil one" (I Jn 2, 14);

2) "*The truth* 'abides' in us, and will be with us forever" (II Jn 2);

3) "Whoever is born of God does not commit sin, because *his seed* 'abides' in him" (I Jn 3, 9);[45]

4) "Let *the anointing* which you have received from him, 'dwell' in you" (I Jn 2, 27; this is the passage that concerns us at present).

This emphasis on the word of God or truth in the first three texts makes it very probable that the statement on the anointing—in a completely parallel structure (always the same expression *menei en*)—is also related to the word.[46]

f) As a final argument, let us mention some parallel texts taken from elsewhere in St. John. According to I Jn 2, 20-21, the function of *chrisma* is to give knowledge of the truth: let us compare this with what St. John says in other places about this same knowledge. He speaks of it in Jn 8, 31-32 and II Jn 1-2: as in the passage in the First Epistle, knowledge of the truth is seen as coming from a reality that abides within us. We transcribe below these two passages and follow them with the one from the Epistle. Each time we shall

Plac., 40 (1937), 159-171, and our own article "L'impeccabilité du chrétien d'après 1 Joh., 3, 6-9," in *L'Evangile de Jean* (Desclée de Brouwer, 1958), 161-177, esp. 172-173 (in the present volume, p. 188f).

45. We have shown elsewhere (*art. cit.*, 170-172; p. 187f. of the present volume) that *sperma* must be understood here as the word of God.

46. All the more so since in the text of the Gospel on the presence of the Spirit (14, 17) the latter is called "the Spirit of truth"; his presence is promised so that the *truth* brought by Christ might enter into men's hearts and be received by them (see 14, 26; 16, 13).

emphasize the words that designate the interior reality by which we know the truth:

1) "If *you abide in my word* . . . you shall know the truth" (Jn 8, 21-32);

2) ". . . all who have known the truth, for the sake of *the truth which abides in us*" (II Jn 1-2);

3) "But you have *an anointing* from the Holy One" ("*let the anointing dwell in you*," adds v. 27) "and you know all things" (I Jn 2, 20-21).

Each time the result is the same: Christians know the truth. The interior reality which explains such knowledge is given a different name in each passage: word of Christ, truth, anointing. The parallelism is too striking for the three words not to designate an identical reality. Here again, *chrisma* appears as being necessarily the word of Christ, the truth "which abides in us."

g) Let us at last return to our opening question: how is *chrisma* translated? Is it an abstract or a concrete word? In English translations, the consecrated term is anointing. Very likely, one of the reasons for the choice of this translation has been, first, the word *unctio* in the Vulgate and the Latin translation; second, the term has been interpreted exclusively as being part of the work of the Spirit. Fr. Bonsirven wrote: "The Holy Spirit . . . is called *anointing*, *chrisma*, an abstract noun designating action produced within."[47] But if *chrisma* signified the action of the verb *chriein*, this would be an exception to the general law of Greek vocabulary, which says that words ending in *-ma* do not indicate action but the result of action, the concrete thing to which the action leads.[48] Moreover, in the Greek words,[49] *chrisma* is always used in this con-

---

47. *Epîtres de saint Jean*, 142.

48. E. Schwyzer, *Griechische Grammatik*, I (Munich, 1939), 522; P. Chantraine, *Etudes sur le vocabulaire grec* (Paris, 1956), 20: "The suffix *-sis* expresses, according to M. Benveniste, the abstract idea of the process conceived of as an objective reality . . . . Words in *-ma* designate the object in which the process is incorporated: *ktēsis* is the fact of acquiring, which can be realized; *ktēma* is the concrete thing which has been acquired." *Chrisma*, therefore, is a concrete noun, designating a *thing*, and not an abstract word which indicates an action.

49. For example, Elien, *Var. Hist.*, III, 13: *chrisma estin autois ho oinos, hōsper allois to elaion*; Joseph, *Antiq.*, III, 197: "He had prepared a

crete way: the word is clearly distinct from *chrisis* (act of anointing) and means: ointment, oil of anointing. Most commentators feel that we should retain all of the concrete sense of the image used in the present text.[50]

Everything we have seen so far leads us in the same direction. *Chrisma* is presented as a *reality*: it was *received* in the past, *abides* in the present, and *is possessed* by men—expressions difficult to explain if they apply to an activity, but understandable if they pertain to Christ's word accepted in faith. It is this word that instructed us in the beginning of our Christian life and continues to do so. It is remarkable that in all of 2, 18-28 the Spirit is not even mentioned; on the contrary, three times it is said that *chrisma* comes from the Holy One, i.e., Jesus. It is the very word of Christ insofar as the Spirit of truth represents it and makes it understood; it is the "oil of anointing" with which the Spirit "anoints" the hearts of believers. The word *chrisma* does not indicate formally the divine action as such, but the word of Jesus in which it is expressed and to which it leads: the word of Christ grasped in the light of faith and source of the interior teaching.[51]

Purpose of the Anointing

What role does St. John attribute to the anointing in the Christian life? Verses 20 and 27 both belong to the last part of the first

---

sweet-smelling anointment (*chrisma euodestaton*)"; Preisendanz, *Pap. graec. mag.*, VII, 874: *chrisēi de autēn kai tōi selēniakōi chrismati*. The only texts cited to give an active meaning to *chrisma* are those of the LXX, where we find several times the expression *elaion chrisma*, a rather "material translation of שֶׁמֶן הַמִּשְׁחָה; this is an insufficient reason for giving a new meaning to *chrisma* used alone, as is the case in I Jn.

50. Weiss, Westcott, Büchsel, Dodd, Michl, Schnackenburg. Let ut note that if Western tradition, starting with the old Latin, has regularly preserved the active word "unctio," we do find twice "unguentum": once in St. Jerome: "Et vos unguentum habetis a Sancto" (*In Habac.*, II, 3; *P.L.*, 25, 1325), and once in the Latin translation (the only one extant) of Didymus of Alexandria (ed. Zoepfl, 50, 18-19; *P.G.*, 39, 1784 C).
51. See R. Bultmann, *Theol. des N. T.*, 406.

section (2, 18-28), where true Christians and the Antichrists are set in opposition. Here we see once more the basic theme of the Epistle:[52] to point out to Christians those people who enjoy divine communion, a reality which of itself surpasses normal experience. St. John proposes a set of criteria[53] by which believers will know it is they and not the heretics who enjoy this communion. In 2. 18-19, he says that the Antichrists have left the Church, thus indicating that they were not really one of us. In v. 22, he proposes another criterion, the doctrinal position of the heretics: they refuse to admit that Jesus is the Christ and must, therefore, reject the Father. Such people are no longer Christians.

In contrast to them are the believers (vv. 20-21). But here the thought process is, so to speak, reversed: John does not move from an external sign to a profound reality; on the contrary, he begins with the interior reality, the anointing, to take into account a sense experience that all men can undergo. In v. 20, this interior reality is indicated; the verse serves as an introduction to v. 21, where all the emphasis is given to "you know," repeated twice. This emphasis on the knowledge of Christians is not intended to soothe the latter against the claims of the Gnostics, who pretend to have a monopoly on "knowledge"; according to this interpretation, John would say to the faithful, "it is you who possess the true and salu-

---

52. In two excellent articles, Fr. M.-E. Boismard has shown very clearly that this is the essential idea of the epistle; see "La connaissance dans l'Alliance nouvelle d'après la première lettre de S. Jean," in *R. B.*, 56 (1949), 364-391; " 'Je ferai avec vous une Alliance nouvelle' (Introduction à la première epître de saint Jean)," in *Lum. et Vie*, n. 8 (February 1953), 94-109.

53. Usually they are indicated by the refrain: "In this we know that . . ." (2, 3, 5; 3, 10, 16, 19, 24; 4, 2, 6, 13; 5, 2), but they are also found under other forms. We can arrange these criteria of the authentic Christian life and communion with God in three categories:

a) *Moral criteria*: the fact of not sinning (3, 6), of walking in the light (1, 7), of observing the commandments (2, 3, 5; 3, 24a; 5, 2b), of practicing justice (2, 29; 3, 10), of practicing charity (4, 6);

b) *Doctrinal criteria*: believing and confessing that Jesus is the Christ, come down in the flesh (2, 23; 4, 2; 5, 2, 10); remaining in the teaching received (2, 24); listening to those who teach the doctrine of truth (4, 6);

c) *Interior criterion* (or rather, the interior source of the two previous criteria): the Spirit, whom Christ has given us (3, 24b; 4, 13).

tary gnosis."[54] Instead, John appeals to the knowledge of Christians
as a criterion that will enable them to discern the truth. In v. 19,
he had given a very clear sign whereby heretics give themselves
away; now he shows that the faithful possess within themselves a
means for making judgments in this area: they have knowledge of
the truth, the "sense" of the truth, a sure instinct for recognizing
it. It was to explain this facility of discernment that he had said
just before that Christians have an anointing;[55] but all our attention is now concentrated on the fact of knowledge.[56]

In v. 27, the same themes are taken up again and made more
specific, but a new idea is added, in line with the spiral-type development so dear to the author. It is no longer said that Christians
merely "have" the anointing, but that the latter "abides" in them.
While in vv. 20-21 the effect of this presence was simply indicated
(they have the awareness of the truth), in 2, 27 this knowledge
is explained ultimately in terms of the active role of the anointing
(it informs believers). In addition to mentioning this, John goes
further than he did in the beginning. It is important to appreciate
the movement and progression of this Johannine phrase. In vv. 20-
21 the movement was twofold: possession of the anointing, sense of
the truth; in v. 27 these first two stages are repeated, then sur-
passed: John adds a third element, "You abide in it" (*menete* is an
indicative). The second movement—which was the last and most

---

54. Such is the understanding of Büchsel, Dodd, Charue, Michl, Schnackenburg, Ross. But in the present context, there is not the slightest allusion
to the heretical claim of possessing "gnosis"; moreover, we see in v. 27
that the "knowledge" about which St. John speaks is essentially oriented
toward a practical attitude: that of remaining in Christ. This is prepared
for in vv. 20-21: there knowledge is felt to be an interior criterion allowing one to discern truth from error (with Westcott, Brooke, Belser,
Lauck, Chaine, Bonsirven). The last few words of v. 21 thus follow
naturally: "no lie is of the truth." St. John is still trying to give *criteria*
to Christians.

55. We translate: *an* ointment, *an* anointing. Here *chrisma* has no article,
since it is a reality not yet identified in the context, and one that will be
recognized only by its effect: *oidate tēn alētheian*. In 2, 27, *to chrisma*
is individualized: the article is anaphorical.

56. Along with Schnackenburg and Bonsirven, we interpret the three *oti*
of v. 21 as declarative; usually, the translation is: "I am writing you
because . . . ." But here it is important to note what Fr. Boismard said

important in 2, 20-21 (the thrice-repeated *oidate*)—is in v. 27 a transition to the third: *hōs didaskei . . . , kathōs edidaxen . . . , menete en autōi.*[57] This is the author's final conclusion in noting the radical opposition between Christians and Antichrists.

But in v. 21 this practical conclusion was not yet in sight. This explains why the knowledge of Christians there appeared more prominent; it was a criterion of discernment. In v. 27, on the contrary, if John refers to the interior teaching, it is in reference to believers themselves: this teaching gives them the certainty of being in communion with God; thus, in v. 28, John invites them to remain united to Christ.

Anointing and the Interior Teaching of the Christian

The interpretation just given allows us to resolve the problem presented by the phrase in 27: "You have no need that anyone teach you." The interesting remarks of St. Augustine on this passage[58] come to mind: only the interior Master can really teach believers; without his "anointing," every preacher's effort is in vain. However, the sovereign importance of the interior teaching does not imply the *non-importance* of that of the Church. Nor is it enough to say, in a negative way, that the author in no way denied the necessity of an exterior teaching, since he himself makes an

(*art. cit.,* 380, n. 2) with respect to 2, 12-14: the object of *egrapsa* indicates the purpose of the letter. We know this purpose (see 5, 15); John is writing so that his fellow Christians may *know* that they possess divine life; here too, the affirmation of knowledge is in the foreground. Therefore, verse 2, 21 is to be taken as a *declaration* of the author.

57. Along with Westcott, Brooke, Windisch, Bonsirven, Chaine, Dodd (in contrast to Belser, Büchsel, Hauck, Schnackenburg), we do not consider the part of the sentence *kai alēthes esti kai ouk estin pseudos* as a first apodosis (parallel to a second: *menete en autoi*), for the second protasis is simply a repeat of the first (*hos . . . didaskei*), the part of the intermediary phrase on the truth of *chrisma* is, therefore, an incision, and does not have the foundation presupposed in the other construction. The whole long sentence is marked by a single movement that carries it forward to its conclusion: *menete en autōi.*

58. *P.L.,* 35, 2004-2005.

appeal to it (I Jn 2, 24; 4, 6; II Jn 9).[59] The problem thus remains: how can John say that believers need no one to teach them? J. Michl expresses himself frankly on this question.[60] His answer is that John is speaking here of the "awareness of the faithful" among Christians. The latter have in their conscience a norm that enables them to state by themselves that heretical doctrines are contrary to the truth.[61]

But again this does not mean that Christians can do without the directives and teachings of the Church, as the verse seems to say. To understand this doctrine, we must recall what the faith means for St. John; it is a dynamic and interior reality which presupposes a constant progression, leading to true communion with God. As a result of this viewpoint, John tends to see the Christian life in terms of its absolute perfection; he describes it as something in which each believer completely realizes his innermost being. This is why he can say in I Jn 3, 9 that the Christian cannot sin: insofar as he heeds the word of God, the divine seed that he bears within him, he becomes really sinless.[62] The more intense and profound the believer's life of faith, the more he can do without the support of an external discipline or law; for him, the attraction of the Father, the word of Jesus, and the call of the Spirit become more and more inviting.[63] It is clear that such a man no longer needs

---

59. De Ambroggi, 244. The author gives an easier response by interpreting *tis,* in 27b, as heretics: you have no need that *anyone of those people* teach you! Such was the interpretation, apologetically oriented, of Bellarmine (*De verbo Dei,* III, 10) and of Cornelius a Lapide, in the antiprotestant controversy. But John will never say that heretics "teach" (Schnackenburg, 161); on the other hand, the interpretation is not related to the context.

60. *Art. cit.,* in *Festschr. Meinertz,* 147-151.

61. This solution is perhaps less new than Michl says: it is already indicated by Belser, Westcott, Brooke, Chaine, and Dodd. But he and Hauck are the only ones to use the felicitous expressions "Glaubensbewusstsein" and "sensus fidelium."

62. See our article "L'impeccabilité du chrétien d'après I Joh. 3, 6-9," 161-171 (see further on in this volume, p. 187f.).

63. Let us confer the no less incisive statements of St. Paul regarding the law: "But if you are led by the Spirit, you are not under the Law" (Gal 5, 18); see Gal 5, 23; Rom 8, 2. In this regard, see the fine study of S. Lyonnet, "Liberté chrétienne et loi de l'Espirt," in *Christus,* n. 4

anyone to teach him: God's word has penetrated him completely, he bears within himself the final source of all teaching, he is taught directly by God (Jn 6, 45). Here John is using the full meaning of the verb *menein*: if the anointing truly "remains" in us, that is, if it is fully effective in us, we no longer need to be taught from without.[61]

The Word and the Spirit

We said at the outset that there were two interpretations of *chrisma* in the two passages from St. John: most commentators see here the work of the Spirit instructing the Christian from within, while Reitzenstein and Dodd understand it as the word of truth accepted in baptism.[65] The analysis we have given leans toward the latter interpretation, while adding to it some important nuances which bring it closer to the common interpretation: the anointing is indeed *God's word*, not as it is preached externally in the community, but as it is received by faith into men's hearts and

(October 1954), 6-27 (in the present volume, Chapter 5). See also the profound remark of St. John of the Cross which he inscribes at the summit of the mount of perfection: "There is no longer any road through here, because there is no law for the just man" (cited by S. Lyonnet, *art. cit.*, 27).

64. This was explained very well by certain past commentators; see in particular A. Salmeron, S.J., *Commentarii . . . T. XVI: In Epistolas Canonicas et Apocalypsim,* (Cologne, 1604), 241-242; esp. 241b: "Et in mysteriis fidei et pure moralibus, perfecte unctus non indiget externa unctione, vel Scripturae lectione de necessitate ordinaria, quia haec oculis claris, et amantibus cernit, et his nutritur, et vivit. Et ante perfectam Unctionem per quam est Verbi et Angelorum discipulus, jam ab homine communiter loquendo didicit necessaria. Et licet non omnes, ad quos scribit Ioannes, perfecti essent, tamen ad hos in ista clausula loquitur: ut cum vocat patres, et cognoscentes . . . . Ideo dixit non esse eis necessariam pro seipsis doctrinam externam, quia iam in eorum cordibus est Lucifer, et aurora praecedens diem gloriae."

65. They had arrived at this conclusion by a comparison of I Jn 2, 20, 27 with later texts, especially that of St. Ignatius of Antioch, *Ad Eph.,* 17, 1-2; on the contrary, we have tried to work directly from the Pauline and Johannine vocabulary.

remains active, *thanks to the work of the Spirit*. Only this synthesis of the various points of view does full justice to the two passages. Reitzenstein saw correctly that v. 27 is directly related to v. 24, and, therefore, that the anointing is related to the teaching received; but his error lay in considering as arbitrary all recourse to *pneuma* to explain *chrisma*. The Spirit, however, plays an essential role insofar as the word is understood in the Church. On the other hand, the traditional explanation quite clearly failed to show the all-important relationship that exists between the teaching of the Holy Spirit and the word of Jesus.[66] St. John himself said clearly that the Spirit would teach only by "bringing to mind" the words of Christ (Jn 14, 26).

As a result, C. H. Dodd was perfectly right in saying that the

---

66. J. Michl (*art. cit.*, 144-145, n. 21) objects to the interpretation of Reitzenstein by saying that John himself distinguishes clearly between "what you have heard from the beginning" (v. 24), that is, Christian doctrine, and "anointing" (v. 20, 27), and that he attributes to these two realities different effects (first, divine communion, and second, knowledge of the truth). Certainly, the doctrine received and the anointing are distinguished in some way; in v. 24, it is a question of the doctrine as *preached* and heard *exteriorly* (*ēkousate*): but John invites Christians (*meneto*) to preserve within them what they have heard. In v. 27, this interiorizing of the word is already presumed to be completed (*menei*) and as such it is now designated as an anointing, capable of teaching us *from within*.

The second objection of Michl is contradictory: knowledge of the truth, he says, is due to the Spirit's anointing, and not to the action of doctrine. But John himself says that "knowledge of the truth" is the direct effect of the presence in us of the *word* (Jn 8, 31-32) or of the *truth* (II Jn 1-2); never does he relate it formally and explicitly to the action of the Spirit; yet, in Jn 14, 26 and 16, 13, we see that he considers this action of the Spirit as indispensable.

R. Schnackenburg had another objection (152, n. 2): if the anointing is doctrine, it is something impersonal; but it "teaches" (v. 27); thus it is probably the Holy Spirit. Now, the difficulty would be a real one in the case of Reitzenstein, who excludes the role of the Holy Spirit. But our own explanation, on the contrary, presupposes it. It is undeniable that the *didaskei* of 27b recalls the *didaxei* of Jn 14, 26, where the future work of the Spirit in the Church is described. But this verse of the Gospel adds the fact that the Spirit's teaching consists of restating the words of Jesus: such words *of Jesus*, made vivid *by the Spirit*, are not an "impersonal" reality!

interpretation of *chrisma* in terms of the Holy Spirit and the interpretation in terms of God's word are perhaps not that much in opposition.[67] They must be taken together. Because the interior illumination of the Holy Spirit has been too often treated independently of the exterior teaching transmitted in the Church, the text of St. John seemed to favor a certain illuminism. This also prevented a satisfactory explanation of the phrase in 27b, "You have no need that anyone teach you." If the exterior teaching given to believers in the anointing is identical to the teaching they have heard (v. 24) and now understand more clearly in the light of faith, there is no problem: there is no longer any opposition between the exterior teaching of the Church and interior illumination.

St. Paul and St. John

To terminate this section, let us briefly contrast this teaching of St. John with the Pauline doctrine discussed earlier. First of all, there is a certain difference in the vocabulary: Paul uses the *verb* "to anoint" and considers the anointing from God's point of view, while John uses the *noun* "anointing," which signifies the effect of divine action in the case of the Christian. The use of the word anointing was, no doubt, customary in baptismal catechesis; thus it was natural to speak of that spiritual reality with which the catechumens were internally "anointed."[68] But the important thing is that each of the two texts (II Cor 1, 21; I Jn 2, 20, 27) leads to an almost identical exegesis. In Paul's text, *chrisas* belonged to a baptismal context and signified the divine action stirring the catechumen to belief in the word; in St. John, *chrisma* is the word itself grasped under the influence of the Spirit. In each case, a *spiritual anointing through faith* is involved.

But here too we see the difference in point of view between

---

67. See the excellent remarks that Dodd makes here in his commentary (63-64).

68. This is not a sufficient reason, we feel, for calling *chrisma* a technical term, as Dodd does (60), relying perhaps too much from Gnostic texts of the second century. In I Jn 2, 20, the noun is used without the article: "You have *an* anointing." If use of the word were already stabilized by usage, should it not be *to chrisma*?

the two authors and the theological progress of St. John over St. Paul. In II Cor 1, 21, the anointing is mentioned only for the past and belongs to the context of *kerygma* and baptism: the faith it arouses is the first adhesion to the truth. John also recalls (v. 24) this beginning of the Christian life, and thereby his text continues perfectly the text of Paul. But he stresses more the permanent function of the anointing: *echete* (v. 20), *menei, didaskei* (v. 27). The word, appearing under the image of the anointing, is the word of Christ as a spiritual reality, it is the truth that *abides* in believers. Similarly, the faith John is thinking of is no longer the initial faith of conversion, but the faith of the Christian in the present reality of the Church. Such Christians are fully conscious of possessing the truth, and thereby can meet the pseudoprophets head-on, for they have within them the true source of all teaching.

There is, therefore, a remarkable refinement of the theme in St. John, due to the fact that he no longer applies it only to the beginnings of the Christian life. In the way he describes it, there are two typically Johannine traits: the anointing is a reality *that abides within us,* and it is this reality that *informs* us about all things.

ANOINTING IN FAITH IN THE ANCIENT PATRISTIC LITURGICAL TRADITION

We cannot attempt to discuss here the entire exegetical history of the two verses. It is rather complicated, being linked to the development and diversity of the rites of anointing in the different Churches. But what is unusual is that there exists an entire tradition that uses the theme of (baptismal) anointing in a simply *metaphorical* sense to designate the faith or supernatural knowledge. More than once, this interpretation of the word *anointing* is referred explicitly to vv. 2, 20, 27 of I Jn. For the adherents of this tradition, *chrisma* signifies not the actual oil used to anoint, either before or after the baptismal immersion, but the Christian truth accepted in baptism, the knowledge of faith. It is this exegesis in which we are now interested as regards the two verses of the New Testament.

The Ointment of Faith

The earliest witness of this tradition is Clement of Alexandria;

his is also the first commentary we have of the First Epistle (unfortunately only a Latin translation remains). There he comments on the verse of I Jn 2, 20: "Illud [= genus electorum] unctionem habet a Sancto, *quae fit secundum fidem.* Qui vero non permanet in fide, mendax est et antichristus."[69] In other parts of Clement's writings, we see that this comparison of faith or the word with an ointment is common to him. In the final chapter of the *Protreptique* he puts on the lips of the *Logos* a solemn appeal to all pagans to come to him: "I will anoint you with the ointment of faith [*chriso humas tōi pisteōs aleimmati*] which will rid you of corruption" (XII, 120, 5; G.C.S., I, 85, 9). Elsewhere, the word of God is described as an ointment for the soul: "The *word* of the Lord abides: it *anoints* the soul and unites it to the Spirit."[70] As far as we know, it is in Clement of Alexandria that the *chrisma* of I Jn 2, 20 is applied for the first time to the idea of an anointing by faith. The theme, however, goes back to Ignatius of Antioch, who urges Christians not to let themselves be anointed (*mē aleiphesthe*) with the bad odor (*dusōdian*) of the teaching of the prince of this world, but to receive instead "the knowledge of God, which is Jesus Christ" (*Ad Eph.*, 17, 1-2). Knowledge of the truth, therefore, is already implicitly compared here to a fragrant ointment with which believers are anointed.[71]

---

69. *Adumbrat.* in 1 Joh., in h. 1. (*P.G.*, 9, 737 B).
70. *Strom.*, III, 17, 103 (*G.C.S.*, II, 243, 31-32); see *Strom.*, VI, 14, 112 (*G.C.S.*, II, 488, 4).
71. The text of the *Protrepticus* of Clement of Alexandria, cited a little while ago, not only repeats the same theme as the passage from Ignatius of Antioch; it is so close to it in expression that it seems to be a restatement of it. In both cases, the gift given is knowledge of God (*gnōsis theou*); if this gift is called *charisma* by Ignatius, Clement uses the verb *charizomai;* both identify this "knowledge" with Jesus Christ, who is the Logos (see Ignatius, *Ad Magn.*, 8, 2): both say that this knowledge should bring incorruptibility (*aphtharsian*). For Clement, this knowledge produces justice, which enables a man to rasie himself up to God; on the other hand, Ignatius said in a negative way that the bad odor of the devil's teaching makes us captives and draws us away from the kind of life that had been planned for us. Thus both authors develop the same theme, that of purification and sanctification by truth. Both also compare doctrine to an ointment. Now, the comparison with a perfume to designate knowledge of the truth goes back to St. Paul (II Cor 2, 14). It appears again in the second and third centuries. See Ignatius of

It is precisely because of this text of the early part of the second century that Reitzenstein and Dodd, as we said earlier, were led to interpreting the *chrisma* of St. John in terms of Christian doctrine.

The interpretation of Clement of Alexandria is found in Origen, in a homily on *Exodus,* where the great themes of baptismal typology are developed. Later on, several of the Fathers will reexamine this doctrine. For these different authors, the anointing with the blood of the paschal lamb on the doors of the Israelites' homes in Egypt (Ex 12, 7) is a figure of the anointing of the soul by faith at the moment of baptism. The *Peri pascha* of Origen[72] explains this verse of Exodus as follows:

> With the blood we anoint our houses, I mean our body, *for the anointing is faith in Christ* [*chrisis pistis estin hē eis auton*]. . . . After being anointed, that is, after beginning to believe in Christ [*meta de to christhēnai hemas, toutesti to pisteusai eis Christon*], we must pass to the eating or consumption of Christ.

This is explained, not in terms of the Holy Eucharist, but in terms of the spiritual manducation of the word of God in the Church.[73] A paschal homily of Pseudo-Chrysostom repeats this

Antioch, *Ad. Magn.,* 10, 2; Clement of Alexandria, *Pedag.,* II, 8 (*G.C.S.,* I, 194, 14).

72. Something should be said of the treatise *Peri pascha* of Origen, discovered in the papyri of Toura. Several passages in this homily coincide with the *Selecta in Exodum* (*P.G.,* 12, 284 C-D), a collection of scholia from Origen (see P. Nautin, *Homélies pascales.* II: *Trois homélies dans la tradition d' Origène,* coll. "Sources chrét." [Paris, 1953], 40, n. 1). In the papyrus of Toura is found the passage that is of interest to us, namely, the commentary on Ex 12, 7 (it is cited by P. Nautin in two fragments, the first: 78, n. 1; the second: 84, n. 1). Our citation is based on these fragments, and whatever has not yet been published from the papyrus is completed by the *Selecta in Exodum.*

73. A no less important text is found in the *Selecta in Ezechielem,* 16 (*P.G.,* 13, 812 A): *kai echrisa se elaiōi Chrisma estin enoikēsis tou hagiou pneumatos en gnōsei tēs alētheias.* This description of "the anointing" is

exegesis and specifies further that "the unspotted blood becomes a salutary sign for those who take part in it, and, seeing it, God will save *those who are anointed with it by means of faith (tous kechrismenous autōi dia pisteōs)*":[74] thus, the anointing with blood on the doors and its salutary effect on the people are applied in a typological way to the anointing of the Christian in faith. The same idea is expressed, although somewhat less clearly, by Procope de Gaza in his commentary on *Exodus*[75] and by Victor of Capua.[76] It is interesting that the same explanation is given in the anonymous homily, based on the treatise on the Pasch of Hippolytus,[77] even though this tradition differs from Origen's on many points. We should, therefore, say that this typological application of the anointing of houses in Egypt to the anointing of the soul at the moment of baptism is very traditional.[78] But in none of these texts is the baptismal anointing an exterior rite; it is always the spiritual anointing of souls, the anointing in faith.[79]

remarkable: for Origen, the *chrisma* is *the knowledge of the truth* provided by the Spirit who lives within us. This close connection between truth and Spirit should indeed be noted .

74. P. Nautin, *op. cit.*, 79, 11-12; see 85, 3-4, where *chrisma* (that is, that which they marked the doors, thus the blood) is explained typologically as the wisdom according to Christ, which allows us to put on the sanctity of Christ. The same explanation of the anointing by faith is also found in two other Easter homilies of Chrysostom: hom. IV (*P.G.*, 59, 731, in medio); hom. V (*ibid.*, 734, 1, 16-17): *tēi pistei tou haimatos hoionei chrisēis kathaper ho Israēl echrie tas eisodous tōi haimati.*

75. *Comm. in Exod.* (*P.G.*, 871, 567).

76. *Libell. de cyclo paschali* (Pitra, *Spicil. Solesm.*, I, 300-301, fgt XII and XVI, *in fine*).

77. P. Nautin, *Homélies pascales. I: Homélie inspirée du traité sur la pâque d'Hippolyte* ("Sources chrétiennes," 27), (Paris, 1950), 143, 18.

78. "The anointing of the doors with the blood of the paschal lamb, a condition of salvation for the first-born of the Jews, was the anticipatory image of the baptismal anointing, by which Christians obtain salvation in the blood of Christ. Such is the unanimous teaching of Christian tradition," P. Nautin, *Homélies pascales. II: Trois homélies dans la tradition d'Origène*, 39-40. But the author does not say what is meant by this "baptismal anointing"; the texts cited show that one should not think of a physical anointing, but of an anointing by faith.

The same teaching is expressed by St. Cyril of Alexandria. With him, however, it is no longer linked, as in the preceding instances, to a typological explanation of *Exodus;* but it is likewise referred to the context of baptism. Cyril describes the moment when a child is brought to be baptized: "When a new-born child is brought to receive *the ointment of catechesis* [*tēs katēcheseōs to chrisma*] or that of the perfecting after holy baptism [*ētoi to tēs teleiōseōs epi tōi hagiōi baptismati*], whoever brings him answers for him: Amen."[80] A double "chrism" is, therefore, distinguished: the one that precedes baptism and signifies metaphorically the catechesis given to the candidate, who must respond to it with a profession of faith. The other follows the baptismal immersion, and most likely refers to the sacrament that completes the initiation and brings it

79. To this series of texts from the Alexandrian tradition, we would like to add the testimony of an anonymous homily from Asia Minor, published by F. Floëri and P. Nautin in the "Sources chrétiennes" (n. 48): *Homélies pascales. III: Une homélie anatolienne sur la date de Pâques en l'an 387* (Paris, 1957), 125, 23. The Jews, who celebrate the Pasch at a different date than do the Christians, are here denounced as *parabatai tou chrismatos.* The editors, for whom this expression has no meaning, say that *chrismatos* must be "a word corrupted in the course of the transmission of the text" and suggest that it be replaced by *boulēmatos.* But there does not seem to be any fluctuation in the manuscript tradition. One should, if possible, retain the expression and translate it not as "transgressores unctionis," as does Migne (*P.G.,* 59, 748, n. 2, 20), but as "bearers of the oil of anointing." On the basis of what was just said these words should be related to the anointing by faith. According to one of the homilies published previously (*Hos. pasc.,* II, 85, 3-4), *chrisma* — that with which one anoints — designates the *sophia kata Christon,* a typological application of the blood of the Paschal lamb, which was used to anoint the doors in Egypt. In the new homily, the words "bearers of the oil of anointing," applied to the Jews, must, therefore, signify "bearers of revealed truth, of the Christian *faith,*" called metaphorically an "ointment for the soul," which in the context makes very good sense.

80. Cyr. of Alex., *In Joh.* 11, 26 (*P.G.,* 74, 49 D). We do not see how one can justify the translation of *tēs katēcheseōs to chrisma* as "the oil of catechumens," a translation which is found in P. de Puniet (art. "Baptême," in *Dict. d'arch. chr. et de lit.,* II/1, 263) and H. Leclerq (art. "Confirmation," *ibid.,* III/2, 2516).

to its perfection, namely, confirmation.[81] Only the first is of interest
to us here. The text belongs to the tradition of Ignatius of Antioch,
Clement of Alexandria, and Origen, but with an important distinction: the ointment is no longer only called *Christian doctrine* or
faith in general, but more specifically *baptismal instruction, catechesis*.[82] This is the theme we encountered above in St. Paul and
St. John.

In placing this text of Cyril alongside another passage from his
commentary on the Fourth Gospel, we will see that the holy doctor
applies this image of ointment to the catechesis, in view of its role
as a source of revelation coming from the Spirit. To confirm the
revelatory work of the Spirit (*to pneuma to agion . . . hēmin apoko-
luptei christon*), he refers to the text of I Jn 2, 27, on "the anointing" that teaches us all things; it is this anointing that gives us
understanding of the truth: *tēn tēs alētheias katalēpsin*.[83]

Anointing and Gnosis

In addition to those writers who explain anointing as faith or as
the word of truth, there are others who interpret it allegorically as

---

81. The noun *teleiōsis* and the verb *teleioō* were used to designate baptismal
    initiation, for example, Athanasius, *Or. II adv. Arian.*, 41 (P.G., 26,
    233 A): *en tēi teleiōsei tou baptismatos*. But the initiation was completed
    only by the anointing that followed baptism; see Cyr. of Alex., *In Joel.*,
    2, 24 (P.G., 71, 273 B): *hē tou elaiou chreia, suntelousa pres teleiōsin
    tois dikaioumenois en Christōi dia tou hagiou baptismatos*. In the process
    of initiation, *teleiōsis* referred more specifically to the postbaptismal rite
    of confirmation (the anointing with *myron*). Cyril's expression *to chrisma
    tēs teleiōseōs*, in contrast to the chrism of the catechesis, seems, therefore,
    to refer to confirmation (see H. du Manoir, *Dogme et spiritualité chez
    S. Cyrille d'Alexandrie*, 402, n. 5, which mentions two interpretations).
    But because of the parallelism with the first use of *chrisma* (in the
    figurative sense), we would think that *to chrisma tēs teleiōseōs* signifies
    not the chrism used in the rite, but the spiritual gift conferred by the
    rite.
82. Let us note that in the text of the *Protrepticus* of Clement of Alexandria
    cited above, the promise of an anointing by faith, made by the Logos,
    was addressed to pagans. There too the *chrisō humas* seemed to signify
    more specifically entrance into Christianity, the moment of baptism.
83. *In Joh.*, 6, 45 (P.G., 73, 556 A-B).

the knowledge of gnosis. It is well known how characteristic of the school of Alexandria this theology of true "gnosis" was. According to the commentary of Didymus the Blind on the Catholic Epistles, the effect of *chrisma* on believers is that they possess the gnosis of all spiritual things.[81] The Alexandrians distinguished two kinds of supernatural knowledge, faith and gnosis: faith pure and simple, proper to beginners, and gnosis or superior knowledge, prerogative of those who are perfect. For Origen, gnosis is "essentially a divine illumination, a religious knowledge that begins in faith and ends in ecstasy."[85] For Didymus, a great admirer of Origen, the word *gnōsis* had practically the same meaning.[86] For him too, it is related to faith, for he calls it *gnōsin tēs pisteōs* (Cramer, VIII, 65, 10-11). Such knowledge includes part of one's experience, as is clear from the definition he gives: *to peiran tinos eschēkenai kai hēnōsthai autōi*.[87] In his commentary on our verse from St. John, this question of experience is also noted, for *chrisma* gives believers a knowledge that enables them to discern in what way the Antichrists are no longer one of them.[88]

Two anonymous texts take up the explanation of Didymus. The first is that of the chain, with respect to I Jn 2, 27: *echontes, phēsi, to pneuma to hagion didaskalon tēs eusebeias gnōseōs, mē prose-*

---

84. "Quicumque sunt participes Christi, in eo permanent, unctionem id est chrisma a sancto percipientes ut possint scientiam spiritualium habere cunctorum" (ed. Zoepfl, 49). The last few words may very likely be retranslated into Greek as follows: *tēn gnōsin echein tōn pneumatikōn hapantōn*.

85. D. Van den Eynde, *Les normes de l'enseignement chrétien dans la littérature patristique des trois premiers siècles* (Gembloux, 1933), 153.

86. See G. Bardy, *Didyme l'Aveugle*, (Paris, 1910), 140-141, 156-157.

87. Cramer (VIII, 111, 16) gives this definition as being anonymous, but it corresponds very well to the Latin text of the commentary of Didymus: thus, the passage is repeated, and correctly so, under the latter's name in his commentary on the Catholic epistles edited by Zoepfl (42-43).

88. At the end of the same paragraph (Zoepfl, 50, 15-20), Didymus says that, thanks to this ointment, believers possess the gift of discernment: "Quia vero secundum aliud quidem ex nobis sunt, accedentes ad scripturam divinitus inspiratam, secundum aliud vero non ex nobis sunt, alium praeter nostrum habentes sensum, palam est ex eo, quod unguentum habent a sancto hi, a quibus recesserunt mali, *ut sciant omnia dogmata ecclesiae recta complecti.*"

chete pneumasi planois (Cramer, VIII, 120, 26-27).[89] The other is a scholia from a later manuscript, which summarizes very well Didymus' interpretation: *chrisma to pneumatikon charisma legei tēs gnōseōs*.[90] Still, we note some small differences: instead of being, as in Didymus or in the chain, a grace that comes from the Holy Spirit, *chrisma* is called here "a spiritual gift" (*charisma*).[91] While in Didymus the effect of the anointing was "knowledge of all spiritual things," and in the chain "gnosis of piety," for the author of the scholia the gift is simply "gnosis" (*hē gnōsis*). In this later text, the term "gnosis" is used in the technical sense. But we still remain in the same Alexandrian tradition: the anointing of believers is explained allegorically; it is supernatural knowledge, gnosis.

Pre-Baptismal Anointing in the Syrian Rite

All the writers mentioned in the two preceding paragraphs belong to the tradition of Alexandria: they interpret the baptismal anointing in a figurative sense. But the other Churches insisted

---

89. The rest of the text, beginning with the words *Ho dieilēphōs epistēmonikōs* . . . (Cramer, 120, 30), is taken from Didymus, as can be seen from a comparison with the Latin text of the Commentary (Zoepfl, 50, 26). On the other hand, the preceding paragraph (Cramer, 120, 26-29), the beginning of which we have cited, differs completely from this commentary. Thus one does not have the right to attribute it to Didymus.

90. This important scholia was published for the first time in the edition of the Catholic epistles of C. F. Matthaei (Rigae, 1782), 120. It comes from a manuscript of the eleventh century (A in Matthaei = 101 in Gregory), which Matthaei regards very highly, in particular, for its very old scholia: "Animadverti, scholia huis codicis a viro docto eodemque scriba et possessore in suos usus *ex vetustissimis Patrum commentariis*, magno cum judicio selecta esse" (*Praef.*, xxx). The scholia of this manuscript, according to Staab, were taken from the chain; see "Die griechischen Katenenkommentare zu den katholischen Briefen," in *Biblica* 5 (1924), 315, n. 2. This can be verified for our scholia on I Jn 2, 27; it seems to be an abridgement of the title that is found in the chain for section 2, 26 - 3, 1 (Cramer, 120, 10-11): *peri theou kai pneumatikou charismatos en hagiasmōi ep' elpidi eis gnōsin*. The scholia repeats the essential words: *to pneumatikon charisma tēs gnōseōs*.

91. For each of the two instances of *chrisma* in I Jn 2, 27, *charisma* is found as a textual variant. No doubt, this favored the explanation of the first word by the second, all the more so since they form a pleasant assonance.

much more on the *rites* of anointing which accompanied baptism. Ordinarily, in the Orient, there was a double anointing with oil: one, before baptism, with the oil of exorcism; another, with the holy, sweet-smelling oil, *myron*, which came afterwards. This post-baptismal anointing was considered in these Churches as the rite of collation of the Spirit, the baptism of the Spirit (confirmation). This we observe in the Constitutions of the Egyptian Church,[92] the euchology of Serapion,[93] and the third mystagogical catechesis of St. Cyril of Jerusalem.[94]

But the Syrian Church—where the ancient Palestinian traditions were often preserved—has a different order. The post-baptismal anointing with *myron* is not in evidence in the ancient period, i.e., before the writing of the *Apostolic Constitutions* (fourth century); before this date, only a *pre-baptismal* anointing is known, and this is of great importance.[95] More than once, this anointing is related to the Holy Spirit, but the problem is to know in what sense. It seems as if the Syrians gave the anointing before baptism a meaning different from the one given by the contemporary Churches of Palestine and Alexandria.

a) This fact of a pre-baptismal anointing in Syria does not cease to intrigue historians of the liturgy. A. Stenzel tries to explain it in terms of non-religious practices or the anointing of kings and priests in the Old Testament.[96] But T. W. Manson, followed by W.

---

92. *Constit. eccl. aegypt.* 18: "... eos fac dignos, qui repleantur spiritu tuo sancto" (ed. Funk, *Didascalia et const. apost.*, II, 110-11); these Constitutions represent the work of Hippolytus of Rome (see B. Botte, *Hippolyte de Rome. La trad. apostolique*, 8).

93. *Euchol. de Sérapion*, XXII and XXV (ed. Funk, *op. cit.*, II, 184-188).

94. *Cat. myst.* III (*P.G.*, 33, 1087-1094). St. Cyril of Jerusalem applies the text of I Jn 2, 20, 27 to this postbaptismal anointing.

95. See two articles from *L'Orient syrien*, I (1956): B. Botte, "Le baptême dans l'Eglise syrienne," 137-155; A. Raes, "Ou se trouve la confirmation dans le rite syro-oriental?" 239-254. One may also consult: B. Botte, "Le vocabulaire ancien de la Confirmation," in *La Maison-Dieu*, n. 54 (1958), 5-22.

96. A. Stenzel, *Die Taufe, Eine genetische Erklärung der Taufliturgie* (Innsbruck, 1958), 128. This comparison with the anointing of kings and priests is found only in the *Didascalia*, III, 12, 2-3 (= *Apost. Const.*, III, 16, 3-4), as we will see a little later on.

Nauck,[97] sought the answer in the right direction: this practice has its origin in the early Church. In the Acts, the gift of the Spirit is not always conferred after baptism (as in the case in 8, 12, 14-17; 19, 5, 6; see also 2, 38) but once *before* (10, 44-48; perhaps also 9, 17?). Manson notes this difference without, however, searching for the internal reason. Several commentators of the Acts have noted the unusual fact of the descent of the Holy Spirit on Cornelius and his people even before they were baptized. But is this really an exception? Of all the examples mentiond, this is the only one that involves the Spirit's coming to *pagans*. The explanation for this apparent anomaly seems to be the following: Cornelius' people heard the message from Peter, but they had first to receive it in faith before they could be received into the Church through baptism (see Mk 16, 16: "Qui crediderit et baptizatus fuerit, salvus erit"). This gift of adhesion to the word in faith is the work of the Spirit. The Acts suggest this interpretation: "The Holy Spirit came upon all *who were listening to his* message" (10, 44). The expression *akouein ton logon* belongs to the vocabulary of *kerygma* and signifies the normal way of acceding to the faith (Eph 1, 13; Rom 10, 8-13).

Before the coming of the Spirit, the pagans and apostles differed in that the latter "believed in the Lord Jesus Christ" (11, 17). Thus, when he must explain the event of Caesarea before the Council of Jerusalem, Peter will say: "God made choice among us, that through my mouth the Gentiles should hear the word of the gospel and *believe*" (15, 7). The gift of the Spirit at Caesarea, therefore, led to the acceptance of the word, which is faith. And yet, Peter assimilates this coming of the Spirit to that which he and the other apostles received at Pentecost (10, 47; 11, 17; 15, 9). We observe, then, that if he gave faith to the pagans, the Spirit at the same time gave them the strength to become witnesses (see Ac 1, 8). If the Spirit thus assimilates these pagans to the believers of the Cenacle, it is because he first "cleansed their hearts by faith" (15, 9):

97. T. W. Manson, "Entry into Membership of the Early Church," in *J. Th. St.*, 48 (1947), 25-33. His explanation was restated and developed further by W. Nauck, *Die Tradition und der Charakter des ersten Johannesbriefes* (Tübingen, 1957), 2 Exk.: Geist, Wasser und Blut, 147-182.

the Acts, therefore, emphasize faith, when they explain this "Pentecost of the Gentiles."

From this we may draw an important conclusion: Luke mentions the coming of the Spirit either before baptism, to lead the pagans to the *faith,* or afterwards (this is the most frequent case), to make of those who already believe, *witnesses* of their faith. The gift of the Spirit, then, is always linked intrinsically to faith: if such faith is already present, the Holy Spirit is given as a source of strength to bear witness; if non-believing pagans are involved, the gift of the Spirit is the grace of faith as well as the strength for witness. But in both cases, this gift is formally distinct from baptism itself, which is the rite by which a man becomes a child of God and enters the Church. These texts contain implicitly, therefore, a clear distinction between the twofold activity of the Spirit: that which takes place in the *act of believing,* in preparation for baptism, and the *gift* of the Spirit, which is normally conferred after baptism, by the imposition of hands. This is the "gift"—the baptism of the Spirit—which will later be called *confirmation.*

For the problem that concerns us here, we should consider the first activity of the Holy Spirit, that which occurs in the origin of faith before baptism. This question also arises, as Manson and especially Nauck showed, in the famous Johannine text on the three witnesses (I Jn 5, 6-7). The Spirit, water, and blood must there be understood in a sacramental sense. According to the explanation given at length by Nauck, we are concerned here, in a very concrete way, with the account of Christian initiation: the water signifies the baptismal immersion, and the blood, the Eucharist; as to the *pneuma,* this indicates the pre-baptismal activity of the Spirit. In mentioning the Spirit *before* baptism, John places himself at the start of this tradition which we will find later on in the Syrian Church. But for I Jn 5, 7, as well as for Acts 10, 44-48, it is not enough to speak of a communication of the Spirit in general, as Nauck does: involved here is the role of the Spirit in relation to *faith.* Indeed, the great theme of the whole section 5, 5-12 (and already, in part, of 5, 1-4) is precisely faith, the faith of baptism. Several baptismal themes appear here:[98] being born of

98. W. Nauck, *op. cit.,* 86-89.

God (5, 4); victory (5, 4, 5); the confession of faith (5, 5, 10), the object of which is the fact that Jesus is the Son of God; finally, the gift of life (5, 11, 12). The role of the Spirit is to be witness, that is, to strengthen believers in their faith vis-à-vis the dangers of the world: to *pneuma esti to marturoun* (5, 6c). To this first witness is added that of water and blood, that is, baptism and the Eucharist. These three sources of witness make up the witness of God. We must accept this witness (5, 9); believers are those who have within them this divine witness (5, 10a); faith is but the acceptance of the Spirit's witness; it is all of a piece with the baptism of water.[99]

We are very close here to the text of II Cor 1, 21, where it is also a question of divine activity in pre-baptismal faith. The difference here is that Paul was comparing such divine activity to an anointing (see I Jn 2, 20, 27). But without using the image of anointing, he speaks elsewhere of an activity of the Spirit among those who respond to preaching with faith (Gal 3, 2).

We have now all the elements needed to explain the origin of this Syrian tradition which attached so much importance to the pre-baptismal anointing. This practice would have come directly from the early Church which, in the context of baptism, spoke of the work of the Spirit *in the genesis of faith* (before baptism) and which compared this divine action to an anointing. What was only figurative language in the New Testament, would become a rite in the Syrian liturgy.

b) If this hypothesis is exact, we should expect that the pre-baptismal anointing of the Syrians has almost the same meaning as the *chrisas* of St. Paul and the *chrisma* of St. John. It does seem that this is the case. In the other Churches, the pre-baptismal anointing was an exorcism; this explains why it was often compared to the anointing of athletes (against the demon). But the texts of the Syrian Church furnish hardly any indication along these lines. In a passage from the *Didascalia* (III, 12, 2-3), repeated in the *Apostolic Constitutions* (III, 16, 3-4), this anointing is compared to that of kings and priests in the Old Testament and could be

---

99. For a more detailed study of I Jn 5, 6-7, from the point of view of witness and faith, see our article "La notion de témoignage dans S. Jean," in *Sacra Pagina*, II (Gembloux, 1959), 193-208 (esp. 202-208).

interpreted as a sort of consecration.[100] But this example is unique. Should we say, along with certain other writers, that the *pre*-baptismal anointing was nothing else but the rite of the collation of the Spirit? This would be surprising, for over the course of centuries this Church would have put the gift of the Spirit before baptism, in contrast to the customary practice of the early Church. Moreover, when the *post*-baptismal rite (confirmation) will appear in the Syrian texts, the anointing before baptism will be continued, without any apparent change in meaning.

No doubt, one passage from the *Apostolic Constitutions* (the one to which we have just referred) could lead us to think that this rite would confer the Holy Spirit: here one explains the anointing with oil as a figure of *spiritual* baptism (*eis typon tou pneumatikou baptismatos*). But this is still not the same thing as the baptism *of the Holy Spirit* (see *infra*). Moreover, most texts, as we will see, are oriented in a different direction. The imprecision of certain expressions should not surprise us: it is understandable that these ancient writers, who spoke of the Spirit but once—regarding the anointing that preceded baptism—would sometimes express what the New Testament says about the gift of the Spirit. Among the New Testament writers themselves, the communication of the Spirit was still more or less indiscriminate, since in Acts 10, 44-48 it designates in an indistinct way the grace of faith and the grace of witness. Thus, the ambivalence and confusion of certain formulas are understandable.

But that the pre-baptismal anointing in Syria does not derive from the "gift of the Spirit" of the Acts seems to us to be proven by a very striking fact: in no Syrian text does one find with regard to this anointing the classical expressions of the Acts of the Apostles to designate the gift of Pentecost or its continuation in the Church (the grace conferred by the imposition of hands). Such expressions are well known: "the gift of the Holy Spirit" (Ac 2, 38; 10, 45; 11, 7); "to receive the Holy Spirit" (8, 15, 17, 18; 10, 47); "to receive the gift of the Holy Spirit" (2, 38; 10, 45); "to receive the power of the Holy Spirit" (1, 8); "to be baptized in the Holy Spirit" (1, 5; 11, 17); "to be filled with the Holy Spirit" (2, 4).

---

100. B. Botte, "Le baptême dans l'Eglise syrienne," 139.

These expressions speak of abundance, total gift, power, plenitude. In the Syrian tradition, on the contrary, when the pre-baptismal anointing is related to the Holy Spirit, this is not to say that the latter is "given" or that a person receives his power; at the most, it is said that one "participates" in the Spirit. But in the prayers accompanying the rite, it is ordinarily a question of something else: either of *witness given by the Holy Spirit, revelation of the mysteries,* or *the truth* signified by the anointing—all of which go back to the *faith.*

c) It is now time to show this in the texts.

In the *Acts of Thomas,* we read at least five times the account of a baptism, and three of these passages explain the meaning of the anointing that accompanies the immersion. After the conversion of the king Gondafor, Thomas, before baptizing the king and his brother, asks Christ to receive them into his flock; the initiation is described as follows: *katharisas autous tōi sōi kai aleipsas autous tōi sōi elaiōi apo tēs periechousēs planēs.*[101] The purpose of the anointing is to guard the faithful against *error.* When he is about to pour the oil on the king's head, Thomas utters a prayer asking the Spirit to come: *elthe hē ta mystēria apokaluptousa ta apokrypha.*[102] Likewise, for the baptism of Mygdonia, wife of a cousin of the king Misdea; she asks the Apostle to pray for her so that she may receive baptism and God may deign to dwell within her. Thomas answers: "I will pray and I will ask for you all . . . that *the word of God* may become fixed [kataskēnōsēi] in everyone and remain there [enskēnōsēi].[103] This way of understanding the grace of conversion as a spiritual possession of the word is very signifi-

---

101. M. Bonnet, *Acta Philippi et Acta Thomae* (Leipzig, 1903), §25, 140, 10-11. Here — a unique exception — the anointing is mentioned after baptism, but that does not signify necessarily an order of chronological succession in the rites: when the latter will be described in their actual development, the anointing will be put in first place. The formula used here simply signifies that the anointing and baptism form one whole.

102. M. Bonnet, *op. cit.,* §27, 142, 16-17 (the verbs are in the feminine because in Syriac the word "spirit" is generally of that gender). See also the euchology of Serapion which, among the graces to be obtained by the prebaptismal anointing, requests: *apokalupsai dia tou aleimmatos toutou* (ed. Funk, 184, 9).

103. Bonnet, *op. cit.,* §88, 203, 4-8.

cant. When the moment of baptism has arrived, Thomas utters, as is the custom, a prayer for the oil: the latter is given "for sanctification," but it is called soon afterwards "a *secret mystery* [*mystērion kryphimaion*] in which the cross has been shown forth." This oil, says the Apostle, "makes clear hidden treasures [*deiknus tous kekrummenous thēsaurous*]."[104] A similar explanation of the anointing is found in the account of the baptism of the son of the kind Misdea, Vazanes, and his sisters. Again the Apostle utters a prayer over the oil: "O fruit more beautiful than other fruits . . . you who *announce* to men [*euangelisamenos tois anthrōpois*] their own salvation, who give light to those who are in darkness . . ."[105]

All these texts emphasize the *knowledge* given by the anointing. However, contrary to what we expect, nowhere is faith itself mentioned explicitly, as was the case in the early catechesis. Rather, the terminology is that of the Apocalypse (*apokryphon, kryphimaion, kekrummenous thēsaurous, apokaluptein, deiknunai, alētheia, planē*), and in particular that of the writings of Qumran. A few authors have shown that the Essene movement exerted an influence on the Syrian Church.[106] This is true in particular, it seems, for the practices of Christian initiation, which are repeated in part in the ritual of initiation of the *Manual of Discipline*.[107] In the Manual, too, purification by truth is a necessary requisite for receiving the ritual purification with lustral water.[108] But in Qumran, mention is never made of an *anointing* in this context; on the contrary, this factor arises in early Christian practice (II Cor 1, 21), regard-

---

104. Bonnet, *op. cit.*, §121, 230, 23-231, 2.
105. Bonnet, *op. cit.*, §157, 266, 11-267, 1.
106. J. Daniélou, *Les manuscrits de la mer Morte et les origines du christianisme* (Paris, 1957), 113-117: "L Eglise syrienne et les sadocites."
107. This was shown very clearly by W. Nauck, *Die Tradition und der Charakter des ersten Johannesbriefes*, 167-169.
108. I QS, 3, 6b-12. In the preceding section (2, 25-3, 6a), it is said that the lustral purification must be forbidden to those who refuse to accept the precepts of the Covenant: The conditions for purification are described as follows: "In the spirit of sanctity, in *union with his truth*, he will be purified of all sin; in the spirit of righteousness and humility, his wrongdoing will be expiated; and by the humility of his soul toward all the precepts of God, his flesh will be purified, when they will sprinkle him with lustral water and when he will be sanctified in the water of contrition."

ing the catechumen who accepts the Christian *message* (see the
kerygmatic expression of the last text cited from the *Acts of
Thomas*: *euangelisamenos tois anthrōpois tēn heautōn sōtērian*).
This leads us to believe that in Syrian practice a conjunctio of influences take place: the tradition coming from the early Church
and another, derived from Qumranian Essenism. Both traditions
are in agreement in putting purification by truth before ritual
purification.

Another document of the Syrian Church, the *Apostolic Constitutions,* is much more important for it is a liturgical document; it thus
has a more official character than the popular and legendary writings of the *Acts of Thomas.* And yet the literary influences seen in
the passages that interest us no longer lead us to the apocalyptic
literature of Qumran, but to the Gospel and early baptismal catechesis. In III, 16, 3-17, 4, the oil used before baptism is related
to the Spirit: it represents the Holy Spirit (*to elaion anti pneumatos
hagiou,* 17, 1); it is an image of spiritual baptism (*eis typon tou
pneumatikou baptismatos,* 16, 4), while the meaning of the anointing with the *myron,* which comes after baptism, is indicated by
the essential word, *babaiōsis tēs homologias* (17, 1), the reinforce-
ment of the profession of faith. To this expression may be related
that of VI, 22, 2, where the use of the *myron* is called "the seal on
the commitment" (*sphragis tōn sunthēkōn*); but for this anointing
which follows baptism, the Spirit is not mentioned. He is, on the
contrary, mentioned for the *pre-baptismal* anointing; in this context, the Spirit is presented as a *witness* of Christ (*tou pneumatos
hē sumparalēpsis hōs marturos,* III, 17, 2, probably a throwback to
I Jn 5, 6, where the Spirit's role is also one of witnessing): the
Spirit, sent by Christ and taught by him, is the one who proclaims
him (*kai ekeinon kērutton,* 17, 4). These texts, inspired by St. John
(Jn 15, 16; 16, 13, 14), show that the role of the Spirit in the anointing that precedes baptism is regarded as a message, a communication of the truth. Another text (II, 26, 6) moves in the same direction: "It is impossible to *believe* in Christ without the teaching
[*didaskalias*] of the Spirit." Thus, if in III, 16, 4 the pre-baptismal
anointing is called an image of spiritual baptism, it would be incorrect, we believe, to see in these words the baptism of the Spirit
in the sense of the Acts. The "spiritual baptism" which is symbolized by the pre-baptismal anointing is rather the grace by which

the Spirit *makes* Christ *known*—the gift of faith; this is why the pre-baptismal anointing is still considered a preparation for the baptism of water (*prokataskeuēn tou baptismatos*, VII, 42, 2).

Another passage from the *Constitutions* (VII, 22, 1-2) refers this teaching and witness of the Spirit to the baptismal catechesis. As in *Didache* (7, 1), which is a direct source for all of book VII, the order to baptize is referred back to the command of Christ in Mt 28, 19-20; it is then explained in detail: "You will first anoint with holy oil; then, you will baptize with water; finally, you will apply the seal with *myron. The oil of anointing (chrisma) makes us participants of the Holy Spirit;* water is the symbol of death; the *myron,* the seal on the commitment." Here again, the anointing precedes baptism. And it is clear that the three elements of the phrase are parallel to the three parts of St. Matthew's verse. The third element, the use of the *myron* as a seal on the baptismal commitment, is an application of the last words of Christ: ". . . to observe all that I have commanded you," that is, a confirmation of the profession of faith. The baptismal immersion itself is the execution of the central command: "baptizing them . . ."; and so, the first element, the anointing with oil, which makes one a participant in the Holy Spirit, corresponds to Jesus' words at the beginning of the verse: *matheutēsate panta ta ethnē* (it is significant that this part of the evangelical citation, missing in *Didache,* has been added in the *Constitutions*).

Thus the anointing that symbolizes the participation of the Holy Spirit signifies that Christians have already taken part in the Spirit in accepting the truth, when faith made of them disciples of Christ. Let us note the words *metochē tou hagiou pneumatos,* which explain the meaning of this anointing. The expression is an unusual one, and seems to be a reminiscence. It probably comes from Heb 6, 4, where it is also presented in a baptismal context: at the reception of baptism, Christians have been illuminated by receiving the faith; they have become *participants in the Holy Spirit (metochous pneumatos hagiou)* and have tasted the celestial gift, the wonderful word of God. This parallelism shows that in the text of the *Constitutions* just cited, the participation of the Holy Spirit is not the eschatological gift of the Spirit in the sense of the Acts, but it is linked with the teaching of Christian truth, the gift of baptismal faith. It is this participation which is symbolized by the anointing with oil which prepares one for baptism.[109]

Our last witness for this Syrian tradition will be St. Ephrem, in his hymns on the Epiphany.[110] One-third of these hymns treat of pre-baptismal anointing; the effect of the anointing that is explained the most is the fact that the oil, symbol of truth, separates Christians from the heretics: "Vos autem, qui grex estis Christi inter ethnicos et impios, *veritas oleo obsignat vos* ut separemini ab errantibus" (no. 3). Again: "Oleum Christi *separat fideles* eius *ab alienigenis.* Illo signo insigniti domestici separantur ab extraneis" (no. 5); the separation of believers and non-believers occurred because the former accepted the truth: here, "the oil of Christ" is the truth. Further on, Ephrem calls this anointing oil "allatae salutis nuntium" (no. 8); finally, in the last doxology (no. 28) the "audientes" and the "obsignati" are put in a kind of parallelism: "[Laus Patri] qui ... dedit *audientibus* intellectum et *obsignati* oleum sanctum." Once more, the anointing oil is related to the truths of faith; it constitutes, therefore, a preparation for baptism, and so we understand how, in the first stanza, Ephrem can say of the Christian who is born to the new life: "concipitur ex

---

109. Important detail: mention of the Holy Spirit's participation occurs again in the euchology of Serapion, but here it is connected with the *post-baptismal anointing* (confirmation); thus it has a different meaning and the formula is modified: *metochoi genōntai tēs dōreas tou hagiou pneumatos kai asphalisthentes tēi sphragidi tautēi diameinōsin edraioi kai ametakinētoi* (XXV; ed. Funk, II, 186-188). Instead of "participants in the Holy Spirit," the text says: "participants *in the gift* of the Holy Spirit," thus repeating the expression of the Acts (2, 28; 10, 45) that designates the gift of Pentecost; the grace requested is strengthening in the faith, deliverance from insults and conspiracies; this is indeed in line with the book of Acts, where the grace of strength to *bear witness* foreshadows a context of hostility. The difference from the simple "participation in the Holy Spirit" (*pre*-baptismal) about which the *Apostolic Constitutions* speak is quite clear. But the fact that this mention of the Spirit is transferred from the prebaptismal anointing to the post-baptismal anointing is of great theological interest: it shows that there is an internal connection between faith and confirmation; see note 114 below.

110. T. J. Lamy, S. *Ephraem Syri hymni et sermones,* I (Malines, 1887), col. 27-44. Our citations are based on the numbered stanzas of that edition.

oleo et nascitur ex aqua." This is, as it were, a throwback to the passages of the New Testament which attribute regeneration, now to truth and faith ("the oil"), now to the baptismal water.

There are, then, excellent reasons for saying that the pre-baptismal anointing in the ancient Syrian rite was not an exorcism as in other Churches nor the rite of the gift of the Spirit as this is understood in the Acts, but a symbol of truth, of the Christian mystery, of the faith—supernatural realities to which the catechumen acceded. It is remarkable that we are thus led back to the tradition of Alexandria, which also spoke of an anointing by faith and considered God's word, accepted in the profession of faith, as a spiritual oil of anointing. There is, of course, an important difference: among the Alexandrians, this anointing was understood allegorically, while the Syrians expressed it in a rite. But on the whole, with or without a visible sign, the same reality is involved: belief in Christian truth.

This convergence of the two great Churches of the East, both of which use either literally or metaphorically the vocabulary of anointing to designate baptismal faith, can hardly be fortuitous. The best explanation for this convergence is that in apostolic times the word of God, heard in baptism, had been called an oil of anointing and that the infusion of faith was described as a divine anointing. On the other hand, this convergence of Alexandrian theological vocabulary and Syrian liturgical practice is an invaluable argument from tradition in favor of the explanation of II Cor 1, 21 and I Jn 2, 20, 27 proposed above.

CONCLUSION

1. In neither of these two New Testament texts should the reference to an anointing be understood in terms of a rite: the anointing signifies neither baptism nor confirmation. However, from all the evidence, *chriein* and *chrisma* belong to the baptismal vocabulary. The distant origin of the theme is the verse of Is 61, 1 on the anointing of the prophet with the Spirit. Jesus used this passage to say that he had been anointed with the Holy Spirit after his baptism. The early Church then used the same theme for Christians, always in regard to baptism. But the anointing received is a purely spiritual anointing.

2. Christ's anointing in the Jordan was closely related to the announcing of the message. For the Christian, too, the anointing is connected with the word of the Gospel: in II Cor 1, 21, it signifies the work of the Spirit arousing in the catechumen adhesion-by-faith to this word of truth. According to I Jn 2, 20, 27, the oil of anointing (*chrisma*) is this same word of Christ perceived in faith; but in recalling expressly the moment of entry into Christianity, John considers this anointing oil more as a permanent reality in the life of believers. The theme of the anointing of the Christian—for St. Paul as well as St. John—therefore signifies the word coming to us from Christ who is made known by the Spirit. No doubt, one of the advantages of this solution is that it leads to the synthesis of the two explanations thus far: *chrisma*, doctrine of Christ, or *chrisma*, grace of the Spirit.

3. This exegesis finds remarkable support in tradition. It is

highly significant that the oldest commentator of I Jn, Clement of Alexandria, sees in *chrisma* an anointing of the Christian by faith and also mentions an anointing by the word. The same interpretation was found in the tradition of Origen and in Cyril of Alexandria. Didymus and the chain spoke rather of gnosis, but here too the anointing oil symbolized a supernatural *knowledge*. On the other hand, the ancient Syrian tradition made of the anointing by oil a pre-baptismal rite, to symbolize the revelation of mysteries, the truths of salvation accepted by the catechumen. This meeting-point of two great Oriental traditions in the use of the vocabulary of anointing to designate the act which prepares one for baptism is probably explained by the texts of Paul and John studied in this chapter.

4. From Paul to John, there is a progression of theme: for Paul, the divine anointing occurred before baptism and pertained to the initial faith. On the other hand, John was thinking of the Christian in his full spiritual maturity: for him, the anointing oil is the truth come from Christ but present internally in the believer as a source of instruction throughout all of his Christian life. This explains St. John's tendency not to insist so much on the baptismal context to which the theme was originally linked.

A similar phenomenon occurs in the development of the exegesis in Alexandria. The two kinds of explanation we have seen—the one represented by Clement, Origen and Cyril of Alexandria, and the one by Didymus and the chain—are related: both interpret *chrisma* in terms of a supernatural knowledge, one simply as knowledge through *faith*, the other as the superior knowledge that is *gnōsis*. Similarly, the Christian of whom St. John is speaking is he who knows all things and no longer needs anyone to teach him, because the word remains in him: for him too, it is the Christian who has moved beyond the initial stage of his life of faith. But in contrast to the Alexandrians, John does not distinguish two groups of Christians, the beginners and the professionals: all are informed by the anointing oil,[111] all have within them since

---

111. This is all the more emphatic if in 2, 20 one accepts the lesson of B and S: *oidate pantes*.

baptism the principle of interior enlightenment. But the degree of spiritual intensity actually presupposed by such habitual direction by the interior word explains the fact that the patristic text preferred in the chains to explain I Jn 2, 20, 27 is not that of Clement, but of Didymus on *gnōsis*.[112] Furthermore, we observe that if the reference to baptism was already less in I Jn, in the exegesis of Didymus and the Alexandrians of the chain it has completely disappeared.

5. The study we have made may clarify to some extent the controversial question regarding the grace proper to the sacraments of baptism and confirmation and the relationship between baptism and faith. The dilemma dividing Anglican theologians is well known: either confirmation is the sacrament of the gift of the Spirit and baptism, therefore, does but remit sins (too negative a view of baptism); or we receive the Holy Spirit in the baptismal immersion, and thus confirmation is no longer a sacrament, but simply a supplementary rite (inadequate explanation of confirmation). This clear-cut opposition rests on too rigid and univocal a view of the Spirit's work.

The passages we have studied force us to speak in a much more subtle way. First, let us say that it is never a question of the *gift of the Spirit* in the baptism properly so-called. What is conferred in baptism, is participation in the death and resurrection of Christ, the remission of sins, justification, the grace of adoptive filiation, and birth to the new life. All that is, no doubt, a grace of the Holy Spirit, which constitutes "the pledge of our heritage" and is essentially part of the work of salvation (Eph 1, 13).

But the *gift* of the Holy Spirit or baptism of the Spirit is a different grace, conferred after baptism, although in close relationship to it. It is participation in the prophetic anointing of Jesus in the

---

112. Furthermore, in a more general way, it is strange that the commentary of Clement has left no certain trace in the chain on Catholic epistles; see K. Staab, "Die griechischen Katenenkommentare zu den katholischen Briefen," in *Biblica*, 5 (1924), 350. On the other hand, Didymus' commentary provided much material for the first compiler of the chain; but in the present state of the latter, these fragments are no longer under his name and have become anonymous.

Jordan, the continuation within the Church of the gift of Pentecost. Here the Acts emphasize the idea of plenitude: by the imposition of hands, the Spirit is truly *given,* and above all is a force. This is why tradition will call this sacrament *teleiōsis,* the "perfecting" of the baptismal grace. But such perfecting should not be understood formally in terms of the divine life of the baptized. It is situated on a different plane, that of a mission in the world: the gift of Pentecost was a power conferred on the apostles, in view of the witness they had to give among men, most often in a hostile environment. Thus, the name *bebaiosis* given to this sacrament. The most frequently used formula is that of the *Apostolic Constitutions* (III, 17, 1): *bebaiōsis tēs homologias,* the reinforcing of the profession of faith (baptismal). The gift of the Spirit, granted by the imposition of hands, strengthens the baptized by transforming them into witnesses of the faith.

Here we see the internal connection between confirmation on the one hand and, on the other, acceptance of the truth and the profession of faith *before* baptism. The New Testament and tradition spoke of an anointing of the Christian in relation to the infusion of such faith. This communication of faith is already a "participation in the Spirit," and not yet the "gift of the Spirit." And yet, it is to this faith of the candidate at baptism that confirmation, conferred after the immersion, essentially refers: the Holy Spirit's "gift" is a force that comes to perfect and "confirm" what the "participation" in the Spirit had begun.[113]

On the other hand, the grace of faith—called in our texts the anointing (prebaptismal) of the Spirit—is also linked intrinsically to the grace of baptism itself, since it *prepares for it*: but then it is in another perspective, that of redemption (Eph 1, 14; 4, 30). In the early Church, it appears that the principal object of the profession of faith was the fact that Jesus was the Son of God:

---

113. This is the probable explanation of the fact that in the ancient tradition it is usually a question of the Spirit, either for the act that *precedes* baptism or the one that follows, namely, faith or confirmation, while immersion is presented as an assimilation to Christ. Both faith and the postbaptismal gift of the Spirit are related to supernatural *knowledge;* on the other hand, the grace of baptism is *objective participation* in the work of Christ: such participation is related to salvation.

Iēsous ho huios tou theou (Heb 4, 14; Ac 8, 37; I Jn 5, 5, 10).[114]
And yet, it is the filiation of Jesus that makes possible the adoptive
filiation of Christians; it is because they have *believed* in the Son
that they themselves could *become* sons of God in baptism (see
Jn 1, 12). The grace of filiation, conferred in the immersion, is,
therefore, God's response to the catechumen's faith; it is truly a
divine "seal" on such faith. Thus, the candidate's acceptance of
truth and God's gift of filiation are the means of entering into
the new Covenant; by this faith and this grace a person becomes
a member of "God's people" (Eph 1, 14). The anointing by which
God causes one to *believe* in his word is intrinsically related to
baptismal regeneration, but on the level of salvation. We understand, therefore, why tradition could call baptism "the sacrament
of faith."

6. Finally, let us compare the teaching of St. Paul and St. John
on the anointing through faith with the later doctrine of spiritual
theology on the anointing of the Holy Spirit. In the New Testament, the anointing of the Christian is not called anointing *of the
Holy Spirit,* as it is later called, nor is it considered an autonomous
teaching of the Spirit. Its object is the word *of Christ* proclaimed
in the Church: this word is the oil of anointing of which St. John
speaks. St. Augustine[115] and St. Gregory,[116] who comment on I Jn
2, 27, stress the necessity of the teaching of the interior Master so
that God's word (understood here as the preaching of the Doctors)
may reach the hearts of the faithful. The connection between spiritual anointing and external word is thus maintained, although in
these writers the word "unctio" signifies directly the Holy Spirit's
work, while in St. John *chrisma* was Christ's word recalled by
the Spirit.

---

114. See W. Nauck, *Die Tradition und der Charakter . . .*, 177-182. But the
author speaks without differentiation of the communication of the Spirit,
either before or after baptism, which confuses everything. Before baptism,
there is the gift of "faith"; afterwards, there is the gift of the Spirit,
which is a "strengthening" of faith, for the purpose of witness.
115. St. Augustine, *In epist. Joann. ad Parthos*, III, 13-IV, 1 (*P.L.*, 35,
2004-2005).
116. St. Gregory, *Hom. in evang.*, lib. II, hom. 30 (*P.L.*, 76, 1222).

In later spiritual theology, the interior anointing will become a classic theme; it will be used independently of the scriptural texts from which it comes, and it will tend more and more to be detached from the theme of God's word to which it was linked in the New Testament. Mystical theology in the West, more psychological and subjective than that of the Fathers, will use the word "anointing" in general to designate all work of interior teaching and illumination done by the Holy Spirit. This we observe in St. Bernard[117] and more clearly in the spirituality of modern times.[118] The Church, it is true, has always maintained the necessity of the teaching and external authority of the magisterium in addition to personal inspiration, to control the latter and preserve it from illusions and from illuminism. Theologians teach that the interior anointing of the *Holy Spirit*, operating in those who lead as well as in those who follow, tends constantly to make the exterior *word* of Christ and the Church accepted among the faithful: in other words, the normal result of the life of faith is the convergence of the two teachings. But it remains true that the word "anointing" itself no longer designates anything but one of the two members of the alternative—the interior activity of *the Spirit*.

117. For example, in the sermons on the Canticle of Canticles, apropos of *Cant.* 1, 2, *Osculetur me osculo oris sui*: "De quo iam osculo nolo vos diutius protrahere, sed sermone crastino audietis quidquid orantibus vobis suggerere mihi inde dignabitur unctio docens de omnibus. Neque enim hoc secretum revelat caro et sanguis, sed is qui scrutatur profunda Dei Spiritus Sanctus" (*Sermo*, Vii, 8; *P.L.*, 183, 810 C). Still, let us note that the anointing is here useful to find out the meaning of a word of Scripture; elsewhere, too, when he calls the sons of God "(illi) quos unctio docet de omnibus" (*Epist.* 107, 3; *P.L.*, 182, 244 B), that is, that they can know the intentions of the Father. In other places, the anointing is simply interior revelation and experience (*De conv. ad cler.*, 13; *P.L.*, 182, 844 A-B; *Serm. in Cant.*, XXI, 11; *P.L.*, 183, 877 C-D).

118. For example, in the prologue of the official directory of the *Spiritual Exercises* of St. Ignatius (1599): "Haec sunt spiritualia documenta, quae . . . non tam ex libris quam ex unctione Spiritus Sancti, et ex interna experientia et usu, noster in Christo Beatus Pater Ignatius composuit. Haec sunt lumina quae ei Dominus in ipso primo conversionis fervore inspiravit, ac deinde in omni progressu eius virtutis et sanctitatis semper confirmavit" (*Proem.*, 2; *Mon. hist. Soc. Jesu*, vol 76, 568).

In the New Testament texts on anointing, the situation is different: here, one should not speak of convergence for the simple reason that the word *chrisma* is not applied exclusively to either of the two teachings, but to both the word of Jesus and the interior illumination of the Holy Spirit. This intrinsic relationship, which St. Paul and St. John stress so well between the objective revelation brought by Christ and the work of the interior Master, seems to us to be of prime importance. It would be desirable to recall this indication in the New Testament when one talks of the anointing of the Holy Spirit: such an anointing is linked intrinsically to faith. The Spirit of truth does but bring to mind what Christ had already taught (Jn 14, 26); he causes it to penetrate within the hearts of believers so that they might thus gain life.

V

Christian Freedom and the Law of the Spirit According to St. Paul[*]

The declaration of St. Paul is unequivocal: the Christian vocation is a vocation to freedom. Christian man is a son, not a mercenary or a slave. "For you have been called to liberty, brethren," writes St. Paul. ". . . But if you are led by the Spirit, you are not under the Law" (Gal 5, 13 and 18).

Such statements, and other similar ones, scandalized not only the Jews, but many of the members of the early Christian Church. If at the start of his missionary activity in Antioch around the year 50, and apparently up to the end of his life, St. Paul was the victim of a latent hostility or, at least, an unfortunate lack of understanding, which echoes throughout his Epistles,[1] it is mainly, if not

---

[*] The text of this chapter, without most of the notes and certain passages, appeared in *Christus. Cahiers spirituels,* no. 4 (1954), 6-27.

1. For example, at Antioch (Gal 2, 4-5; Acts 15, 1-3), in Galatia (Gal 1, 6, 10; 4, 16-20; 5, 7-12), at Corinth (II Cor 1, 17, 23-24; 2, 4; 3, 1; 4, 1-2; 7, 5; 10-13), in Jerusalem (Rom 15, 30-31; Acts 21, 20-26), in Rome (Phil 1, 15, 17, unless the epistle was written from Ephesus), in Rome, at

entirely, because of his attitude toward the law and his preaching on Christian freedom. This is what continues to alienate him from those Jews who, in our own day, are empathetic toward the person of Christ. Certainly, in a given situation he could become all things to all men, even Jewish toward the Jews in order to win them over.[2] But when the principle of Christian freedom was involved, nothing could deter him from his course (Gal 2). In his opinion, this was not a secondary teaching or an inconsequential point; it involved everything connected with the religion of Christ.

It remains for us to understand the exact nature of the freedom Paul preaches. Several times, especially in the Epistles to the Galatians and the Romans, he had the opportunity to express his thought fully; but since he generally addressed himself to special circumstances, his writings may seem to discuss problems that have today been transcended. With little effort, we believe, one can draw from Paul's statements a doctrine whose relevance or importance is undeniable. It can be summarized as follows: the Christian animated by the Spirit is freed in Christ not only from the Mosaic law insofar as it is Mosaic, but also from the Mosaic law insofar as it is law, in fact, from any law which constrains man from without (I do not say, which obliges him), without his becoming an amoral being, above and beyond good and evil. Despite appearances, such a doctrine is perfectly consistent, clear, and simple. It is discussed again and again in Catholic tradition, and notably by St. Augustine and St. Thomas Aquinas. And yet, it always seems new to us because, in the practices of daily life, we tend to overlook it.

FREEDOM FROM LAW

When he talks of law, St. Paul is evidently thinking first of all of the law which for him and his Jewish contemporaries merited

---

any rate, during the second captivity (II Tim 1, 17; 4, 16). See below, Chapter 9, p. 261f.

2. See I Cor 9, 20. Thus there is no reason to doubt the account of the Acts regarding the circumcision of Timothy (Acts 16, 3) or the attitude of Paul at Jerusalem, yielding to the urging of James (Acts 21, 23-26).

the title par excellence, namely the legislation of Sinai. To get an idea of the scandal which his statements must have caused among his former coreligionists, we have only to recall the veneration, the cult, with which they surrounded the Torah. Identified with divine Wisdom, it said in the book of Ecclesiastes:

> Before all ages, in the beginning, he created me, and through all ages I shall not cease to be.... Come to me, all you that yearn for me, and be filled with my fruits.... He who eats of me will hunger still, he who drinks of me will thirst for more; he who obeys me will not be put to shame, he who serves me will never fail.
> All this is true of the book of the Most High's covenant, the Law which Moses commanded us... (24, 9, 18, 20-22).

It was God's word, the water that satisfies man's thirst, the bread that gives life, or the vine that brings forth excellent fruits, that which contains the treasures of wisdom and knowledge—in short, what St. John and St. Paul will say precisely about Christ.[3]

And yet, Paul declares the Christian to be freed from this law: "You are not under the Law but under grace" (Rom 6, 14). Just as a woman is bound to her husband as long as he is alive, and is so completely free of the law which bound her to her husband that on the day he dies she does not commit adultery in becoming the wife of another, so the Christian, along with Christ who died and rose again, has died to the law, become free of the law, and is no longer subject to it (Rom 7, 1-6).

Did the law have a role in the history of the Chosen People? It would be the hardly enviable role of the jailer or the pedagogue who was assigned not to teach, but to lead the children to their master (Gal 3, 23-24). In still stronger terms, this law, which the Jews thought of as bringing a person to life is, according to Paul, imposed by God to lead man to death; it was a regime not of benediction, but malediction (Gal 3, 10)!

---

3. Col 2, 3, and St. John, *passim*. Fr. Bonsirven has written very correctly: "A Christian often has the feeling that for the rabbi the Torah is in large part what Christ is for him" (*Le judaïsme palestinien*, I, 249).

"Why then was the Law?" he asks in the Epistle to the Galatians (3, 19), and he answers: "It was enacted on account of transgressions. . . ." A scandalous declaration, even for Christians, which well-intentioned copyists very soon tried to correct.[4] A number of ancient commentators, both Greek and Latin, will have the Apostle say, in spite of the context, that the law had been established to repress, diminish, seal off transgressions.[5] This is an impossible distortion: it is not a question of repressing transgressions but of provoking them.

Exaggeration? Paradox? Not at all. The Epistle to the Romans does have various levels of meaning; the Apostle's thought here has a fullness, a balance which the impassioned tone of the polemic prevented him from attaining right away.[6] But the teaching remains the same. What is more, the dialectic of the Epistle underscores it. Liberation from the law is one of the essential links, indeed, the last one, in the argumentation: freed from sin, death, and the flesh, the Christian could not be saved without being freed from the law. Only this ultimate liberation will deprive sin of the control it exerts over man: "Sin shall not have dominion over you, since you are not under the Law but under grace" (Rom 6, 14). Being under the law is equivalent to being under the power of sin. Never had Paul been so incisive.

Although such assertions were and are scandalous to the Jews, they may seem of small importance to the modern Christian who has never experienced a strong attachment to the Mosaic law and is relieved to be no longer subject to a complicated ritual and a mass of observances that are in his eyes without any strictly religious value: circumcision, minute regulations for the Sabbath and for the preparation of food, or contact with the pagan world. If

---

4. The oldest witness of the direct tradition, the Chester Beatty papyrus, contains a text in which the word "transgression" disappeared: "Why then the law of works until descendents come?" Others understand: "Why then the law of works? It was added (or established) until descendents come . . . ."

5. Cornely cites a good number: Chrysostom, Theodoret, Jerome, Pelagius, Pseudo-Primasius, Nicholas of Lyra, Denys the Carthusian, Cajetan, and more recent ones like Bernard of Pequigny and Palmieri.

6. For example, Rom 5, 20-21, esp. 7, 7-14.

St. Paul were not thinking of any other liberation for the Christian, his statement would hardly raise any difficulties; nor would they be of any great interest to contemporary man. But they would be a caricature of the Pauline teaching. Supposing that such an interpretation had been seriously defended,[7] the context of the Epistle to the Romans, if not that of the letter to the Galatians, would be so much in contradiction that no exegete would think of proposing it.

Under the term "law," Paul included that part of the Mosaic legislation that concerns the moral life, properly so called; the Epistle to the Romans directly speaks only of it. In chapter 7, which discusses the question *ex professo,* if he is thinking of the Mosaic law, Paul is considering it "not in terms of its rites or ceremonies but in its permanent moral content."[8] In other words, it is a question of the Mosaic law as a positive expression of the natural law. Paul, moreover, is explicit: the "law of sin and death," that is, the one which provokes a man to sin and leads him to death, and from which he proclaims us freed in 8, 2,[9] is formally designated in 7, 7 with the help of a commandment of the Decalogue: "Yet I did not know sin save through the Law. For I had not known lust unless the Law had said, 'Thou shalt not lust!' "

To go one step further: the English and Latin translations could suggest that here the Apostle is thinking of a particular law, the one forbidding carnal lust, in short, the so-called "Tenth Commandment." But this is not so. Not only is the context of Exodus (20, 17) or Deuteronomy (5, 21), from which the phrase comes,

---

7. Sometimes there are ambiguous formulas that could *suggest* an analogous interpretation: for example, Paul rejects the old law in *its positive aspect,* but not the moral law founded on the nature of man. We will see that in a certain sense nothing is more exact; but the Mosaic law did not make any distinctions, nor did St. Paul.

8. J. Huby, *Saint Paul, Epitre aux Romains* ("Verbum Salutis"), 234. Likewise, 231: "There is no allusion either to circumcision or to the other rites of Judaism." The interpretation of Rom 7, 7ff. presupposed here, was developed at length in the article "L'histoire du salut selon le chapitre VII de l'Epitre aux Romains," in *Biblica,* 43 (1963), 117-151, and in a brochure (Pontificio Instituto Biblico, 1962, same pagination).

9. "For the law of the Spirit of the life in Christ Jesus has delivered me from the law of sin and of death" (Rom 8, 2).

in opposition, but the Greek verb *epithumein* and the noun *epithumia* almost never in the Septuagint signifies carnal concupiscence. Indeed, the commandment of the Decalogue forbids, in the most general sense, all lust for the goods of another.[10] Similarly, Ecclesiasticus summarizes the whole of Jewish law in a single precept: "Avoid all evil" (17, 12). Moreover, for the son of Sirach, this law seems to summarize not only the legal code of Sinai, but all of God's wishes proclaimed to man since his creation and synthesized in a unique law and covenant.[11] Thus, it is not surprising that Paul should choose the most universal formula, capable of being applied to all divine law or, if you will, encompassing all, including the command—the type of all others— that was promulgated to our first parents. Wishing to describe

10. "You shall not covet [Greek *epithumein*, Hebrew root *ḥmd*] your neighbor's house. You shall not covet your neighbor's wife, nor his male or female slave, nor his ox or ass, nor anything else that belongs to him" (Ex 20, 17). "You shall not desire [Greek *epithumein*, Hebrew root *ḥmd*] your neighbor's wife. You shall not desire [Greek *epithumein*, Hebrew root *'wh*] your neighbor's house or field, nor his male or female slave, nor his ox or ass, nor anything that belongs to him" (Dt 5, 18; Vulgate 21). Likewise, the place named *Kibrot-hattavah* "graves of greed" (Greek *epithumia*, Hebrew root *'wh*) recalls the episode of the quail and the punishment inflicted by God on the people "seized with desire" (Greek *epithumētēs*, Hebrew root *'wh*). See Num 11, 34 and 33, 17. In I Cor 10, 6, St. Paul summarizes under the term of "lust" all of Israel's sins in the desert and, for the Targum, the pagans are essentially "those who lust" (Targum of Ex 20, 17, and Dt 5, 18). See *Histoire du salut*, 145.

11. Some commentators see two sections in this passage from Ecclesiasticus: the first (17, 1-10) would be concerned with the creation of man, while in the second (17, 11-14) "the author would pass from man in general to the Hebrew people in particular" (J. Bonsirven, in Crampon's edition of the *Sainte Bible*, 1952). The conditional tense used by Fr. Bonsirven suggests that he does not take this explanation at face value. At any rate, the transition is imperceptible and v. 11, which is concerned with the Mosaic law (see vv. 12 and 13), very probably evokes the two trees in the garden of Eden, as Dom Calmet remarked: "It gave them knowledge, it bestowed on them the law of life." On the other hand, v. 7 evokes the precept given to Adam in the very terms that summarize the law of Moses in Deuteronomy. We need only compare the two texts: "With wisdom and knowledge he fills them; good and evil he shows them" (Sir 17, 7); "I have set before you life and prosperity, death and doom" (Dt 30, 15). See St. Justin, *I Apol.*, 44, 1.

how man becomes conscious of sin and the essential role played by the law, Paul automatically thought of the biblical description of sin par excellence—the type of all sin—which the successive generations of men continue to commit, each in their own way.[12] In fact, as has been noted for a long time,[13] more than one detail of the text evokes the story of Genesis; at any rate, it is perhaps enough to have this in mind in order that this passage, which is puzzling at first sight, may become quite clear.

Adam and Eve are living in divine friendship; but the serpent comes and persuades them that they will be like gods if they taste of the tree of knowledge of good and evil. At once the fruit, now seen as a means of obtaining this divine privilege, takes on a hitherto unknown charm in Eve's eyes. The Bible emphasizes this in particular: "Now the woman saw that the tree was good for food, pleasing to the eyes, and *desirable* for the knowledge it would give" (Gen 3, 6).[14] And yet no sooner have they transgressed

12. See Rom 5, 12 and the notes of the *Jerusalem Bible*. On the close connection between original sin and actual sins, underscored in the Greek tradition and in St. Thomas, see the *Supplément au Dictionnaire de la Bible*, VII, in particular, col. 510, 546-551, 562-563 (article "Péché dans le N. T."). Not that Paul wants to describe here Adam's sin in itself: he writes not as an historian, but as a theologian. However, contrary to some interpretations, his source of information is not psychological introspection, but the Bible. See *Histoire du salut*, 130, 147.

13. Thus, among the ancients, Methodius of Olympus (*De resurrectione*, II, 1-8), Theodorus of Mopsuestia, Severian of Gabala, Theodoret, Genadus of Constantinople, etc. K. L. Schelkle thinks that such was the interpretation "by far the most common" among the Fathers (*Paulus, Lehrer der Väter*, 1956, 238). Likewise, in the sixteenth century, Cajetan and, among the moderns, Lietzmann, Lagrange, K. Prümm, etc. Among the former who reject it, a good number at least admit that Paul took the account of Genesis as a model. Thus F. J. Leenhardt wrote: "The relationship of v. 7 to v. 12 with Genesis 3 shows that the Apostle thought out the scene he constructed starting with the person . . . who was Adam" (*L'Epitre de saint Paul aux Romains*, 1957, 106). Likewise, P. Bläser, *Das Gesetz bei Paulus*, 1941, 115, n. 77, and A. Feuillet, who speaks of "traits clearly borrowed from the scene of Adam and Eve's disobedience in the earthly paradise, an offense that was in a way the type of all those that followed" (*Lumière et Vie*, no. 14, 1954, 222). See J. Huby, *Epitre aux Romains*, 2d ed., 601-604, and *L'histoire du salut*, 132-134.

14. Note that the Hebrew terms translated here as "seductive" and "desirable"

the law than they see themselves reduced to nudity, deprived of everything that heretofore brought them happiness. Formerly friends of God, they now hide from him, are afraid of him, and flee him. They are then dismissed forever from Paradise (i.e., divine intimacy), forbidden to enter therein—both themselves and their descendants—by the Cherubim with their flaming sword. If God had not mercifully intervened, they would have been prevented from ever entering upon the road to the tree of life, that life which is enjoyed by God alone and by those who are united to him. God's command, of course, was good, holy, of a spiritual nature, and divine (Rom 7, 13-14). It is not his command, but the serpent that is responsible for all the misfortunes of Adam and Eve. And yet, according to the biblical narrative, the divine command played a part—the serpent used it to induce our first parents to disobey. Intended to preserve life in them, the commandment became, in fact, a cause, at least an occasion, of death.

This is precisely, we feel, what St. Paul wants us to understand in this controversial passage. Only one of the participants changes: sin is personified in the role of the serpent.[15]

What shall we say then? Is the Law sin? By no means! Yet I did not know sin save through the Law?[16] For I had not known lust unless the Law had said, *"Thou shalt* not lust." But sin, having thus found an occasion, worked in me by means of the commandment all manner of lust, for without the Law sin was dead (Rom 7 7-8).

(roots '*wh* and *ḥmd*) are the very ones found, in the case of the first, in the expression "graves of greed" and, for the second, in the commandment of the decalogue: "You shall not covet" (see note 10 *supra*).

15. Diodorus of Tarsus noted: "He seems to call the devil sin" (*Pauluskommentare aus der griechischen Kirche,* ed. K. Staab, 87). One may also compare Rom 5, 12: "Therefore as through one man sin entered into the world and through sin death . . . ," with Wis 2, 24: "By the envy of the devil, death entered the world."
16. "Know" in the sense of spiritual experience. See *Verbum Domini,* 40 (1962), 163.

Sin met death like a crushed serpent, notes Fr. Huby.[17] Better yet, according to the text of Paul, sin died like a cadaver which has lost its strength (*nekros*). And Paul continues: "Once upon a time I was living without law" (7, 9).

This is truer of Adam than of any other man, of Adam and Eve before sin, in the guise of the serpent, conquered them, creating in their heart that complicity which will be the desire to become like gods, a desire which will become specific in the wish to taste of the forbidden tree.[18] But, to a certain extent, this applies also to the circumcised Jew, to every baptized Christian, indeed, to every man, insofar as in any free act he is not yet oriented to his final end.[19] The Apostle continues, "But when the commandment came, sin revived" [*anezēsen*]: until then a cadaver [*nekros*], it became [*ana-*] alive [*ezēsen*], "and I died," that is, I lost that eminently divine privilege which is life. "And the commandment that was unto life was discovered in my case to be unto death. For sin, having taken occasion from the commandment, deceived me" —as the serpent "deceived" Eve[20]—"and through it killed me" (Rom 7, 9-11). So for Paul, as well as for the author of Genesis and of

---

17. In his commentary published in 1941, Fr. Huby rejected the explanation of Fr. Lagrange, which he had at first taught, to adopt the explanation called "heilsgeschichtlich." The one that is presupposed here is no less "heilsgeschichtlich"; but it makes this "history of salvation" start with the creation of man, like the Bible, and not only with his sin. See Huby, 2d ed., 605-607, and *Histoire du salut*, 147-148. St. Paul thus seems to be opposed to the Jewish view that attributed Adam's justice to observation of the law: according to the Targum, he had been placed in paradise "to observe the law" and not "to cultivate the garden" (Targ. of Gen 2, 15), and "the tree of life" was formally identified with the law (Targ. of Gen 3, 23). See *Histoire du salut*, 137-138. Similarly, in Rom 4, Paul opposed the Jewish view of Abraham's justification by the works of the law.

18. What St. Paul says of every "spiritual" Christian, namely, that he is not "under a law," pertains even more so to Adam and Eve, in paradise, despite the command "not to taste of the forbidden tree." In fact, Adam and Eve disobeyed the commandment only when the serpent reminds them of its existence; previously, they obeyed the command just as a mother obeys the fifth commandment, forbidding her to kill her child. See *Histoire du salut*, 141.

19. See St. Thomas, *Summa theol.*, I-II, q. 89, a. 6, and parallel passages.

20. See Gen 3, 13; St. Paul certainly alludes to it in II Cor 11, 3 and I

Wisdom (2, 24), the one who is responsible for death is not the law or God, its author, but the serpent or the devil or sin. The conclusion follows: "The Law indeed is holy and the commandment holy and just and good" (Rom 7, 12).

But how can we explain this strange behavior of God? If he wishes only life, why give man a law which will lead him to death? Paul poses the problem and then provides the answer: "Did then that which is good become death to me? By no means! But sin, *that it might be manifest as sin,* worked death for me through that which is good, *in order that sin* by reason of the commandment *might become immeasurably sinful*" (Rom 7, 13).

The important word is pronounced. The Jews imagined that the law conferred life.[21] But a law, as such, even if it proposed the most sublime ideal, could not transform a being of flesh into a spiritual being, who lives the very life of God. Or this would be to suggest that man did not need to be saved, that he can save himself! Far from conferring life, that is, destroying in man that power of death which is sin, or even repressing it, sealing it off, the Law's aim is to allow him to give vent, so to speak, to all his virulence, and thereby exteriorize and unmask itself. It does not take away sin; but it reveals to man his state as sinner.[22] Likewise in Paradise, by inducing the woman to violate the divine command, the serpent, whom she took to be a friend and honest counselor, revealed his true self: he was the worst of enemies, supremely sin-

Tim 2, 14, and in both cases he uses, as here, the compound verb "eksapatan" instead of the simple "apatan" of the Septuagint.

21. See the expressions "the law of life" (Sir 17, 11; see note 11 in this chapter), "the path to life" (Ps 16, 11) etc., and more generally the assimilation of the law in Wisdom (see above, p. 146f.). This is exactly what Paul presupposes in Gal 3, 21: "For if a law had been given that could give life, justice would truly be from the Law" and thus would be contrary to the economy of the promise (where justification depends on a promise given unilaterally, as in a testament).

22. "For by the works of the Law no human being shall be justified before him, for through law comes the recognition of sin (Rom 3, 20). The statement makes way for Rom 7, 7-14, which explains what Paul means by "the recognition of sin."

ful, a liar and murderer, as St. John says, separated and separating from God who is life.

Let us note in passing that, strictly speaking the law does not provoke sin but transgression. No doubt, it has been customary to make the two ideas identical and, in order to emphasize better its religious aspect, so profoundly inculcated by the Bible, to define sin as the violation of a divine law. Paul certainly regards sin as opposition to God. But he usually does not confuse it with simple transgression; in this he follows the teaching of Genesis which places Adam and Eve's sin above and beyond disobeying God's law, in their desire to be like God; in this regard the serpent, without transgressing any formal law, sinned most seriously since, of the three persons involved, he is the most severely punished and the only one irrevocably cursed.

Paul thinks of transgression as the expression and exteriorization of a much more radical evil, *hamartia*: evil power personified, which is often reduced to carnal concupiscence alone, but which in reality corresponds better to that deep-rooted egotism by which man, since the time of original sin, instead of orienting himself to God and others, orients everything to himself; in short, what St. Augustine will call "love of self," builder of the city of evil, and what Paul calls explicitly "hostility to God" (Rom 8, 7).[23] It is this "sin" which must be destroyed in us. By itself, the law cannot do so; but in permitting "transgression," it enables sin to reveal its true identity and man, enlightened by this unfortunate experience, to have recourse to his only Savior. Thus Paul understands the role of the law—its indispensable, ultimately beneficent, and salutary role—a role which cannot be the privilege of a particular code of law, even if it be the Mosaic law. Paul's view is consonant with everything that brings to perfection the notion of law, with

---

23. Going a different route, Fr. Gilleman arrives at the same conclusion: "In the case of sin, transgression of the law formally specifies the nature and deformity of sin, but the malice comes, properly speaking, from one's deviation from charity .... The transgression is only the moral, external aspect of a present decrease in our capacity to love." Similarly, "moral obedience to the law is the external aspect and necessary expression of our true and fundamental life which is love" (*Le primat de la charité en théologie morale* [Lessianum Museum, 1952], 256).

every norm imposed from without on the human conscience. Thus it is from the "legal domain" as such that the Christian is declared free by St. Paul.[24]

THE LAW OF THE SPIRIT

Is the Christian a man without law? A being who is above and beyond good and evil? St. Paul understands the objection perfectly and answers no. "What then? Are we to sin because we are not under the Law but under grace? By no means!" (Rom 6, 15). Nothing would contradict more clearly the teaching of all the Epistles. The paradox, however, remains to be solved. Chapter 8 of the Epistle to the Romans, which takes up the arguments expressed briefly in the Epistle to the Galatians, provides, we think, all the elements of the solution. Indeed, the most authoritative commentators in the Catholic tradition are content to repeat the statements of St. Paul without trying to mitigate them. For so delicate a question, we may invoke the testimony of such commentators especially St. Thomas Aquinas, who proposed in his commentary on the Pauline epistles the final expression of his thought.[25]

---

24. The fact that St. Paul refrains from saying that the Christian is not "under *the* law," but says that he is not "under *a* law" (*upo nomou*), without the article, is perhaps not without meaning. Of course, the use of the article in Koiné Greek, and especially in the Greek of the papyri, varies and does not have the precise meaning it has in classical Greek. Nevertheless, St. Paul is far more educated than most of the writers of the papyri; he handles the Greek language with a skill that is evident, for example, in the subtle use he makes of particles or prefixes (thus Rom 2, 1; 12, 3; 14, 22-23; Phil 18-19). In particular, the passage from Rom 2, 14ff., where St. Paul contrasts the Jew violating *the Mosaic law* and the pagan observing *a law*, namely, the law of his conscience(with the grace that does not fail if he is of good faith and which alone justifies a man in Paul's eyes), provides a series of examples where, without unusual subtlety, one notices in each instance the presence or absence of the article.

25. This is especially true of the commentary on the Epistle to the Romans which alone he had the time to complete. The rest, beginning with I Cor 7, 14 (or more precisely 10, 1) is a "reportatum' of Brother Reginald, based on the lectures given by his teacher at the papal court of Orvieto between 1259 and 1265.

Chapters 5, 6, and 7 of the Epistle to the Romans describe the conditions necessary for the Christian to be saved: liberation from sin, from death, from the flesh, and, last but not least, freedom from the law. These chapters show that the successive forms of liberation are experienced by the Christian in Christ, and in Christ alone. Thus chapter 8 can begin with a triumphant cry: "There is therefore now no condemnation for those who are in Christ Jesus." And Paul explains why: "For the law of the Spirit of the life in Christ Jesus has delivered you from the law of sin and of death" (Rom 8, 2). Thus from this law which in the Bible had been the instrument of sin and death, man is freed by something which St. Paul also called, rather surprisingly, a law—the law of the Spirit who gives life. What does this mean? Would Christ be content with replacing the code of the Mosaic law by another code, one which was more perfect or less complicated but which was largely similar and thus would keep the Christian under a legal regime? By no means. Paul was not opposing the Mosaic law to another law, but to grace: if sin no longer exerts its control over you, he explained, "you are not under the law but under grace" (Rom 6, 14). Did he change his thinking? Not at all. The formula changed, but not the idea.

Tradition has been aware of this, and St. Thomas, for example, summarizes it all with a clarity and conciseness that leaves no doubt. "The law of the Spirit," he writes in his commentary on the Epistle, "is what is called the new law"—a phrase to remember when one tries to interpret exactly the passages where St. Thomas Aquinas, as a theologian, will explain in the two *Summas* the treatise on the "new law." "But," he adds, "it is identified either with the very person of the Holy Spirit or with the activity in us of this same Spirit." And to prevent any misunderstanding of the meaning of these words, he adds a comparison with the old law, saying that "the Apostle had said of it, somewhat before, that it was a spiritual one." Paul did in fact describe it as being *pneumatikos* in Rom 7, 14, that is, "given by the Holy Spirit."[26]

---

26. *In Rom* 8, 2: "Quae quidem lex potest dici: *a*) uno modo Spiritus Sanctus ... qui mentem inhabitans non solum docet quid oporteat fieri in-

The "law of the Spirit," therefore, is not distinguished from the Mosaic law—and *a fortiori* from any other non-revealed law, even if it is considered as an expression of the divine law—only because it would propose a more elevated ideal, would impose greater demands, or, on the contrary, would offer salvation much more easily, as if Christ had substituted an "easy morality" for the intolerable yoke of the law code of Sinai. The law of the Spirit is by its very nature radically different from the old law; It is no longer a code, even if "given by the Holy Spirit," but a law "accomplished in us by the Holy Spirit"; not a simple, external norm of action, but what no other code of laws as such could be, a principle of action, a new, interior dynamism.

If, to designate this spiritual dynamism, the Apostle used the term "law" instead of "grace" (Rom 6, 14) as elsewhere, it is probably in reference to the prophecy of Jeremiah, cited here even by St. Thomas, which announced the new Covenant, the "New Testament." For the prophet also spoke of law: "But this is the covenant which I will make with the house of Israel after those days, says the Lord. I will place my law within them, and write it upon their hearts" (Jer 31, 33). A few years later, Ezekiel took up the very words of Jeremiah, substituting for the word "law" that of "spirit": "I will put my spirit within you" (Ez 36, 27), that Spirit who is capable of giving life to "dry bones" (Ez 37, 4) and of transforming them into a "vast army" (Ez 37, 10).[27] Thus each time St. Thomas will evoke this "New Testament," the same formulas will reappear: "It is proper for God to act by

tellectum illuminans de agendis, sed etiam affectum inclinat ad recte agendum; *b*) alio modo lex Spiritus potest dici proprius effectus Spiritus Sancti, scil. *fides per dilectionem operans* (Gal 5, 6), quae quidem et docet interius de agendis ... et inclinat affectum ad agendum .... Et haec quidem lex Spiritus dicitur lex nova, quae vel est Spiritus Sanctus vel eam in cordibus nostris Spiritus Sanctus facit. De lege autem veteri supra dixit quod erat spiritualis (Rom 7, 14), id est a Spiritu Sancto data" (lect. 1; ed. R. Cai, no. 602-603).

27. See "Rom 8, 2-4 à lumière de Jérémie 31 et d'Ezechiel 35-39," in *Mélanges Eugène Tisserant*, I, 1964 (Studi e Testi, 231), 311-323, and "Le N. T. à la lumière de l'Ancien," in *Nouv. Rev. théol.*, 87 (1965), 561-587.

operating within the soul, and it is thus that the New Testament was given since it consists of the infusion of the Holy Spirit"; "The Holy Spirit himself is the New Testament, effecting within us love, the plenitude of the law."[28] Thus, for the Church and its liturgy, the promulgation of the new law dates not from the Sermon on the Mount, but from the day of Pentecost, when "the finger of the right hand of the Father, *digitus paternae dexterae,*" inscribed its law in men's hearts: to the code of the ancient law given on Sinai corresponds not a new code, but the gift of the spirit.[29] As Cardinal Seripando said so well, it is this which the Christian "receives under the guise of a law."[30]

Far from falling into amoralism, the Christian, receiving this Spirit who acts within him, or what is practically the same thing, receiving this activity of the Spirit, becomes capable of "walking according to the Spirit," that is, in conformity with what the law —it too "spiritual"—demanded in vain from him. So true is this that Paul, having proclaimed man's liberation by the law of the Spirit thanks to Christ's redemptive work, can assign to this work the

---

28. *In Heb* 8, 10: "Modus tradendi est duplex: *a*) unus per exteriora, sicut proponendo verba ad cognitionem alicujus; et hoc potest homo facere; et sic traditum fuit vetus testamentum; *b*) alio modo interius operando, et hoc est proprium Dei . . . , et hoc modo datum est novum testamentum, quia consistit in infusione Spiritus Sancti, qui interius instruit . . . ; item ad bene operandum inclinat affectum . . . . *In corde eorum superscribam eos* (Jer 31, 33) id est super cognitionem scribam caritatem" (lect 2; ed R. Cai, no. 404). *In 2 Cor* 3, 6: "Spiritus Sanctus, dum facit in nobis caritatem, quae est plenitudo legis, est testamentum novum" (lect. 2; ed. R. Cai, no. 90). This was precisely the interpretation given by St. Augustine to the oracle of Jeremias: "Quid sunt ergo leges Dei ab ipso Deo scriptae in cordibus, nisi ipsa praesentia Spiritus Sancti, qui est digitus Dei, quo praesente diffunditur caritas in cordibus nostris, quae plenitudo legis est et praecepti finis?" (*De Spiritu et littera,* 21; P.L., 44, 222).

29. See J. Lécuyer, "Pentecôte et loi nouvelle," in *Vie spirituelle,* May, 1953, 471-490.

30. 30. *In Rom* 8, 2: "Haec lex spiritus vitae est Dei Spiritus, quem humana mens legis vice accipit." Far from being an unqualified theologian, Seripando was made cardinal to preside over the meetings of the Council of Trent as a legate in place of Cardinal Cervini, who had become Pope Marcellus II. See H. Jedin, *Papal Legate at the Council of Trent, Cardinal Seripando* (London, 1947), 562-577.

following aim: "in order that the requirements of the Law might be fulfilled in us, who walk not according to the flesh but according to the spirit" (Rom 8, 4), with the idea of completeness which the verb "fulfill" contains, somewhat as a prophecy is fulfilled in its realization, or the type in the antitype.[31] The verb here is in the passive, so aware is Paul of the fact that while it remains a free act of man, this "fulfillment" is much more an act of God, of the Spirit who works within man.

From this fundamental doctrine everything else follows, and in particular the fact that Christian morality rests necessarily on love, as Paul the disciple teaches, in imitation of the Master: "For the whole Law is fulfilled in one word: Thou shalt love thy neighbor as thyself" (Gal 5, 14). "He who loves his neighbor has fulfilled the Law. *For Thou shalt not commit adultery, thou shalt not kill, thou shalt not steal, thou shalt not covet;* and if there is any other commandment, it is summed up in this saying, *Thou shalt love thy neighbor as thyself.* . . . Love therefore is the fulfillment of the Law" (Rom 13, 8-10). Love is not primarily a norm of conduct, but a force, a dynamism. Because it was not a form of love, says St. Thomas, the law—as law—could not justify man: "Thus it was necessary to give us a law of the Spirit, which, effecting love in us, can give us life."[32]

Thus we understand how a Christian, that is, a man animated by the Holy Spirit (Rom 8, 14), can be freed from all external law, not be "under a law," and yet lead a perfectly moral and virtuous life. St. Paul explains it in lucid terms in the Epistle to the Galatians, soon after having reduced all law to love: "Walk in the Spirit, and you will not fulfill the lusts of the flesh" (Gal 5, 16). Nothing is more evident, he says, since these are two antagonistic

---

31. See A. Descamps, *Les justes et la justice dans les Evangiles et le christianisme primitif,* 112ff.
32. *In 2 Cor* 3, 6: "Et ideo [because 'littera occidit, Spiritus autem vivificat'] necessarium fuit dare legem Spiritus, qui caritatem in corde faciens, vivificet" (lect. 2; ed. R. Rai, no. 90). The "dilige et fac quod vis" of St. Augustine seems to be at first a practical principle of conduct regarding fraternal charity. See J. Gallay, *Recherches de Science Religieuse,* 1955, 545-555.

principles: if you follow one, you can only be opposed to the other. But "if the Spirit animates you, you are not under the law." Indeed, what would you need it for? A spiritual man knows clearly what is carnal, and he will avoid it almost instinctively if he is spiritual: "immorality, uncleanness, licentiousness, idolatry, witchcrafts, enmities, contentions, jealousies, anger, quarrels, drunkenness, carousings, and suchlike" (Gal 5, 19-21a).

To do such things would indicate that a person is not animated by the Spirit. "And concerning these I warn you, as I have warned' you, that they who do such things, will not attain the kingdom of God" (Gal 5, 21). But a person will not commit these wrongs, once he is spiritual. The fruits he will produce are those of the Spirit, or rather "the fruit" for there is only one fruit, which has many facet: "charity, joy, peace, patience, kindness, goodness, faith, modesty, continency" (Gal 5, 22); in short, in whole body of Christian virtues which are, in St. Paul's eyes, but expressions of charity:

> Charity is patient, is kind; charity does not envy, is not pretentious, is not puffed up, is not ambitious, is not self-seeking, is not provoked; thinks no evil, does not rejoice over wickedness, but rejoices with the truth; bears with all things, believes all things, hopes all things, endures all things (I Cor 13, 4-7).

Without needing any law, which constrains him from without, the Christians, animated by the Spirit, fulfills all law in the full freedom of the sons of God.

Thus it is surprising that Fr. Prat should find it "difficult to see in St. Paul a directive principle of moral teaching" and could criticize the morality of Paul for having made *tabula rasa* of the Mosaic law and not saying clearly what it was replacing it with.[33]

THE CODE OF CHRISTIAN LAWS

Many a reader will share Fr. Prat's concern. The difficulty

---

33. *Théologie de saint Paul,* II, 6th ed., 376-377.

he poses is not an imaginary one. The Christian religion, without doubt, contains positive laws. Paul himself does not refrain from promulgating them, even some very specific ones. The morality of the New Testament, including the Pauline morality, has nothing to do with a "morality without obligation or sanction."[34] To the catechumen seeking baptism, the Church, like the synagogue, imposes a code of morality, which is less complicated, more sublime, but still presented as a code of laws. Moreover, when a person talks of "new law," as opposed to "old law," is he not usually thinking primarily of this aspect?

Ordinarily, perhaps, and it is this, no doubt, that Fr. Prat was thinking of. But not St. Paul, I believe. He speaks twice of the "law of Christ,"[35] but to the ancient law he generally opposes grace or, what is the same thing, the law of the Spirit. St. Thomas too is aware of the classic opposition between old and new law, but in trying to define the latter, he resists calling it primarily a code of laws: "The new law is chiefly the very grace of the Holy Spirit, given to Christians."[36] Thus, he adds, it is an "unwritten law," and therefore "it justifies." But insofar as it is a code of laws, insofar as it contains "the teachings of faith and the moral precepts directing the attitude of men and their acts," the new law does not justify men any more than the old law did, for it is not of another nature: a norm of conduct, yes, but not a principle of action. Thus, recalling, as St. Augustine did, the expression of St. Paul, "the letter kills" (II Cor 3, 6),[37] Thomas states without the slightest hesitation: "Under the term of letter, one must understand all law exterior to man, even the precepts of evangelical morality."[38]

---

34. On this particular aspect, see the excellent remarks of G. Salet, "La loi dans nos coeurs," in *Nouv. Rev. théol.*, 79 (1957), 449-462, 561-578.
35. Gal 6, 2 and I Cor 9, 21: the expression is understood perfectly in light of what we have just said.
36. *Summa theol.*, I-II, q. 106, a. 1, corp.: "Principaliter lex nova est ipsa gratia Spiritus Sancti, quae datur christifidelibus."
37. See St. Augustine, *De spiritu et littera*, ch. 14, 17, 19, *passim* (*P.L.*, 44, 215- 222).
38. I-II, q. 106, a. 2: "Ad legem Evangelii pertinent: *a*) unum quidem principaliter, scilicet ipsa gratia Spiritus Sancti interius data; *b*) aliud ... secundario, scilicet documenta fidei et praecepta ordinatia affectum human-

The same idea arose after the Protestant Reformation, for example, in St. Robert Bellarmine. Commenting upon the Pauline antithesis between "law of works" and "law of faith" (Rom 3, 27),[39] he says in line with St. Augustine's *De Spiritu et littera*:

> The law of works in the Apostle's mind is that which commands what one must accomplish; the law of faith is faith itself, which obtains for man the grace to accomplish what the law of works commands.... The law of works provides a light for our conscience; the law of faith enables us to accomplish.... The law of works is the letter which kills ..., and the law of faith is the Spirit who gives life....
>
> Thus, not only the law of Moses but also the law of Christ, insofar as it commands something, is the law of works; while the law of faith is the spirit of faith by which not only we Christians but also the patriarchs, prophets, and all just men have obtained God's grace and, justified gratu-

um et humanos actus. Quantum ad primum, nova lex justificat; quantum vero ad secundum, nova lex non justificat. Unde Apostolus dicit: *Littera occidit, Spiritus autem vivificat* (II Cor 3, 6). Et Augustinus exponit quod per litteram intelligitur quaelibet scriptura extra homines existens, etiam moralium praeceptorum, qualia continentur in Evangelio. Unde etiam littera Evangelii occideret, nisi adesset interius gratia fidei sanans." St. Thomas did not look askance at the expression "sola fides," which will be abused later on. Commenting on St. Paul's expression in I Tim 1, 8: "Scimus quia bona est lex, si quis ea legitime utatur," he explains that the Apostle means the moral precepts of the Decalogue and that "legitimate usage" means not attributing to them more than they contain: "Horum legitimus usus est, ut homo attribuat eis plus quam quod in eis continetur. Data est lex ut cognoscatur peccatum .... Non est ergo in eis spes justificationis, sed in sola fide." Involved here is the "fides per caritatem operans" (Gal 5, 6) so often mentioned by St. Thomas. Furthermore, he does not hesitate to support his statement by invoking the famous verse of Rom 3, 28 where Luther will add the adverb "solum": *Arbitramur justificari hominem per fidem sine operibus legis* (*In 1 Tim* 1, lect. 3; ed. R. Cai, no. 21). On the justification "solum per fidem," see *Quaestiones in epist. ad Rom*, I, 2d ed., 114-120.

39. In Rom 3, 27, Paul contrasts the law that consists of performing works with the one that consists of believing. See St. Augustine, *De Spiritu et littera*, ch. 13; *P.L.*, 44, 213-215.

itously by this same grace, have observed the commandments of the law.[40]

But then why does the religion of Christ contain a code of
laws? Why, alongside this primary, unwritten element which
justifies man, maintain a secondary, written element which does
not justify? Already foreign in the old economy, does it not become
incomprehensible in the economy of grace? Not at all.

The Pauline principle remains: "The Law is not made for
the just, but for the unjust" (I Tim 1, 9). If all Christians were
just, there would be no need to constrain them with laws. As a
general rule, the law intervenes only to repress an existing disorder.
As long as Christians received frequent communion, the Church
never thought of obliging them under pain of sin to receive communion once a year. But when fervor decreased, in order to remind them that a man cannot possess divine life unless he is
nourished on Christ's flesh, it promulgated the law of Easter communion.[41] Actually, although all are bound thereby, the law is not
aimed at the fervent Christian who continues to receive communion during the Easter period, not "in virtue of the Lord's precept,"[42]
but in virtue of the interior drive which motivates him throughout
the year to receive communion each Sunday or even every day.
Not that he ceases to be bound by this precept; but as long as he
feels this interior demand—a fruit of the Spirit who animates him—
he will fulfill the law without even thinking about it, just as a
mother by nature obeys the law of the Decalogue which forbids
her to kill her child. Indeed, like that mother, he will fulfill it
"superabundantly," in the sense of the Greek verb *plēroun*.[43] On the

40. St. Robert Bellarmine, *Controversia de justificatione impii*, I, 19; *Opera
    omnia*, Naples, 1856-1862, IV, 492.
41. It is said, for example, that in the thirteenth century the devout king of
    France, St. Louis, attended several masses each day and recited the
    breviary, but that he received communion only three times a year. At
    the same time, St. Catherine of Siena suggested to one of her com-
    patriots a spiritual plan of life as follows: daily Mass with the recitation
    of the little office of the holy Virgin and monthly confession, but com-
    munion only at major religious feasts and at least once a year (see, C. Butler,
    Wege christlichen Lebens [Einsiedeln, 1944], 127).
42. The expression is that of St. Thomas. See the text cited below, p. 172.
43. Apropos of Rom 8, 4, see above, p. 160.

other hand, as soon as the interior urge is no longer felt, the law will be there to compel him and thus warn him that he has ceased to be animated by the Spirit.

Thus it will serve him the same way the Mosaic law served the Jews.[44] As a pedagogical instrument leading him to Christ, not only does it make up for the light no longer provided by the Spirit, but above all it enables him to become aware of his sinful state, that is, a man who has ceased being animated by the Spirit. Such an awareness, in St. Paul's view, is the first requirement for being healed. Thus we understand why the law was instituted for sinners.

And yet, the law is not without usefulness for the just themselves. For even when in the state of grace the Christian, as long as he remains on this earth, has only a pledge (Rom 8, 23; II Cor 1, 22). As long as he lives within a mortal body, he is never so freed from sin and the flesh that he cannot fall back under their control at a given moment (see Rom 6, 12). In this unstable condition, the written, external law, objective norm of moral conduct, will help his conscience, so easily confused by the passions—for the flesh continues to struggle against the Spirit (Gal 5, 17)—to distinguish the works of the flesh from the fruit of the Spirit and not to confuse the inclination of his own nature, weakened by sin, with the interior movement of the Spirit.

Paul does not consider it superfluous to remind the Christian of the kind of inspiration the Spirit gives the truly spiritual man and to add to his doctrinal explanations an exhortation intended to direct his moral life. Until the Christian attains full spiritualization in the land of his Father, his freedom remains imperfect and initial.[45] Alongside the principal element, grace, which

---

44. Fr. Huby has remarked: "The Christian . . . can again live according to the flesh and let sin gain the upper hand over him; he is then no longer under grace but under the law. The law becomes once again what it was for him before his union with Christ" (*Epitre aux Romains,* 233).

45. In *Mystiques paulienne et johannique,* 1946, 57-58, J. Huby says: "In order that divine law may become completely interior to man, all feeling of opposition disappear, every occasion of conflict between God's and man's *will* be radically suppressed, the body would have to cease being a weight, an obstacle, to the soaring drive of the spirit, that it cease being a mortal body to become a completely spiritualized one: this will

alone justifies, there will also be a secondary element, not more capable of justifying him than the ancient law, but indispensable to sinners and in no way superfluous for the imperfectly just that all men are.[46]

Nevertheless, it must remain secondary and not tend little by little, as happened with the Jewish law in the time of St. Paul, to assume the role of principal element. To resist this always threatening danger, it is fitting for us to recall a fundamental principle, a simple corollary of the doctrine explained so far and one which St. Thomas, in particular, expressed with his usual clarity: *the external law can only be the expression of the interior law.*

Considering, in the treatise on the law in the *Summa theologica,* whether the new law should impose or prohibit external works, in other words, should include a code of positive laws, St. Thomas begins by reaffirming the doctrine that the main element in the new law is the interior grace of the Holy Spirit. The works imposed can exist only in relationship to this interior grace. Either these will be works which put us in communication with Christ's humanity, from which comes all grace, and thus produces in us that dynamism that consists of faith acting in charity, or they

be accomplished only at one's glorious resurrection." See also J. Mouroux, *L'experience chrétienne,* 145-146, 202-203; *Le sens chrétien de l'homme,* 166.

46. Against the objections of Kant and Scheler contrasting love and law, Fr. Gillen invokes the statement of Kierkegaard: "However joyful and indescribable love is, it feels the need to be bound. It is only when love is a duty that it is eternally certain. This certainty given by eternity dissipates all iniquity and makes love perfect. For instantaneous love, satisfied with its present existence, can arise only from an anxiety, that of being able to change. On the other hand, true love, which has absorbed eternity within itself in becoming a duty, never varies. Only when love is a duty, is it eternally free, in a state of blessed dependence" (L. M. Gillon, "La théologie morale et l'ethique de l'exemplarité personnelle," in *Angelicum,* 34 [1957], 257, n. 2, according to Kierkegaard, *Vie et règne de l'amour,* trans. Villadser, 1946, 39-49). Thus, far from destroying love, the institution — even a human one — alone allows it to escape, at least partially, contingency — so much the more the divine institution of the sacrament of marriage, with the grace it provides. Such is also the meaning, for example, of "religious vows" or commitment to perpetual celibacy.

will be works which translate and express this interior dynamism. If they are a necessary expression, they are prohibited or imposed in the code of the new law. If, on the contrary, they do not have this necessary link with the interior law, they are neither imposed nor prohibited in the new law, such as Christ and the apostles promulgated it, but are left to the discretion of the legislator who will impose or prohibit them where in a particular situation this necessary link with the interior law of charity will pertain to a group of Christians or the whole Church, in other words, when such works become a necessary, concrete expression of this law.[47]

It follows, then, that for a Christian a purely external violation of the law, that is, one without any relationship to the internal law, cannot be a real violation. The concept of "involuntary sin," which is so important in the Mosaic legislation, since the Levite's "sacrifices for sin" were intended precisely to expiate errors of this kind, does not make any sense to the Christian. Purely material sin can, no doubt, have grave effects in view of the habits it creates and its social repercussions; strictly speaking, however, it cannot be an offense which needs to be pardoned.

On the other hand, an observance that is empty of love is also without any significance. Whoever considers observance as a value in itself will try to maintain it at any price and can imagine himself obeying the law, even if he succeeds in distorting it, or, as the Pharisees said, "playing with it."[48] Whoever, on the contrary, sees the external observance as but the expression of the internal law, can no longer think of such a process as having any meaning. Its sole aim being to assure the Christian's internal dynamism, the external law derives all its value from the latter, and not conversely. The essential point is not the observance of this or that

---

47. I-II, q. 108, a. 1: "Utrum lex nova aliquos exteriores actus debeat praecipere vel prohibere"; see a. 2: "Rectus usus gratiae est per opera caritatis."

48. The Gospel furnishes a typical example with the question of "corban": see Mk 7, 10-13. It has even been said that sometimes knowledge of the law had become "knowledge of the way in which the just man can act so as to achieve his aims without breaking the law" (J. Dupont, *Gnosis*, 256). For some Christians, there is a way of observing certain laws, such as those of abstinence, which is very similar (see the following note).

penitential practice but the penitential spirit, not this or that exercise in piety but the spirit of prayer, since such a practice or exercise is imposed only to assure such a spirit. Without neglecting the letter, the Christian will be concerned, first of all, with the spirit and will not think of truly observing a law before he has penetrated its meaning,[49] that is, before he has reflected as to how it will translate in a concrete way the interior drive that he feels or should feel.[50]

It also follows that the external law will usually not offer him an ideal he may delight in attaining, but only a limit beyond which that dynamism which makes him a Christian will not be available to him. This explains why the code of the new law, while containing a series of positive prescriptions and commands, offers the Christian a norm of another kind—the imitation of Christ's person

---

49. Thus we understand how important it is to explain to Christians not only the objective content of the law, but also the aim of the legislator in promulgating it. For example, it is clear that in imposing on every Christian attendance at Sunday Mass, the Church does not mean to prescribe only an external act, but an act that is at the same time the expression of adoration and cult. No doubt, the same is true of laws of fast and abstinence. At least this is certainly how they were understood in the beginning: it was a question of honoring Christ's passion by an authentic form of penance, even a penance that was at the same time a act of charity toward one's neighbor. Thus, according to St. Leo, "the abstinence of the faithful must become the building up of the poor," and Pope St. Gregory, in his *Regula Pastoris,* advises Lenten preachers to warn those who were about to observe Lenten regulations that "their abstinence will please God only if they give to the poor the food from which they will refrain." Abstinence has always been considered a mitigated form of fasting. See A. Guillaume, *Jeûne et charité dans l'Eglise des origines au XIIe s., en particulier chez saint Léon le Grand,* 1954, *passim* (the texts cited here will be found on 117f.; 153); likewise, "Abstinence du vendredi et charité fraternelle," in *Nouv. Rev. théol.,* 83 (1961), 510-521.

50. See G. Gilleman, *Le primat de la charité en théologie morale,* 255: "The Christian way of envisaging the law as the exteriority of love and moral order, shows that the substance of the moral life is not obedience to a law but charity toward people; that obedience, however indispensable it is, is second in relationship to love .... The law of grace is no longer a heavy yoke imposed from without, it is but the exigency and necessary determination of charity."

and especially his charity, which is itself the reflection of the charity of the Father. Such a norm is an equally objective one, since Christ is not a product of one's imagination, but a historic figure whose actions are portrayed in the Gospel.[51] In fact, St. Paul refers to hardly any other norm, and in imitation of Christ commanding his disciples to be perfect as their heavenly Father is perfect, he reminds his followers again and again to contemplate Christ and imitate him:

> On the contrary, be kind to one another, and merciful, generously forgiving one another, as also God in Christ has generously forgiven you.
> Be you, therefore, imitators of God, as very dear children and walk in love, as Christ also loved us and delivered himself up for us ... (Eph 4, 32-5, 2).

The whole morality of marriage, for example, is said to revolve around one precept: "But just as the Church is subject to Christ, so also let wives be to their husbands. ... Husbands, love your wives, just as Christ also loved the Church, and delivered himself up for her, that he might sanctify her ..." (Eph 5, 24-26).

The pious Jew, devotee of the law, tried always to understand it better in order to follow it in the smallest details. The manual of the Qumran sect states that "wherever there is a group of ten members, there will be someone who searches through the law continually, night and day, in order to find out the duties of each member."[52] For the Christian, the whole law is Christ in his person, not only as regards the main element which is the Spirit of Christ communicated to him, but also as regards the secondary element, which, in the final analysis, goes back to the imitation of Christ, according to the magnificent formula of Fr. de Foucauld: "Your rule? Follow me. Do what I would do. Ask yourself in all instances: what would our Lord have done? And do it. This is your only rule, but it is your absolute rule."[53]

---

51. See G. Salet, *art. cit.,* 575; L. M. Gillon, *art. cit.,* 376-377.
52. *Manuel de discipline,* col. VI, lines 6-7. While their piety is undeniable, the Qumran sect pushes legalism to the extreme. See, for example, L. Cerfaux, *Le chrétien,* 442-443.

Finally, it follows that under these conditions the Christian is free. For "where the Spirit of the Lord is, there is freedom" (II Cor 3, 17). A favorite theme of St. Augustine's it is no less favored by St. Thomas, who comments:

> The free man is he who belongs to himself; the slave is one who belongs to his master. Thus, whoever acts spontaneously, acts freely; but whoever acts on the impulse of another, does not act freely. Therefore, whoever avoids evil, not because it is wrong but as a result of a commandment of the Lord, is not free. On the other hand, he who avoids evil because it is wrong, is free.[54] But this is due to the work of the Holy Spirit, who perfects our spirit from within by giving it a new dynamism, so that it refrains from evil because of love, as if divine law was commanding it; and so such a person is free, not that he is not subject to divine law, but because his interior dynamism moves him to do what divine law commands.[55]

53. *Ecrits spirituels,* 171. See the practical commentary given by Fr. Voillaume in the "message of Beni-Abbès" of Feb. 23, 1950 (*Au coeur des masses,* 1950, 42-45) and which Fr. de Foucauld himself wrote in his *Diaire,* dated May 17, 1904: "In case of doubt about my way of life and following of the rulés of the Little Brothers of the Sacred Heart of Jesus, I must always conform to Jesus' conduct at Nazareth and on the cross, since the first duty of the Little Brothers of the Sacred Heart and mine, the first article of their vocation and mine, of their rule and mine, which is written for them and for me by God, *in capite libri,* is to imitate Jesus in his life at Nazareth and, when the time comes, to imitate him on the way of the cross and in his death" (cited by J. F. Six, *Itinéraire spirituel de Charles de Foucauld,* 306). For a Jew, to know one's religion consisted essentially of knowing perfectly a code of laws; for a Christian, it is a question of knowing a person, Christ, of loving and following him. In spite of the etymology, the "disciple" is not someone who "learns" (*discere*) a lesson, however sublime it may be, but someone who "follows" the Master by participating in his Passion and resurrection (see Mk 8, 34).

54. For St. Thomas, sin would not be an "offense against God," if it were not opposed to the good of man: "Non enim Deus a nobis offenditur, nisi ex eo quod contra nostrum proprium bonum agimus" (*Contra Gentiles,* III, c. 122).

In the *Summa Contra Gentiles*, Thomas expresses the same idea, always in reference to the Pauline expression.[56] And Sylvester de Ferrare comments in turn:

> The just are under the divine law, which obliges them without constraining them, in that they observe the precepts of the law in a completely free and voluntary way and not as if they were compelled by fear of punishment and the orders of the superior, like the wicked, who would not obey the law if there were no precepts to oblige them and if they were not afraid of being punished for having transgressed it.[57]

---

55. *In 2 Cor* 3, 17: "Liber est qui est causa sui; servus autem est causa domini (see I, q. 96, a. 4: "ordinatur ad alium."). Quicumque ergo agit ex seipso, libere agit; qui vere ex alio motus, non agit libere. Ille ergo qui vitat mala, non quia mala, sed propter mandatum Domini, non est liber; sed qui vitat mala, quia mala, est liber. Hoc autem facit Spiritus Sanctus, qui mentem interius perficit per bonum habitum, ut sic ex amore caveat ac si praeciperet lex divina; et ideo dicitur liber, non quin subdatur legi divinae, sed quia ex bono habitu inclinatur ad hoc faciendum quod lex divina ordinat" (lect. 3; ed R. Cai, no. 112). See I-II, q. 108, a. 1 ad a. See also the four degrees of human freedom and dignity which, apropos of I Tim 1, 9, St. Thomas establishes in his commentary on Rom 2, 14: *"Justo lex non est posita* (I Tim 1, 9), id est exteriori lege non cogitur . . . . Et iste est supremus gradus dignitatis in hominibus, ut scilicet non ab aliis sed a seipsis inducantur in bonum. Secundus vero gradus est eorum qui inducantur ab alio sed sine coactione. Tertius autem est eorum qui coactione indigent ad hoc quod fiant boni. Quartus est eorum qui nec coactione ad bonum dirigi possunt" (*In Rom* 2, lec. 3; ed. R. Cai, no. 217).

56. *Contra Gentiles*, IV, c. 22: "Since the Holy Spirit enables us to love God, we are also in some way moved by him to fulfill the laws of God according to Rom 8, 14, not as slaves but as free men . . . . But we act freely when we act by ourselves . . . . Thus the Holy Spirit influences us in such a way that he enables us to act voluntarily, according to the expression of St. Paul: *Where the Spirit of the Lord is, there is freedom* (II Cor 3, 17), and also: *If you are led by the Spirit, you are not under the Law* (Gal 5, 18)."

57. Franciscus de Sylvestris Ferrariensis, *Comment. in Libros Quattuor contra Gentiles S. Thomae de Aquino*, lib. IV, c. 22, 4: "Justi non sunt sub

Such is the traditional teaching of the Church, common to all schools of spirituality. It is precisely that of a St. John of the Cross, observing to perfection St. Paul's formula, so often repeated by St. Thomas: "There is no longer any road here, since there is no law for the just."[58] And the editor of the works of St. John of the Cross, Fr. Lucien Marie de Saint-Joseph, also comments on his master's thought regarding the freedom of the saints:

> Such souls are free because, psychologically speaking, if they do good, it is not because of the order which enjoins them, but because of the force of the interior movement which makes them wish for the fulfillment of God's will as a requirement of their love. So great is their love that they cannot not wish what the Beloved wishes. But the commandment does not bind them, nor does it constrain them. . . . The

divina lege tanquam coacta . . . . Sunt sub lege obligante, non autem cogente, in quantum libere et voluntarie omnino quod est legis observant, non autem coacti timore poenae et superioris mandato, sicut mali qui quod legis est non observarent nisi esset divinum praeceptum, et nisi timerent pro legis transgressione puniri." Related to this is I-II, q. 93, a. 6 ad 1, where St. Thomas explains that the Christian, animated by the Spirit, is not under the law, according to Gal 5, 18: "Duobus modis viri spirituales non sunt sub lege: *a*) quia per caritatem, quam Spiritus Sanctus cordibus eorum infundit, voluntarie id quod legis est implent; *b*) in quantum hominis opera qui Spiritu Sancto agitus, magis dicuntur esse opera Spiritus Sancti quam ipsius hominis; unde cum Spiritus Sanctus non sit sub lege, sicut nec Filius (a. 4 ad 2), sequitur quod hujusmodi opera, in quantum sunt Spiritus Sancti, non sint sub lege (2 Cor 3, 17: *Ubi Spiritus ibi libertas*)." In different terms, this is the pure doctrine of St. Augustine, for example, in *De Spiritu et littera*, c. 14 (26): "Quod mandatum, sit fit timore poenae non amore justitiae, serviliter fit, non liberaliter, et ideo nec fit. Non enim fructus est bonus, qui de caritatis radice non surgit. Porro autem si adsit fides quae per dilectionem operatur, incipit condelectari legi Dei secundum interiorem hominem: quae delectatio non litterae sed Spiritus donum est, etiamsi alia lex in numbris adhuc repugnat legi mentis, donec in novitatem quae de die in diem in interiore homine augetur, tota vetustas mutata pertranseat, liberante nos de corpore mortis hujus gratia Dei per Jesum Christum Dominum nostrum" (*P.L.*, 44, 217).

58. *Ascent of Carmel*, frontispiece.

prohibition does not bother them either and it is not because of the prohibition that they avoid evil. They see themselves as fulfilling the prophetic promise of Jeremiah, repeated in the epistle to the Hebrews: "I will place my laws in their spirit and engrave them in their heart."[59]

The same principle underlies the whole legislative work of a St. Ignatius Loyola. The latter expresses it as clearly as possible in the beginning of his Constitutions, by proclaiming the primacy of what he calls "the interior law of love and charity which the Holy Spirit is accustomed to imprint within men's hearts," an interior law which is irreplaceable and which should be sufficient for all situations. Throughout the Constitutions, the same principle is repeated again and again. If, for example, the legislator gives directives for the admission of candidates, for the formation of young Jesuits for the apostolate, for the selection of apostles and the works to be given them, he always hastens to note that the true guide in all this will be "the holy anointing of divine Wisdom," "the sole anointing of the Holy Spirit and that discretion which the Lord is accustomed to give those who entrust themselves to his divine Wisdom," "the sovereign Providence and direction of the Holy Spirit." And if he demands from his disciple intimacy with God, more than competence and human gifts, it is precisely "so that he may be led by the divine hand."[60]

But let us return to St. Paul. In the Epistle to the Galatians, an Epistle devoted entirely to defending and exalting Christian freedom, he summarizes in an incisive way the mystery of this freedom: "For you have been called to liberty, brethren; only do not use liberty as an occasion for sensuality, but by charity serve one another." The idea of "serving others" is expressed very strongly: *douleuete allēlois*, "make yourselves the slaves of others!" For, as

---

59. "La liberté des saints," in the *Bulletin des Fraternités Charles de Foucauld*, 86 (1952), 25ff., or in *Eglise et liberté* (Week of Catholic Intellectuals, 1952), 255. The author shows perfectly how "the goal is never attained fully here below; it remains relative; thus the freedom of the saints should be defined as a state of tendency, rather than as a state of fixed repose."

60. *Constitutiones*, Pars I, c. 2, n. 13; IV, c. 8, n. 8; VII, c. 2, decl. F; X, n. 2.

Paul adds, "the whole Law is fulfilled in one word: 'Thou shalt love thy neighbor as thyself'" (Gal 5, 14).

Is the Christian life, therefore, a form of slavery? Yes, but a slavery born of love, a fruit of the Spirit, and thus sovereign freedom: "By love, make yourselves slaves of one another!"

That Messianic people has for its ... heritage ... the dignity and freedom of the sons of God, in whose hearts the Holy Spirit dwells as in his temple. Its law is the new commandment to love as Christ loved us" (Dogmatic Constitution on the Church, II, 9).

VI

The Impeccability of the Christian According to I Jn 3, 6-9[*]

In an article on "the impeccable Christian," Father Galtier wrote that vv. 6 and 9 of the third chapter of I Jn are reputed to be the most obscure or at least the most controversial in the New Testament.[1] Indeed, it is enough to survey the various commentaries to see how many divergences exist in the interpretation of this passage.

We shall not present here an entirely new interpretation, but rather we will reexamine and synthesize the elements of a solution already indicated. We would like above all to study better than has been done until now the historical and literary context of these verses. We shall see that the doctrine of impeccability belongs to the sapiential and eschatological traditions. We shall therefore

---

[*] A part from a few new references and one or more corrections, this chapter reproduces the text of a study that appeared in *L'Evangile de Jean. Etudes et problèmes* ("Recherches bibliques," 3), Desclée de Brouwer, 1958, 161-177.

1. P. Galtier, "Le chrétien impeccable" (I Jn 3, 6, 9), in *Mél de sc. relig.*, 4 (1947), 137-154.

first consider this area and clarify it by means of new texts taken from the manuscripts of Qumran. Then we will examine the immediate principles of impeccability indicated by St. John: the divine seed in us and the new birth of Christians. But first it will be helpful to recall briefly the solutions to our problem so far proposed.

Despite differences in point of view, the Greek Fathers offer a remarkably similar exegesis. Developed above all by Severus of Antioch, Didymus the Blind, Maximus the Confessor, and Photius, it became classic, thanks to the linkings,[2] and has been taken up again by a few moderns. We can summerize it as follows: the seed of God is an interior force by which the soul ceases to be oriented toward sin; allowing itself to be led by this interior dynamism, the soul becomes truly incapable of choosing evil.[3]

The Latin exegesis, which is largely that of Augustine,[4] moves in a much less felicitous way in trying to define the meaning of the Johannine expression: it is not every sin that John declared to be impossible for the Christian, but a specific sin, namely, violation of charity. Nowhere, however, does the context speak of charity, and the statement of St. John has a very general meaning.

---

2. J. A . Cramer, *Catenae graecorum Patrum in Novum Testamentum*, VIII, Oxford, 1844, 124-127. This edition, where we find the extracts of Severus of Antioch and Maximus the Confessor, is very defective. The same fragments are better presented in the commentary of Euthymius Zigabenus on the Pauline epistles and on the Catholic epistles, ed. Nik. Kalogera, Athens, 1887, II, 612-615. For the text of Maximus the Confessor, it would be better to go directly to the *Quaestiones ad Thalassium*, VI, from which it is taken (*P.G.*, 90, 279-289); for Photius, see *Ad Amphilochium*, VIII (*P.G.*, 101, 112B — 113C). The commentary of Didymus the Blind, has been edited by F. Zoepfl: *Didymi Alexandrini in epistolas canonicas brevis enarratio* (Ntl. Abh., IV, 1), Munster, 1914.

3. See, for example, the beautiful phrase of Oecumenius: "When someone who is born of God gives himself to Christ, who dwells within him by filiation [*heauton ekdous tōi enoikounti en autōi dia tēs huiothesias Christōi*], he remains beyond the attacks [*anepaphos*] of sin" (*In ep. Iam Joannis*, c. 7; *P.G.*, 119, 684).

4. St. Augustine, *In epistolam Ioannis ad Parthos*, tract. V, 3 (*P.L.*, 35, 2013). His interpretation is taken up by Venerable Bede (*P.L.*, 93, 101-102); it is summarized in the *Glossa ordinaria* (*P.L.*, 114, 679): "Non de omni peccato, sed de violatione caritatis."

Among modern commentators, attempts at a solution abound. Some look for explanations similar to St. Augustine's: John is speaking of some very serious sin, which for the Christian would be practically impossible. Thus, Belser thinks of impurity,[5] Galtier of inveterate sin, moral perversion, which consents to deliberate sin; others think it is a question of habitual sin. But all these considerations are foreign to the context; besides, they do not resolve the problem any better than the Augustinian solution, for none of these interpretations explain the fact that John can say: *ou dunatai hamartanein.* Nor is it enough to say that the text simply affirms the incompatibility of grace and sin, which would be a banality, almost a tautology, and would not explain St. John's expression any better. A number of exegetes,[6] we have said, return to a solution based on the Greek Fathers; they express it in this phrase of Augustine's: "In quantum semen Dei in ipso manet, in tantum non peccat,"[7] that is, insofar as we are submissive to grace, we become incapable of sin. This solution is excellent on theological grounds and contains the beginnings of a profound spiritual doctrine. But is it sufficient to explain historically the thought of St. John?

What is characteristic of all the preceding explanations is that they try to interpret the text in itself, logically and psychologically, while ignoring the fact that St. John is the inheritor of a long tradition. Windisch,[8] Dodd,[9] Schnackenburg,[10] and above all Preisker[11] have succeeded in putting the doctrine of impeccability

5. J. E. Belser, *Die Briefe des heiligen Johannes,* Freiburg im Breisgau, 1906, 77-79.
6. Above all, J. Bonsirven, *Les Epîtres de saint Jean* ("Verb. salutis," IX), new ed., Paris, 1954, 158-162, and A. Charue, in *La Sainte Bible,* XII, Paris, 1938, 537-538. This was formerly the solution preferred by Cornelius a Lapide.
7. *In epist. Joannis,* IV, 7, apropos of I Jn 3, 6 (*P.L.,* 35, 2010).
8. H. Windisch, *Die katholischen Briefe* (Handb. zum N. T., XV), Tübingen, 1951, 121-122: "grundlegend ist die Beziehung auf die jüdische Eschatologie."
9. C. H. Dodd, *The Joannine Epistles* (The Moffatt New Test. Comm.), London, 1946, 78-81.
10. R. Schnackenburg, *Die Johannesbriefe* (Herders theol. Komm. zum N. T., XIII, 3), Freiburg, 1953, 169-170, and the Excursus XII, 252-258.
11. H. Preisker, in the *Anhang* of the third edition of the Windisch com-

in its true context, that of Judaeo-Christian eschatology. One must also add here the influence of the sapiential tradition. Let us review quickly, in this twofold tradition, the main texts which constitute the antecedents of the Johannine theme.

IMPECCABILITY IN THE BIBLE, IN JUDAISM, AND IN THE NEW TESTAMENT

The doctrine that emerges quite clearly from the body of texts we shall cite is this: at the end of time, the chosen people will be a holy people, a people without sin; this sanctity, this impeccability, will be due to the active presence of the Spirit, wisdom, and law within the hearts of the chosen ones. From their relationship with God they will receive the strength to sin no longer and the gift of life.

The Old Testament

Long ago, Deutero-Isaiah had prophesied of the Messianic people: "Your people shall all be just" (Is 60, 21), and Daniel had described the Israel of the future as the people of the holy ones of the Most High (7, 18, 27; 8, 24). Ezekiel declared that an interior renewal would characterize the Messianic era; it would result from an overflowing effusion of the Spirit within the hearts of men, who would thereby become capable of observing the law faithfully: "I will put my spirit within you and make you live by my statutes, careful to observe my decrees. . . . I will save you from all your impurities" (36, 27, 28).

The sapiential tradition showed whence this strength against sin comes: from openness to wisdom and law, present in the just man's heart. In Ecclus 24, 22, it is said that "He who serves me will never fail" (*hoi ergazomenoi en emoi ouch hamartēsousin*). In Prov 9, 6, in conclusion to the passage where men are invited to the banquet of wisdom, the gift of life is presented as the reward

mentary cited above (note 8), 166. See also his work *Das Ethos des Urchristentums*, Gutersloh, 1949, 206ff.

of those who accept this invitation. Similarly, this text of Deutero-Isaiah, in the sapiential tradition: "Come to me heedfully, listen, that you may have life" (Is 55, 3). The psalms clearly refer this moral integrity to the action of *the law*, which has become interior to the just man: "The mouth of the just man tells of wisdom . . . ; the law of his God is in his heart and his steps do not falter" (Ps 37, 30-31); and more explicitly: "Within my heart I treasure your promise, that I may not sin against you" (Ps 119, 11). Thus it is the word of God, the interior law, that gives the just man the strength to sin no more.

The Jewish Apocrypha

The apocryphal literature develops the same doctrine: "Now I am going to sow my law within your hearts; it will bear fruit within you" (IV Esdr 9, 31); "This law, which is within us, will aid us, and the outstanding wisdom which is within us, will assist us" (*Bar. syr.*, 48, 24). "And in the time of his priest [the Messiah], the nations on earth will advance in knowledge and will be illuminated by the Lord's grace . . . ; in the time of his ministry sin will disappear, and the wicked will cease doing evil" (*Test. de Levi*, 18, 9). A text of *Jubilations*, exactly as is the case in St. John, sees impeccability as the result of a new nature: "And for all his works he made a new and proper nature, so that they could never in their nature sin, but each one would be completely just in its own species" (5, 12). Finally, the book of *Enoch*, in a text that perfectly summarizes this whole tradition, attributes this privilege to the work of wisdom: "Then will wisdom be given to the elect, and they will all live, and they will no longer sin [*ou mē hamartēsousin eti*] either by disregard or by pride" (6, 8).

The Texts of Qumran

In the writings of Qumran, which bear witness to an even more ardent eschatological anticipation, the idea of "people without sin" appears often. It is remarkable that we find here the same duality, the same apparent contradiction as in St. John: the children of the Covenant are both sinners and without sin. But just as in St. John, the two series of statements belong to different contexts. In the *Manual of Discipline*, the members of the Covenant mention their sins only in regard to their attitude toward God—for example, in the final psalm. As is to be expected, we find these contrite feelings above all in the hymns, e.g., "What will man say regarding his sin? How will he plead, with all his iniquities?" (I *QH*, 1, 25).

On the other hand, when they see themselves vis-à-vis the children of darkness and know that they are the chosen community, the ideal Israel, the tone is completely different. They then assume a whole series of titles to describe the sanctity of their Covenant: they are "the holy ones of the Most High" (*CD*, XX, 8); "holy men" (I *QS*, V, 13; VII, 17, IX, 8); "the holy community" (I *QS*, IX, 2); "the council of the holy" (I *QH*, IV, 25); "the foundation of the dwelling-place of holiness" (I *QS*, X, 8); "the men of perfect sanctity" (*CD*, XX, 2, 5, 7; I *QS*, VIII, 20); "the children of truth" (*passim*); "the children of light" (*passim*). When they describe the Messianic age, they designate themselves as "those who walk in the ways of light" (I *QS*, III, 20); "those who walk as perfect men" (*ibid.*, IX, 6); "a house of perfection and truth in Israel" (*ibid.*, VIII, 9). These texts are all influenced by the eschatological dualism of the sect.

The apparent contradiction between these statements and the one that precedes can be resolved only by an awareness of a difference of perspectives. The members of the Covenant, filled with the spirituality of the psalms, know they are sinners before God; but at the same time they are very much aware of being the object of God's choice, or, as they themselves say, "the children of his good will" (I *QH*, IV, 32-33). They form the Messianic community, one which could only be a community without sin. There is, therefore, among the children of the Covenant a certain tension between the two ways in which they look at themselves, both of which ways are equally real.

Can we be more specific? Let us consider, in the texts of Qumran, what the instrument that Messianic purification will be. A very important passage in the *Rule of the Community* tells us:

> Then, by his truth, God will purify all of man's works, and he will refine, for himself, man's body, to suppress every spirit of iniquity in his flesh and to purify it *with the spirit*

> *of sanctity* from all acts of impiety; and he will pour over
> him *the spirit of truth* like a lustral water, to wash him of all
> deceitful abominations, . . . to give the just understanding of
> *the knowledge of the Most High,* and to teach the perfect
> *the wisdom* of the sons of heaven. . . . No longer is there
> any iniquity: all deceitful works will become a source of
> shame (I QS, IV, 20-23).

This text is remarkable. Faithful to the teaching of the prophets
(Is 44, 3; Ez 36, 25-28; Joel 3, 2), it announces that the Messianic
age will be characterized by an effusion of the Spirit. But here,
as before, the Spirit is presented as the one who causes a purification from sin (see Is 4, 4); for this reason, he is called the Spirit
of sanctity, and his work is compared to that of a lustral water
(see Ez 36, 25). Not that such work is the direct result of a particular rite. The Spirit will act by means of his truth, that is, by
teaching perfect men knowledge of God and heavenly wisdom.
Is this not the same as saying that such knowledge, such wisdom,
such truth will have the virtue of an interior transformation?
Thus we remain within the prophetic and sapiential tradition
described above. The only new element is the equivalence between the ideas of truth, knowledge, and wisdom, to designate the
instrument of Messianic purification.

The New Testament

Finally, let us note a few passages of the New Testament in
which the same theme reappears. In the Epistle of James (1, 21),
Christians are exhorted to receive the word implanted in them,
for it can save them; because of this salvific power, the word is
called "the perfect law of liberty" (v. 25). The First Epistle of
Peter states that Christians have purified their souls "by obedience
to truth" (1, 22), those who have been regenerated by an incorruptible germ, God's word. A passage from the Second Epistle of
Peter speaks more in general about the grace proper to the Christian vocation: "Therefore, brethren, strive even more by good
works to make your calling and election sure. For if you do this,
you will not fall into sin at any time" (1, 10). The fact is stated:
Christians will not sin if they strengthen within themselves their

vocation and their election. Note here the continuity with the doctrine of Qumran: just like the children of the Covenant, Christians, by becoming conscious of their election and vocation, receive the strength and capability of avoiding sin. Another text, the start of the final doxology of the Epistle of Jude (v. 24), is similar to the preceding one: "Now to him who is able to preserve you without sin and to set you before the presence of his glory, without blemish. . . ." Once again, the possibility of avoiding sin is affirmed, but this time the principle is the power of Christ. The eschatological point of view of the text is, as before, quite evident.

Finally, let us cite a passage from St. Paul: "Walk in the Spirit, and you will not fulfill the lusts of the flesh" (Gal 5, 16). For the Apostle, the great reality of the Christian life is the presence of the Spirit, an interior principle of action and thus the distinctive sign of the children of God: "For whoever are led by the Spirit of God, they are the sons of God" (Rom 8, 14). Insofar as they are faithful to the law of the Spirit, Christians have the assurance of no longer yielding to carnal lust. Within their own selves, they possess, in the gift of the Spirit, the very principle of impeccability.

Looking at the theme of impeccability as a whole, we see several lines of preparation from the biblical and Jewish traditions converging. The theme is, first of all, an eschatological one: with an amazing consistency, the texts of the various periods describe impeccability as a privilege of Messianic times. Next, the chosen ones will owe this to divine election, their vocation, the new nature which will be conferred on them, and the gift of the Spirit. But most often, this liberation from sin is situated clearly in a sapiential rather than a cult perspective: the Spirit of sanctity will purify souls by the word of truth, interior law and wisdom, and the gift of knowledge. It is natural that in the New Testament this sanctifying action should be attributed to the power of Christ, for he is the one who confers all these favors. As to man, the only condition that is stipulated for obtaining victory over sin is complete openness and submission to the teaching and guidance of the Spirit.

IMPECCABILITY IN THE FIRST EPISTLE OF JOHN

Let us now pass on to St. John. In the same Epistle, there are two quite clear, apparently contradictory statements. On the one hand, man is deceitful if he says he is without sin (I Jn 1, 8, 10); on the other, it is said that the Christian does not and cannot sin. The answer to this seeming contradiction must be found here too in the difference of themes treated and the point of view proper to the particular context. The affirmation of sin among Christians belongs to a kerygmatic passage: *kai esti autē hē angelia hēn anangellomen humin* (1, 5). In the original *kerygma* sin, redeemed by Christ, had an essential place (see Ac 2, 38; 3, 19-26; 5, 31; 10, 43; 13, 38). This point of view is eternally true in pastoral preaching. On the other hand, when St. John says that the Christian does not and cannot sin, it is always in the theological context of his eschatological dualism, where he contrasts the children of God and the children of the devil.

Eschatological Content

The verses under discussion do, indeed, develop an eschatological theme. Already at the end of chapter 2, this point of view is very clear: the final hour has come, for many Antichrists have risen up (2, 8) and try to lead Christians astray (2, 26). The latter must remain in Christ and thus will be able to present themselves to him at the Parousia (2, 28). Let us note that the technical term *parousia* (very indicative of an eschatological context) is found only here in all of the Johannine literature.

The section which follows (2, 29-3, 10) forms a very definite literary unit, surrounded by an inclusion. The theme is stated clearly in the last verse: "In this the children of God and the children of the devil are made known." This is the theme of the eschatological opposition between the forces of good and evil. Two spiritual realities are present, recognizable by specific signs. In vv. 1-2, the reality of divine filiation under its twofold aspect is indicated: present now, yet still hidden, it must one day be fully manifested. The *nun* of v. 2 underscores the present reality of the last days. Then, in vv. 3-10, are described in parallel series the external signs which permit one to recognize the two groups, the children of God and the children of the devil, namely, the moral conduct of each one.

We will not spend more time here on the group of those who

commit sin. Let us remark only that it too is placed in an eschatological light; this is the meaning of the parallel verses 4 and 8:
"Everyone who commits sin commits iniquity also"; "he who commits sin is of the devil." *Anomia,* in v. 4, no longer has the classic
meaning of transgression of the law which is too often given to
it; it signifies instead the state of eschatological hostility toward
the Messianic kingdom, toward Christ, under the domination of
Satan.[12] As for the children of God, their distinctive qualities are
pointed out in vv. 3, 6, 7, 9: they sanctify themselves, practice
justice, do not sin, are incapable of sinning. The theme appears
again under a very similar form in 5, 18-19: "We know that no
one who is born of God commits sin; . . . the evil one does not
touch him. We know that we are of God, and the whole world is
in the power of the evil one." Again we find ourselves in the same
context of eschatological opposition between the children of God
and the evil world.

The Johannine Eschatology

If the theme of impeccability is an eschatological theme, we
should clarify it in terms of the general characteristics of the Johannine eschatology. A good number of critics wanted at one time to
exclude all eschatology from the writings of St. John, but there
has been a reaction against this, and for good reason. Kümmel,[13]
Menoud,[14] Barrett,[15] but above all G. Stählin[16] and G. Eichholz[17]
have analyzed the characteristic traits of the eschatology of the
Fourth Gospel and the Epistles. On the one hand, the realities of

---

12. For more details, see our article "Le péché, c'est l'iniquité" (I Joh, 3,
    4), in *N. R. Th.,* 1956, 785-797 (see here Chapter 2).
13. W. G. Kümmel, "Die Eschatologie der Evangelien," in *Theol. Blätter,*
    15 (1936), 135-139.
14. Ph. H. Menoud, "L'originalité de la pensée johannique," in *R. Th. Ph.,*
    1940, 233-261.
15. C. K. Barrett, *The Gospel according to St. John,* London 1955, 56-58:
    "Eschatology."
16. G. Stählin, "Zum Problem der Johanneischen Eschatologie," in *Z. N. W.,*
    33 (1934), 225-254.
17. G. Eichholz, "Erwählung und Eschatologie im I. Joannesbrief," in *Ev.
    Theol.,* 5 (1938), 1-28.

salvation are present in Christ; with the manifestation of the light that is Christ, the world is already judged by the choice it makes and thus it is divided into two camps; victory over the world and the prince of this world is already won; the children of God, by their new birth, already possess eternal life. On the other hand, in addition to this eschatology already achieved, there is a tension directed toward the future; this is not, however, a tension directed toward future rewards, but only toward a future manifestation of realities already present in Christ. This twofold aspect of the rewards of salvation—present and future at the same time, but with a very definite accent on their present possession—is the most characteristic trait of Johannine eschatology.

What these traditional eschatological realities are, which the synoptics describe as future, is clear; but for St. John they have become present in the life and historical work of Jesus:

a) First, the resurrection: "I am the resurrection," said Jesus to Martha (11, 25); and to the Jews: "The hour is coming, and now is here, when the dead shall hear the voice of the Son of God" (5, 25).

b) The judgment is also a present fact: "Now is the judgment of the world" (12, 31). In effect, for St. John, the judgment is the confrontation with Christ-the-light; by the choice it makes, the world judges itself.

c) The result of this judgment is also present: "The prince of this world has already been judged" (16, 11). Jesus conquered the world (16, 33); similarly, "he who does not believe is already judged" (3, 18). On the other hand, the believer is not judged (*ibid.*), the son of God is conqueror of the world (I Jn 5, 4), he already possesses eternal life (Jn 3, 36; 6, 47). While for the synoptics eternal life is still a future reward, for St. John it is already salvation possessed.

Impeccability, An Eschatological Theme

Given the above, the question of the Christian's impeccability very nearly ceases to be a problem. For such impeccability constitutes a privilege of the last days. Already anticipated in Christ like the other realities of this order, it permits St. John to say that the child of God sins no more, and even no more can he sin; for he already belongs to the future era: "We know that we have passed from death to life" (I Jn 3, 14). On the other hand, it is true, the Christian is still in the present age; he is, therefore, a sinner. From the moment of baptism, he belongs to two worlds. This is why the line of demarcation between the children of God and the children of the devil does not simply pass between two groups of men, the baptized and the non-baptized, Christians and heretics. It distinguishes rather two attitudes, two spiritual zones, light and darkness, to which each man may belong in different degrees. This line passes within the deepest part of ourselves, for it is by our personal decision that we opt for one group or the other. Insofar as we sin, we belong to iniquity and are children of the devil; insofar as we practice justice and "do the truth," we enter into the light (see Jn 3, 21) and manifest ourselves as children of God.

Thus, to resolve the problem of Christian impeccability, we must revert to a twofold aspect of Johannine eschatology:

a) the first aspect, that the eschatological realities are *present* realities for John; if the privileges of the future life are realized in the person and work of Christ, this holds true for impeccability, a privilege of the final days of man's life;

b) second, eschatological *dualism* (for the dualism of St. John is essentially linked with his eschatology).

In opposing so clearly one group against another—the children of God against the children of the devil—John no longer considers them under their empirical aspect, but according to the more profound theological reality which they bear within them, that is, divine life or adherence to Satan. These two realities characterize two diametrically opposed camps, which will confront one another openly at the end of the world. Thus John leaves subtleties aside and brings face to face the two groups and that which distinguishes them, truth and iniquity, light and darkness.

GOD'S WORD AND IMPECCABILITY

Is the problem now resolved? Not completely. By turning to

eschatology, we have brought the doctrine of impeccability back to its historical foundation, but we must still explain, on the *psychological,* and *theological* levels, how St. John could present, with such force, impeccability and the other realities of salvation as being already present in Christ. What is the reality which specifically makes the Christian impeccable, and in what sense can we say that he already truly enjoys this privilege, which seems to be reserved for the future life?

The principle of impeccability for St. John is a twofold one: *a)* the new birth of the Christian; *b)* the fact that he remains (with special emphasis on this verb *menein*) in a new state; this is expressed in two complementary formulas: the Christian remains in Christ (v. 6); the divine seed remains in him (v. 9).

The Seed of the Word

How should the seed *(sperma)* be understood? Most modern critics understand it in terms of the Holy Spirit, the principle of divine life, because John says elsewhere that we are born of the Spirit. But nowhere is this life of grace as such compared to a seed. Others have interpreted *sperma* in the concrete sense of descendance, understanding it as either descendance from God in general (Christians) or descendance from Christ, who is the "Seed" par excellence.[18] But such an interpretation would require the article *(to sperma),* as it is in fact found in the texts used for support (Gal 3, 16; Apoc 12, 17; see I Jn 5, 18), but it does not fit the context very well.

Along with B. Weiss,[19] Büchsel,[20] and Dodd,[21] we feel it is neces-

---

18. A. W. Argyle, "I John 3, 4," in *Exp. Times,* 65 (November 1953), 62-63; he interprets *sperma* as descent in general. The *Jerusalem Bible* applies the seed to Christ in the first edition of the section of St. John; the second edition accepts the identification: seed = the word of God.

19. B. Weiss, *Die drei Briefe des Apostels Johannes* (Krit. - ex Komm. über das N. T., XIV), Göttingen 1899, 93.

20. F. Büchsel, *Johannes und der hellenistische Synkretismus* (B. z. F. chr. Th., II, 16), Gütersloh, 1928, 59. On the other hand, in his commentary (Theol Handkomm., XVII, Leipzig, 1933, 52), he returned to the common opinion.

21. C. H. Dodd, *The Johannine Epistles,* 74-78.

sary to return to the interpretation of a good number of older commentators,[22] for whom the seed is *the word of God*. This image was familiar to the Jewish and Christian traditions. We cited above several texts[22] where the seed designates the interior law in the just man's heart or the word of God. The comparison is developed at length by the synoptics in the parable of the sower.

But the text of John itself shows us what this seed meant to him. In several places, he designates explicitly and without the use of images the interior principle of moral purification: "You are already clean because of *the word* that I have spoken to you" (Jn 15, 3). Likewise, in the Epistles: "*The word* of God abides in you, and you have conquered the evil one" (I Jn 2, 14); "As for you, *let that which you have heard from the beginning* abide in you" (*ibid.*, 2, 24); "the truth abides in us" (II Jn 2). All these formulas are equivalent. It is thus very probable that the *seed* which abides in us according to 3, 9, just like *the anointing oil* of 2, 27, designates the object of faith presented at baptism to new believers: the Christian truth, the word of God, source of regeneration and sanctification. Let us recall once again St. Paul's expression: "For in Christ Jesus, through the gospel, did I beget you" (I Cor 4, 15), and the text of Enoch cited above: a new *wisdom* will be given to the elect, and they will sin no more.

The Word That "Remains" in Us

But the most important word in the verse is the verb *menein*, which is very characteristic of John's style.[24] It occurs 112 times in the New Testament, 67 times in the Johannine writings. It is seen

---

22. Clement of Alexandria, *Adumbrationes in I epist. Johannis* (*G.C.S.*, III, 214; *P.G.*, 9, 738); Photius, *Ad Amphilochium*, VIII (*P.G.*, 101, 112 C): *toutou dē tou despotikou spermatos ētoi didaskalikou logou;* St. Augustine, *In epist. Ioannis*, V, 7 (*P.L.*, 35, 2016); Bede (*P.L.*, 93, 102). This interpretation was restated by Luther in his *Vorlesung über den I. Brief Johannes*, 1527 (Wemar, ed., XX, 705): "semen dei i.e. verbum." This is also the formula of Augustine.

23. *IV Esdras*, 9, 31; *Apoc. syr. de Baruch*, 48, 24; I Pet 1, 23-25.

24. G. M. Pecorara, "De verbo manere apud Johannem," in *Div. Thom.* (Plac.), 40 (1937), 159-171.

most frequently in the allegory of the vine (Jn 15): 11 times, in vv. 4 to 16. The allegory of the branches united to the vine shows already that the verb "to remain" indicates not an inert state but a vital union, achieved through a real communication of life.

When *menein* is applied to supernatural realities, it is found in two forms, which the Germans call "Indikativ" and "Imperativ," that is, the hortatory use (to which one may add the conditional use), and the declarative (absolute) use, where the fact is stated that such and such reality remains. This twofold usage manifests again the Johannine concept of Christian salvation. The hortatory or conditional series, when it pertains to "impersonal" realities (that is, when they do not apply directly to God or Christ), is always concerned with the word of Christ or charity. The three texts concerning the teaching or word of Jesus are as follows:

> As for you, let that which you have heard from the beginning *abide in you* (I Jn 2, 24).

> *If you abide in my word,* you shall know the truth, and the truth shall make you free (Jn 8, 31-32).

> *Anyone who does not abide in the doctrine* of Christ, has not God; *he who abides in the doctrine,* he has both the Father and the Son (II Jn 9).

In these texts and others which could be cited, the profound supernatural realities (deliverance from sin, union with the Father and the Son) are made dependent on the fulfillment of two commandments, two conditions, which are always the same: abiding in the word and abiding in charity.

In another series of passages, the "declarative" series, this abiding in the word is presented as an indisputable fact, with the result that victory already seems certain:

> I am writing to you, young men, because you are strong and *the word of God abides in you,* and you have conquered the evil one (I Jn 2, 14).

> *The truth abides in us, and will be with us* forever (II Jn 2).

Here we should cite the passage we are dealing with in this chapter: "Whoever is born of God does not commit sin, because *his seed abides in him*" (see also I Jn. 2, 27).

How can this usage of *menein* help us to resolve the problem of impeccability? Let us show by drawing three conclusions from the preceding analyses.

God's Word and Impeccability

1. First of all, the use, now hortatory, now declarative, of *menein*, shows that St. John speaks from two points of view: the human, pastoral point of view, where he knows that Christians are always in danger of sinning (that is why he must exhort them to remain in the word and in charity); and the divine point of view of supernatural reality, of God's word which, in fact, abides in us with its permanent power of sanctification. The two points of view are juxtaposed in the verse under discussion: in v. 6 ("*Whoever abides in him,* does not commit sin"), this permanence, seen from man's point of view, is presented as a condition to be fulfilled. In v. 9, on the other hand ("Whoever is born of God does not commit sin *because his seed abides in him*"), the permanence is considered from the point of view of divine action; it is no longer conditional, but stated simply as a fact: this action is always at our disposition. Let us note that this constant tension between the two points of view—the rewards of salvation already granted by God and yet ever threatened by our infidelity—is a fundamental trait of early eschatology.

2. If John is talking here of impeccability, it is because of his dynamic and very biblical concept of the word and of life. Thus he belongs to that whole tradition described above which said that in Messianic times wisdom and law would be interior to the just, that they would give them the strength to avoid sin and would become a principle of life. This is why John presents the word of God as a divine seed that grows, produces fruit, operates within us and sanctifies us, provided we let ourselves be formed by it.

The fact that in v. 9 impeccability is attributed to both the new birth and the divine seed is very significant; St. John is thereby restating once again the traditional doctrine of early Christianity:

we are born to the new life as a result of God's word (I Cor 4, 15; Jas 1, 18; I Pet 1, 23). The apocryphal writings (*Jubilations*, Enoch) also had announced a twofold principle of impeccability: a new nature and the gift of wisdom. In the Christian context, the two principles are really but one: we receive the new nature by our acceptance of divine truth.

This recourse to the efficaciousness of divine action to explain the fact that the Christian can become sinless, is really the basic principle of the Greek interpretation of the passage in question (although it gave less emphasis to the role of *the word* as such). This principle is summarized perfectly in the phrase of Cornelius à Lapide, commenting on this verse: "Semen . . . dat nobis potentiam et robur, qua possimus non peccare, et vincere omne peccatum, si velimus ei cooperari."

3. Third, John's attitude regarding supernatural realities (divine life and God's word) and, correspondingly, sin, can and must be characterized as a mystical attitude. What does that mean? In the strict sense, the mystical way is normally defined in terms of the experiential knowledge of supernatural realities; the emphasis on "knowledge" in the Epistles, the use of the formulas "we know" and "you know," seems to imply an experience of this kind. But as Fr. de Guibert stated in an excellent study on the meaning of the word "mystical," the term can also be understood in a larger sense: "*Mystical* designates the aspect of passivity that is found again and again in every interior life."[25] The mystical attitude in the life of grace will, therefore, consist of directing one's attention less on the human effort than on the divine action and our openness to it: here, docility is primarily important. This is what St. John invites us to: "Et erunt omnes docibiles Dei" (Jn 6, 45).

In an article on Johannine mysticism,[26] Fr. Braun says very aptly that, strictly speaking, St. John did not leave a morality but a mysticism, and that his morality is implicitly contained in his mysticism. This is confirmed rather strikingly in his exhortations regarding sin:

25. J. de Guibert, "Mystique," in *R. A. M.*, 7 (1926), 3-16, esp. 14.
26. F.-M. Braun, O.P., "Morale et mystique à l'école de saint Jean," in *Morale Chrétienne requêtes contemporaines* (Cahiers de l'actualité relig.), Casterman, 1954, 71-84, esp. 82.

we do not find in his writings, as in St. Paul's, those urgent appeals to avoid sin, in order that Christians may remain in communion with God (which would be the moral point of view); there is only one such text (I Jn 2, 1). Ordinarily John uses the very opposite approach: he invites Christians to remain in Christ and his word; for if they fulfill this condition, they will no longer sin (the mystical point of view): "Whoever abides in him does not commit sin." Is this not like an echo of the verse from St. Paul already cited: "Walk in the Spirit, and you will not fulfill the lusts of the flesh" (Gal 5, 16)? All this is but a corollary of the preceding conclusion: the dynamism and efficacity of the word must be accompanied by an attitude of docility on the part of the Christian.

Here we find at last the true solution to the problem of impeccability. Msgr. Charue stated it in his commentary: "The principle of impeccability . . . [is] not a simple theoretical norm of moral goodness, but a mystical participation in divine being."[27] Let us add that, for St. John, this interior principle, considered objectively, is not so much divine action in general as that of God's word taught by the Spirit. "And as for you, let the anointing [= Christ's word taught by the Spirit] which you have received from him, dwell in you, and you have no need that anyone teach you" (I Jn 2, 27). From the subjective point of view, this principle is nothing else but openness to the word, permanence in divine communion. It is not surprising that this mystical aspect of impeccability was very well understood by the Greek Fathers[28] and that the most fruitful commentary was made by one of the greatest representatives of Oriental spirituality, St. Maximus the Confessor.[29]

---

27. In his commentary, 537.
28. For example, by St. Gregory of Nyssa; but he develops this theology of victory over sin by means of Platonic categories. See W. Völker, *Gregor von Nyssa als Mystiker*, Wiesbaden, 1955, 109-112. Since sin is an *amathia*, an *agnoia*, we must try to fight it by *mathēsis, epistēmē*. Scripture, assimilated in prayer, plays an all-important role here, according to Gregory: the Word of God, like a plow, penetrates into the depths of the soul and pulls out the unseen roots of sin.
29. See *supra*, note 2. It may be interesting to compare with this commentary the interpretation given this text by a spiritual writer of the 16th century, Jerome Nadel, S.J., in his *Orationis Observationes* (Monum. histor. Soc. Jesu, Epist. P. Nadel, IV, 684) L: "Scio quemdam [it is himself], qui

One final question arises: what is the connection between this mystical principle of impeccability and its character as an eschatological privilege, which we discussed in the second part of this chapter? Full emphasis must be given to this eschatological character, for the impeccability of the elect will be fully realized only in the final phase of the kingdom; here on earth, we remain sinners. But the important thing is that the privilege of impeccability of the next life will not be given to us as something new and superadded, in an extrinsic way, so to speak. The principle of impeccability is given, as of the present moment, in the divine life of the baptized, in their submission to interior truth. On earth, however, it is put into effect imperfectly and in varying degrees. Here we grasp the meaning of the Johannine teaching for our present life: if the divine "seed" produces fruit in the life of the Christian, the latter does not really sin, and the more active and important the seed becomes, the more incapable he becomes of sinning. It is by our openness to the word, and to the extent of this openness, that it becomes impossible for us to still opt for evil. For then we already truly belong to the kingdom of the future, where "there shall not enter anything defiled" (Apoc 21, 27).

sibi post confessionem generalem videbatur confirmatus, ne peccare posset mortaliter; quod arbitrabatur fore frequentissimum, nisi hominum segnicies et indispositio obstaret. Hoc consuerunt sancti de vera poenitentia, definientes poenitentiam esse, praeterita deflere, nec alia praeterea admittere; et hoc D. Joannes dixit de eo qui per gratiam baptismi ex Deo natus est. *Haec sensus spiritualis gratiae atque eius virtutes ostendunt de facto, nisi ex nobis defectus sit;* alioque tamen semper est possibilitas peccandi de lege communi, etc." The words italicized, expressed somewhat awkwardly, bring us back to the interpretation developed above: impeccability comes from the force and effects of grace (*eius virtutes*), to which the Christian must try to become completely subject (*nisi . . . indispositio obstaret, nisi ex nobis defectus sit*). Provided he does not put any obstacle in the way of this force and lets himself be directed by it, he acquires a spiritual sense by which he feels himself incapable of sinning. We may note the experiential aspect of this solution (*sensus spiritualis gratiae*), well in the line of that of the Greek Fathers. See also St. Thomas, *Summa theol.*, II-II, q. 24, a. 11, in corp. et ad 1.

CONCLUSION

To understand St. John's teaching on the Christian's impeccability, we have made use of two principles. First, his concept of eschatology already realized in Christ: impeccability is one of the rewards promised for the Messianic era. No doubt, it will be realized completely and definitively only when we will see the Son of God face to face; but it is already actualized in a very real way in the Christian life, because its source—divine life and knowledge of God—is given to us as of now. It follows from this that the Christian can conquer sin and can become, strictly speaking, sinless, provided he remains united to Christ and lets the word operate within him; he will commit sin only when he ceases to obey the truth. This is the second principle of explanation which we have used: the efficacity and force of the divine seed which abides within us.

As is evident, the two principles are necessary ones. The first (eschatology) alone enables us to place St. John in his historical context; it alone shows the exact place and precise meaning of Christian impeccability in the two great phases of the economy of salvation; it alone explains that sort of dialectic by which St. John can call the Christian both sinner and sinless. On the other hand, his teaching on divine life and the efficacity of God's word is also essential, for it provides us with the formal explanation of impeccability.

Thus it is meaningless to pose the dilemma: "mysticism or eschatology?" For the Johannine mysticism is rooted in its eschatology; it is centered on the person and historic work of God's Son, with whom the final era of the world has begun.

Let us make one final comment. If we compare this solution to the different explanations mentioned in the beginning, we will see that it is an attempt at synthesis. It belongs essentially to the exegesis of the Greek Fathers, restated in the Renaissance and by certain modern commentators: "In quantum in ipso manet, in tantum non peccat." What is lacking in this interpretation, which is theologically perfect, is the fact that it was not sufficiently established on historic grounds and did not show the place of impeccability in the total structure of salvation history. It was necessary to situate it in the currents of thought of Judaism and early Christianity, namely, in the currents of eschatological expectation and the sapiential tradition. These trends we have tried to describe in a more precise way by significant texts from Qumran. We trust that our attempt to synthesize the positive contributions of recent research on Johannine eschatology and the always important conclusions of Patristic exegesis has clarified to some extent the idea of Christian impeccability.

VII

The Christian Vocation to Perfection
According to St. Paul[*]

Rather than search through the letters of St. Paul for a response
to questions raised in this chapter, we shall instead attempt to clarify the questions which the Apostle posed to himself. The response
he in fact gave regarding the fulfillment of the Christian life was
seen in Chapter 6 above as essentially a life of which the Holy
Spirit is the principle. In other words, we shall now try to determine
the teaching of the Apostle in view of the problematic which was
his. Very often this problematic will arise from the more special
needs of the communities he addresses (notably in II Thess, Gal,
I-II Cor); occasionally, he is but responding to a series of questions
presented by those he corresponded with, thus passing in review
"matters of conscience" that were submitted to him (I Cor 7ff.).
But in the solutions offered and the many counsels accompanying
them, the major preoccupations of Paul already appear; these be-

---

[*] The text of this chapter appeared, without the notes, in the volume entitled: *Laïcs et vie chrétienne perfaite* (Collection "Laïcat et Sainteté,"
I), Herder, 1963, 15-32.

come much clearer in other letters, and especially in the letters to the Romans and the Ephesians, which are less influenced by the historical circumstances of their composition.

I

On several occasions the Apostle speaks of "perfect" Christians, not to distinguish them from those who hypothetically would not be called to perfection, but to contrast them with those who are still only "infants." Such is the clear meaning of the adjective *teleios* wherever Paul uses it—the first three times the term is presented, namely, in the First Epistle to the Corinthians. He explains to the faithful of Corinth that if he did not speak to them as he does to the "mature" (I Cor 2, 6), it is because they are still "little ones" (*nēpioi*, 3, 1): they could tolerate only milk, not the solid food of adults (v. 2). Likewise, in chapter 13, vv. 10 and 11 mention two parallel contrasts, first, between "perfect" and "imperfect," then, between "child" and "man"; the same contrast is found again in 14, 20: "Do not become children . . . but mature," that is, "men," "adults." The other examples all confirm this fundamental sense, in particular, Phil 3, 15; Col 1, 28; Eph 4, 13. "Perfection," therefore, is the normal state which every Christian can attain, under pain of remaining a child. Moreover, we will see that this state is less a condition acquired once and for all than the pursuit of a goal not yet attained. About himself, St. Paul will say explicitly that he is no longer a "child," a *nēpios*, but an "adult," a *teleios*. "We who are perfect" (Phil 3, 15), says Paul, without seeing any contradiction with what he had declared three verses earlier: "Not that I have already obtained this or already have been made perfect" (*teteleiōmai*, Phil 3, 12). Paul is "perfect," but "he has not yet arrived at the summit of perfection," as Fr. Huby says;[1] he has not yet attained all the perfection to which he has been called, "that for which he has been seized by Christ Jesus."

What does the Apostle mean by a "perfect" man? The examples already given furnish one answer. The Corinthians are still "chil-

---

1. J. Huby, *Saint Paul. Epîtres de la captivité* ("Verbum Salutis"); 34.

dren" because they still give evidence of "jealousy and strife"; their conduct is entirely "human" (I Cor 3, 3); they follow first Paul, then Apollos (v. 4), as if these were not simple servants of Christ (v. 5), who alone died for them and in whom they have been baptized (1, 12-13). In short, they are still not "spiritual" men (3, 1). Likewise, the fact that they are dazzled by the most attractive charisma, instead of aspiring to higher goods and starting out on the royal road of charity, which surpasses us all (I Cor 12, 31), is another sign of their childishness, of a sense of judgment that lacks maturity (14, 20).

In the Epistle to the Ephesians, the emphasis put more perhaps on the solidity of Christian convictions: "Until we all attain to the unity of the faith and of the deep knowledge of the Son of God, to perfect manhood, to the mature measure of the fullness of Christ," instead of "being tossed to and fro and carried about by every wind of doctrine devised in the wickedness of men, in craftiness, according to the wiles of error" (Eph 4, 13-14). But Paul hastens to add that firmness in the faith must be translated into a moral life "according to truth and in love" (v. 15). Epaphras, according to Paul, expressed precisely the same wish for the Christians of Colossae whom he had converted: "that you may remain perfect and completely in accord with all the will of God" (Col 4, 12). That is what Paul was aiming at when he strove "to make every man perfect in Christ" (Col 1, 28).

Rom 12, 2 offers some further important details. After a long dogmatic discourse, carried on over eleven chapters, Paul, as is his custom, draws some practical applications. But it is significant that the first requirement listed by the Apostle is an interior "renewal" of spirit which makes the Christian capable of "discerning what is the good and acceptable and perfect will of God" (12, 2). Just as in Judaism, "what is perfect" is identified with "what pleases God," what "conforms to his will." But that will is no longer identified with a code of law given once and for all.[2] The "perfection" of the Christian, like that of the Jew, will be characterized by openness to the divine will; it will be a submission, an obedience.[3] But it will

---

2. See above, p. 169.
3. For St. Paul, faith itself, by which man is justified, is conceived of as a

be an obedience to a divine will which must be sought out, discerned, and whose demands cannot be measured in advance. Thus Paul writes to the Colossians that he "prays for them unceasingly and asks God that they may be filled with knowledge of his will, in all spiritual wisdom and understanding, so that they may walk worthily of God and please him in all things" (Col 1, 8). Just as Abraham, responding to God's appeal, "went out, not knowing where he was going" (Heb 11, 8), so the Christian, seeing "the good and acceptable and perfect will of God," starts out on a road whose end is not yet discerned.

II

One thing, however, is certain: for the Christian, the road will lead to the question of love. For "the full knowledge of the divine will," which will enable the Colossians to "walk worthily of the Lord," is none other than "the mystery of the divine will" which the Apostle evokes for the Ephesians, "this his good pleasure he purposed in him to be dispensed in the fullness of the time" (Eph 1, 9-10), the mystery of men's salvation announced in the Scriptures but revealed only in Jesus Christ (Rom 16, 25-26). For St. Paul, as well as for St. John, this mystery is first and foremost a threefold mystery of love:

Mystery of the love of the Father, who "has not spared even his own Son but has delivered him for us all" (Rom 8, 32; see Jn 3, 16); for the proof that God loves us is that "when as yet we were sinners, Christ died for us," for "impious" men, for "enemies" (Rom 5, 6-10; see Eph 2, 4);

Mystery of the love of the Son for men, the one who "loved me and gave himself up for me" (Gal 2, 20; Eph 5, 2 and 25); for "greater love than this no one has, that one lay down his life for his friends" (Jn 15, 13);

Finally, *mystery of the love of the Son for his Father* since he

form of obedience; see below, p. 210f. Conversely, for him Abraham's obedience is, first of all, an act of faith: Rom 4; see Heb 11, 8-19. See *Quaestiones in epistulam ad Romanos,* I, 2d ed., 93.

goes to his passion precisely so that "the world may know that I love the Father, and that I do as the Father has commanded me" (Jn 14, 30; see Phil 2, 8; Rom 5, 19; Heb 5, 8).

This is why, according to St. John, just as the only divine wish of the Son was that he should give his life for us in a supreme act of love, so the only wish of God for men is expressed in the unique teaching of Christ: "As I have loved you, you also love one an-ther" (Jn 13, 34), a sign by which they show themselves to be his disciples (v. 35), indeed, proof par excellence that his own mission was from God (Jn 17, 21). But St. Paul is no less explicit: "For the whole Law is fulfilled in one word," he declares to the Galatians (5, 13), as he says again to the Romans: "He who loves his neighbor has fulfilled the Law" (Rom 13, 8), with the meaning that the event "fulfills" the prophecy in always surpassing it; for "love is the fulfillment of the Law" (Rom 13, 10). Christ himself had expressed the same idea when he summarized "the law and the prophets" in the "golden rule" of love (Mt 7, 12) and presented to his disciples, as an ideal to be imitated, the very perfection of the heavenly Father: "You therefore are to be perfect, even as your heavenly Father is perfect" (Mt 5, 48), where the context shows clearly that it is a question of the perfection of disinterested love, the love even of one's enemies (vv. 44-47), so that St. Luke dares to say: "Be merciful, therefore, even as your Father is merciful" (Lk 6, 36).[4]

In his letters, St. Paul returns unceasingly to this commandment of love of neighbor: there is none in which it does not occupy an important position, and sometimes the sole important one. Indeed, it is the point of convergence of all the others, which are mentioned as so many different kinds of love or as conditions of love. For ex-ample, if he invites Christians to humility, it is because they cannot love their brothers efficaciously, cannot "serve" them, as Christ served them, without "regarding the others as their superiors" (Phil 2, 3, which introduces the solemn exhortation to disinterested love, following the example of Christ, "becoming obedient to death, even

---

4. Luke's formula seems to be the original one: see J. Dupont, *"Soyez parfaits"* (Mt 5, 48). *"Soyez misericordieux"* (Lk 6, 36), in *Sacra Pagina*, II (1959), 150-162.

to death on a cross," vv. 5-10). In order to put himself at the service of the community of which he is a member, the Christian must rid himself of all pretension (Rom 12, 3ff.). If the "luxury-seeking" person is often mentioned in connection with the "greedy one," the one who "desires above and beyond his own needs" (*pleonektēs*), it is because each one treats his neighbor as an instrument of pleasure or profit, using him instead of serving him.[5] Likewise, the law of work is not imposed in the name of some abstract order, but "so that no one may be a burden to any of you" (I Thess 2, 9; II Thess 3, 8), or better yet, "so that one may have something to share with him who suffers need" (Eph 4, 28). Paul himself wanted to give an example of this (I Thess 2, 9; II Thess 3, 8): "We toil, working with our own hands" (I Cor 4, 12). As he tries to remind the priests of the Church of Ephesus who had come to greet him at Miletus, he wanted thereby "to show them that by so toiling you ought to help the weak,"[6] reminding us of those words of the Lord Jesus: "It is more blessed to give than to receive" (Ac 20, 34-35).

The Apostle urges us to charity toward the neighbor not for the sake of maintaining purity of doctrine or of fostering prayer. At his departure for Macedonia, he bids Timothy "stay on at Ephesus that thou mightest charge some not to teach novel doctrines, and not to study fables and endless genealogies which beget controversies rather than godly edification, which is in the faith" (I Tim 1, 3-4). But he specifies that "the purpose of this charge is charity, from a pure heart and a good conscience and faith unfeigned" (v. 5). Along the same lines, he had warned the Corinthians that "knowledge puffs up," while only "charity edifies," that is, "builds up" the local community (I Cor 8, 1) and the whole Church which is "the

---

5. I Cor 5, 10-11; Col 3, 5; Eph 5, 3-5. On the sin of *pleonexia*, see *Supplément au Dictionnaire de la Bible*, VII, col. 498-500.

6. These "weak" are "those in need," such as those one always thought of in connection with Nicholas of Lira in the sixteenth century. The idea that Luke would have thought of Christians "weak in faith" appears only when the clergy have long since stopped earning their living by manual work. If Luke did not write "poor" but "weak," that is, "sick" or "infirm" (see below, p. 248), it is because the "poor" in question are such because their physical strength no longer allow them to work. Fr. D'Aragon studied the history of the interpretation of this passage in *Sciences Ecclésiastiques*, 7 (1955), 5-22.

body of Christ" (Eph 4, 12). As to prayer, he thinks of it as a struggle in which the Christian participates with God for the good of souls entrusted to his care (Col 4, 12; Rom 15, 30). We are all aware of the place such "apostolic" prayer has in the letters of Paul.[7]

Besides, all we need do is to go back to the description he gave of *agapē* in the hymn to charity in I Cor 13, notably vv. 4-7, to see that in his eyes the body of Christian virtues are but different expressions of the unique *agapē*:

> Charity is patient, is kind; charity does not envy, is not pretentious, is not puffed up, is not ambitious, is not self-seeking, is not provoked; thinks no evil, does not rejoice over wickedness, but rejoices with the truth; bears with all things, believes all things, hopes all things, endures all things.

On the other hand, the Epistle to the Galatians contrasts with the "works of the flesh" the unique fruit of the Spirit which is "charity, joy, peace, patience, kindness, goodness, faith, modesty, continency" (Gal 5, 22-23). Finally, the Epistle to the Colossians summarizes this whole teaching when, at the end of a long exhortation, the Apostle adds: "But above all these things have charity, which is the bond of perfection" (Col 3, 12). Charity is the link that "brings together, as in a cluster, the virtues which constitute perfection."[8]

III

The above citations do not by any means exhaust the demands

---

7. Such a struggle obviously was not intended to exert "pressure" on God to "bring him to want what he at first did not want" (St. Thomas), but according to the teaching of the Angelic Doctor who borrows the idea from St. Augustine, to "render man ready to receive what God wants to give him." It is intended to change man and not God. See "Un aspect de la prière apostolique d'après saint Paul," in *Christus. Cahiers spirituels,* no. 19 (1958), 222-229. In Scripture, the intercession for Aaron, model of all others, consists essentially of reminding God of his promises (Wis 18, 21-25, interpreting the episode told in Num 17, 11-13, and which, it seems, inspired Heb 7, 25; 9, 24).

8. J. Huby, *op. cit.,* 91, n. 1.

of charity. The law of love is not a law that a person can fulfill once and for all. St. Paul remarked that, as regards love, the Christian will always be "indebted" to his neighbor (Rom 13, 8). Recommendations or prohibitions are but a guideline to help the Christian become "perfect." For St. Paul, the true law of love, and hence of perfection, is a norm of a very different kind: imitation of Christ's person, namely, of his charity, which is itself a visible reflection of that of the Father—a norm as objective as would be a code of regulations, for Christ is not a creation of fantasy but an historical figure whose deeds and acts are recorded in the Gospels. This is the norm to which the Apostle refers, always implicitly and sometimes explicitly, as was explained.[9]

Indeed, this fundamental principle of Christian perfection is presupposed throughout: "Let every one of you please his neighbor . . . for Christ did not please himself" (Rom 15, 2-3). "Wherefore receive one another, even as Christ has received you" (Rom 15, 7). "Do not look to your own interests. . . . Have this in mind which was also in Christ Jesus" (Phil 2, 4-5).[10] But in this respect nothing is more illuminating than the use of the term *agapē*. In St. Paul it designates the love of God or Christ for us or the love we must show our neighbor; and so convinced is the Apostle that the first is the rule of the second that the same qualities are used to describe each one. Our love for our neighbor will be marked by goodness and kindness (Gal 5, 22; I Cor 13, 4; Col 3, 12; Eph 4, 32), like that of God (Rom 2, 4; 11, 22; Eph 2, 7; Tit 3, 4); by mercy (Rom 12, 8), compassion (Col 3, 12), patience (I Cor 13, 4; Gal 5, 22), just as God is merciful (Tit 3, 5), compassionate (Rom 12, 1), patient (Rom 2, 4; 9, 12); it will be faithful (Gal 5, 22), as God is faithful (Rom 3, 3; I Cor 1, 9). Above all, it will be disinterested (I Cor 10, 24 and 33; 13, 5; Phil 2, 3; Rom 12, 20-21), like that of God who loved us even though we were his enemies (Rom 5, 6-10), and thus will it be universal (Rom 12, 16-18), just as God does not make exception of persons (Rom 2, 11; Gal

---

9. See Chapter 5, p. 168f.
10. Absolutely identical teaching in St. John: "As I have loved you, you also love one another" (Jn 13, 34) and in the synoptics (Mt 5, 48, and Lk 6, 36), cited above, p. 201.

2, 6; see Mt 5, 45) but desires the salvation of all men (I Tim 2, 4).

Still, the Christian does not imitate God or Christ as an artist strives to reproduce the characteristics of his model, or even as the Christian can try to reproduce the attitudes or sentiments he admires in saints who always remain exterior influences, whereas God "is more interior to us that we are to ourselves." The love of charity in the Christian is a participation in God's love; it is even that love communicated to the Christian. So profound is his union with Christ that every Christian can say with Paul: "It is now no longer I that live, but Christ lives in me" (Gal 2, 20).[11]

Such is the effect of this union that in the same Epistle, in the following chapter, the Apostle attributes to baptism the fact that every one of the baptized and all the baptized together form with Christ "a single living being" (*eis* in the masculine), so "one" that all the differences that separate men—social (slave, free man), religious (Jew, Greek), even those inherent to our nature as God created it (man, woman) —are transcended in a higher unity (Gal 3, 27-28).[12] In the Epistle to the Romans he will say that the baptized man has become with Christ "a single being" (*sumphytos*,

---

11. All the more so, since Paul is speaking in the name of all baptized Christians. One could not say more explicitly how profound is the union of the Christian with Christ and with God: the Christian life is not only a "life for God," that is, a life completely dedicated to God (*theōi zēn;* see II Cor 5, 15), nor even a "life in God in Christ Jesus" (Rom 6, 11); it is in all truth "a life of Christ in me." From this text, Cajetan concluded: "Thus, all my vital actions, such as understanding, thinking, loving, rejoicing or sorrowing, wishing, working, are no longer my actions; they no longer come from me; they come from Christ in me. Indeed, whoever is crucified with Christ, has Christ as an explanation of all his acts, and so much does Christ direct, dispose of, and use his interior and exterior forces that one may rightly say that it is Christ who lives in him" (*In Gal* 2, 19; cited by E. Mersch, *Le corps mystique du Christ. Etudes de théologie historique,* II, 257).

12. "More one than if they constituted a single body," explains St. John Chrysostom in commenting on Eph 4, 3 (*P.G.,* 62, c. 72). Concerning this text, Fr. Mersch wrote: "The strongest of formulas (Pauline) is not that we are the body of Christ. The latter, as strong as it is, does not express a unity as intimate as those short phrases in which Paul says that we are all *unus* in Christ, one single mystical person, one single mystical Christ" (*op. cit.,* I, 151). The expression "mystical person" is

Rom 6, 5). In baptism is given to us the Spirit of Christ, in whom Father and Son love one another and love men, so that Paul does not hesitate to define the Christian, a son of God, in terms of the gift of the Spirit: "For whoever are led by the Spirit of God, they are the sons of God" (Rom 8, 14); "led" (*agontai*), not guided, driven, conducted, as from without, but animated by him:[13] those in whom the Spirit prays to the Father (Gal 4, 6; see Rom 8, 15) and who, being the Spirit of the Son, puts on their lips and in their hearts the very prayer of the only Son: *Abba,* attesting thereby that we are children of God (Rom 8, 16), loved by the Father with the same love by which he loves his own Son.[14] Thus Paul can say that "the love of God"—that with which he loves us, as the context indicates—"is poured forth in our hearts by the Holy Spirit who has been given to us" (Rom 5, 5). The "sacerdotal" prayer of Christ has been answered: "I have made known to them thy name, and will make it known,[15] in order that the love with which thou

from St. Thomas, who uses it to explain the vicarious satisfaction of Christ: "Caput et membra sunt quasi una persona mystica" (*Summa theol.,* III, q. 48, a. 2, ad 1).

13. Both the Greek and Latin traditions will not cease to recall this truth, especially with regard to the conception of Christ or Gal 4, 6. Thus St. Thomas: "Ad hoc terminata est incarnatio ut homo ille qui concipiebatur esset sanctus et Filius Dei: utrumque autem horum attribuitur Spiritui Sancto." And after having cited Gal 4, 6 and Rom 1, 4, he concludes: "Sicut ergo alii [i.e., homines] per Spiritum Sanctum sanctificantur spiritualiter, ut sint filii Dei adoptivi, ita Christus per Spiritum Sanctum est in sanctitate conceptus, ut esset Filius Dei naturalis" (*Summa theol.,* III, q. 32, a. 1 corp.).

14. Thus tradition likes to discern in the proclamation of Christ's filiation after his baptism or his transfiguration, the announcement of our own filiation. St. Hilary, for example, whom St. Thomas cites, explains that "the Holy Spirit descended on the baptized Jesus and the voice of the Father was heard to say: This is my beloved Son; the result is that we realize that through Christ the Holy Spirit comes down from heaven in baptism to dwell within us and that by adopting us the Father's voice makes us sons of God" (III, q. 39, a. 8 ad 3). Such is also the explicit teaching of the liturgy of the Transfiguration, as is evidenced in the prayer of the feast: "Deus qui ... adoptionem filiorum perfectam voce delapsa in nube lucida mirabiliter praesignasti."

hast loved me may be in them, and I in them" (Jn 17, 26).

We can go further. In Romans, St. Paul reminds his audience that baptism united them not only to Christ's person but also to his death and resurrection (Rom 6, 3-5). It united them to Christ in the very act of freedom by which "he loved us and gave himself up for us" (Gal 2, 20, etc.), "he laid down his life for us" (Jn 10, 11, etc.), and "having loved his own who were in the world, loved them to the end" (*eis telos*, Jn 13, 1[16]), he fulfilled what St. John calls here his "Passover," his return to his Father (Jn 13, 1). Thus St. Paul sees in this love of Christ, as is shown to us by his death, the essence of every apostolic life. To the Corinthians who had accused him of acting for human motives, the Apostle makes known the principle that directs all his activity: "The love of Christ impels us" (II Cor 5, 14). What does this mean? Certainly Paul was passionately seized with love for Christ; how else could a Christian react toward one who loved us so much? But is this what the Apostle means here? Why would the term "love of Christ" have a different meaning from the one given everywhere else, where it always signifies the very love with which Christ loved us, and, more exactly, died for us?

It is this love that has the Apostle "bound" and "hard pressed"[17] and driven to give himself to the work to which Christ called him, the work which God had entrusted to his Son, and which must be completed: the reconciliation of the world (vv. 18-20). Moreover, the Greek verb *sunechein*, which we have translated "to press," had taken on in the terminology of the common philosophy of the time

---

15. He will do so by his presence among his followers, which will enable all men to share in the love that exists between the Father and the Son (see the *Jerusalem Bible*).

16. The term appears again in 19, 30 in the verb *tetelestai*, which "corresponds to the *eis telos* of 13, 1" (C. Spicq, *Agapè*, III, 144). At that supreme moment are consummated the loving aim of the Father, contained in Scripture, and the Son's love received from the Father. See below, p. 249.

17. The expression is Fr. Huby's *Saint Paul. Epîtres de la captivité*, 283, apropos of Phil 1, 23, where Paul uses the same verb. For the meaning of *sunechein* in this passage in Corinthians, see the excellent remarks of C. Spicq, *Agapè*, II, 128-136.

a very precise meaning, which is seen, for example, in the book of Wisdom which says that in filling all the world, the Spirit "is all-embracing" (*sunechon;* Wis 1, 7), that is, from the multiplicity of elements he makes one unity, one being. The role which the Stoics attributed to that substance which was imminent to the world and was called by them *pneuma,* and which the Wise Man attributed to the very Spirit of Yahweh, is assigned by Paul to Christ's love for us, to that "remarkable charity in which his death in some way immobilized him."[18] This is what was given to the Christian in baptism, is sustained in him by the Eucharist,[19] and from which he lives and with which he loves: the charity which Paul put alongside faith and hope in the "triad" which will be known as the "theological virtues" (I Cor 13, 13), that is, according to the definition of St. Thomas, "those which unite us immediately to God."[20] And if Paul ranks charity above the other two, it is because it unites us to what is in God, what is, so to speak, the "most" God since "God is love" (I Jn 4, 8).

IV

But in reserving the term *agapē* for the love of God or Christ for us and the love of men among themselves, St. Paul evidently does not intend to exclude our love for God from the components of Christian perfection. In declaring twice that "the whole Law is fulfilled in one word: Thou shalt love thy neighbor as thyself"

18. *Ibid.,* III, 149.
19. In the Eucharist, sacrament and sacrifice, the Christian participates in the very act of love by which Christ offered himself. Thus St. Cyprian declares that "sacrificium dominicum legitima sanctificatione non celebratur, nisi oblatio et sacrificium nostrum responderit passioni" (cited by Pius XI in the encyclical *Miserentissimus*). We can understand why it is "sacramentum caritatis," just as baptism is "sacramentum fidei" (III, q. 73, a. 3 ad 5) and why the "res hujus sacramenti" is "unitas corporis mystici" (*ibid.,* corp.) or that "caritas non solum quantum ad habitum sed etiam quantum ad actum" (q. 79, a. 4, corp.).
20. *In 1 Cor* 13, 13: "Haec tria conjungunt Deo; alia autem non conjungunt Deo nisi mediantibus istis" (lect. 4; ed. R. Cai, no. 805).

(Gal 5, 13; Rom 13, 9), he certainly did not intend to contradict Christ's teaching on "the first and greatest commandment." It suffices, however, to note that after having answered the scribe's question by reciting the opening part of the profession of faith which every Jew repeated each morning and evening: "Listen, O Israel! . . . Thou shalt love the Lord your God with your whole heart . . . ," Jesus himself adds, although the question was not asked, that to this "first" commandment must be added a "second" (Mk 12, 31), "like unto the first" (Mt 22, 39). St. Luke unites the two commandments in a single one, encompassing at one and the same time both loves (Lk 10, 25), while the parable of the Good Samaritan, intended clearly as a commentary on the Lord's teaching, retains only the "second" precept, like St. Paul (Lk 10, 29-37). At any rate, Christ intended to summarize the essence of the Christian's duties in this twofold attitude toward God and men.

St. Paul offffers a formula that expresses, though in different terms, this same twofold attitude regarding God and one's neighbor: often, and especially in the prayer of thanksgiving with which most of his letters begin, he speaks of the faith of his correspondents in God or in Christ and of their charity toward one another: "We are bound to give thanks to God always for you, brethren. It is fitting that we should, because your faith grows exceedingly and your charity each one for the other increases" (II Thess 1, 3). And to the Colossians: "We give thanks to God . . . for we have heard of your faith in Christ Jesus and of the love that you bear towards all the saints" (Col 1, 4; likewise, Eph 1, 15). And if in the Epistle to Philemon he thanks God for what he "hears of thy charity and of the faith that thou hast in our Lord Jesus and towards all the saints" (Phm 4), the parallelism of the other formulas shows that the Apostle is having recourse to a well-known rhetorical figure and wants to talk of Philemon's faith in the Lord Jesus and his charity toward all the saints.[21] St. John, moreover, expresses himself in the same way: "And this is his commandment, that we should believe in the name of his Son Jesus Christ, and love one another"

---

21. Fr. Spicq who denies this interpretation, reads here: "I have heard of your Christian faith and charity toward the saints, made for their benefit" (*Agapè*, II, 266-267).

(I Jn 3, 23).

Furthermore, it is enough to reflect on what St. Paul and St. John mean by "believing in God or in Christ," to understand how they could see in faith the exact correspondent to the "first commandment. In effect, the Pauline and Johannine faith, the faith that justifies, is what later theology will call "living faith," including, therefore, at the very least what it calls "love of God." For Paul, as well as for John, this is the adherence of the intelligence to truths (Rom 10, 9), but even more so, adherence of one's whole being to a Person (Rom 3, 22; Gal 2, 16; etc.). Like Abraham's faith, it implies trust, abandonment, a lucid confidence, founded on the conviction that God is truthful, that he can neither be deceived nor deceive us. It "stakes" everything on God's truth, fidelity, omnipotence (Rom 4, 21), and love: "And the life that I now live in the flesh, I live in the faith of the Son of God, who loved me and gave himself up for me" (Gal 2, 20).

This was already the meaning of the Hebrew verb which the Septuagint translated by *pisteuein*:[22] derived from the root *'aman*, it expresses solidity, fidelity, strength, all qualities proper to God, in contrast to the inconstant, unfaithful man, unstable as the moving sands on which nothing can be built. "Yahweh is a sure God [*ne 'eman*] on whom we can rely completely (Dt 7, 9). . . . To believe is to rely on One who, of his very nature, deserves unlimited trust: we rely on God absolutely because he is what he is (Gen 15, 6). Faith is precisely that attitude of total surrender."[23] Ruling out, by definition, all self-sufficiency (Rom 3, 27), faith is essentially for St. Paul a submission, an "obedience":[24] if this is the only attitude proper to a creature vis-à-vis God, from whom he can only "receive," how much more will it be the attitude when it is a matter

---

22. The New Testament borrowed this highly religious expression from the Septuagint and not from current language where, then as now, the verb "to believe" is used in connection with things of which a person is not sure: the object of *pistis* is *doxa*, that is, uncertain opinion, precisely the contrary of what the object of "faith" is.

23. A. Gelin, "La foi dans l'A. T.," in *Lumière et Vie*, no. 22 (1955), 433.

24. Rom 1, 5; 16, 26, where the formula *hupakoē pisteōs* signifies: "the obedience that is faith," *pisteōs* being a "genitive of definition." See also Rom 10, 16.

of the most gratuitous gift of all, the very life of God. In commenting on Rom 4, 5, St. Thomas will see, quite rightly, in the justifying faith of Paul a consent on man's part to the work God does in him: "In believing in God who justifies, man submits to that activity and thus receives its effect."[25]

But St. Paul is not content to juxtapose these two essential components of the Christian life. Besides adding to them hope, most often in third place (I Thess 1, 3: 5, 8; II Thess 1, 3-4; Col 1, 4-5; etc.), he states, at least in one passage, the relationship that unites faith and charity: he speaks of "the faith which works through charity" (Gal 5, 6: *pistis di' agapēs energoumenē*). No doubt, the formula is open to different interpretations; the Greek participle can be explained as a passive one or as a deponent, and the term *agapē* can signify, although St. Paul does not use it elsewhere in this sense, the love with which we love God. But put alongside numerous passages where Paul juxaposes faith and charity, the formula of the Epistle to the Galatians offers a rather obvious meaning.[26] The act of faith being precisely, according to the Apostle, that by which the Christian receives within him the gift of divine life, or, as he says elsewhere, that by which "Christ dwells in your hearts" (Eph 3, 17), it is not surprising that this life, which is at the same time love, is carried out under the form of love: the sole authentic faith, which is, in effect, the reception of the Trinitarian life, is that which "works through love, *fides per dilectionem operans*," according to the translation St. Thomas gives in preference to the one in the Vulgate.[27]

Even under the supposition that charity means in St. Paul love of neighbor, one still could not then reduce the Pauline concept of perfection to a simple "moralism." This would be to forget the fact that if charity is "the way that surpasses all others," in man, here

---

25. *In Rom 4*, lect. 1: "Ex eo enim quod credit in Deum justificantem, justificationi ejus subicit se, et sic recipit ejus effectum" (ed. R. Cai, no. 331).
26. Thus the *Ambrosiaster* understood: "Fides caritate fraterna debet muniri, ut perfectio sit credentis." See *Biblica*, 40 (1959), 1043.
27. In question 108 of the I-II, the formula occurs at least three times in the body of article 1. "Dead" faith is that which is not operating, which is "inactive" like a corpse, according to the meaning of the Greek term *nekros*, and also that of the context of Jas 2, 17 and 26.

on earth, it is conditioned by faith; it is through faith that love, a participation in the love of God and Christ, is communicated to man: "Faith works through love." But by that very fact we understand how capable such a love is of uniting us to God and how it therefore deserves the name "theological." In theological language, God, and more precisely God's love, is the unique "formal object": "id quo diligimus."[28]

Let us add that by virtue of the incarnation Christ, and consequently God, is also in a real sense the material object: a true love of friendship, implying "mutual exchange,"[29] a love in which man, as unthinkable as it may appear, not only "receives" from God but "gives in return," becomes actually possible. Through the incarnation, God became man, finite, and thus capable of "receiving." During his earthly life, Christ did not only "go about doing good" (Ac 10, 38); a real man, he needed other people; he gave but he also "received," and when, sitting at the well of Jacob, he asked for a little water to quench his thirst, he was not pretending with the woman of Samaria (Jn 4, 7).

But Christ continues to "receive" in his brothers, men on earth: "Amen I say to you, as long as you did it for one of these the least of my brethren, you did it for me" (Mt 25, 40). He wished to remain present with us not only in the Eucharist but also in the members of his Body, two kinds of presence whose relationship is noted expressly by St. Paul: "Because the bread is one, we, though many, are one body, all of us who partake of the one bread" (I Cor 10, 17). And as we know, this teaching will be used again and again by the Greek and Latin Fathers who love to unite these two forms of presence. As St. John Chrysostom says:

> Do you wish to honor the body of Christ? Do not neglect it when it is exposed. Do not honor it here with veils of silk, to neglect it outside where it suffers from cold and exposure.

28. See the formula of St. Thomas: "Homo participat cognitionem divinam per virtutem fidei . . . et amorem divinum per virtutem caritatis" (I-II, q. 110, a. 4).

29. In his *Spiritual Exercises,* St. Ignatius, in the preamble to the "Contemplation to obtain divine love," notes that "love consists of a mutual communication" (no. 231).

For he who said: "This is my body"..., is he who said: "When I was hungry, you did not give me to eat," and: "As long as you did it for one of these the least of my brethren, you did it for me. . . ." What good is it if the table of Christ is filled with chalices of gold, when he is dying of hunger? Begin by feeding the hungry and then, with what is left over, decorate his table. . . . In decorating the house, please do not neglect your afflicted brother, for this temple is more precious than that one.[30]

And a Latin interpreter like St. Leo the Great, the "Doctor" of the mystery of the incarnation, is not less explicit; his formulas, more compact and more "theological," are all the more significant. Thus he reminds Christians:

Since the Lord himself said: "Unless you eat the flesh of the Son of Man, and drink his blood, you shall not have life in you" (Jn 6, 53), you should receive communion at this holy table in such a way that you doubt in no way of the reality of Christ's body and blood. . . . But he is also worthy of praise who, distributing garments and food to the poor, knows that he is nourishing and clothing Christ, since he himself said: "As long as you did it for one of these the least of my brethren, you did it for me" (Mt 25, 40).

And he concludes by affirming the unity of the two natures in the unique person of Christ:

---

30. *In Mat,* hom. 50; *P.G.,* 58, 508-509. Commenting on chapter 9 of II Cor, he compares the altar of whoever gives alms, "altar made up of the very members of Christ," altar which is "the very body of the Lord," not only with the altar where the priests of the old law sacrificed victims, but also with the altar where the priest of the New Testament offers the Holy Sacrifice; he also adds: "This altar is more august than that one. The first is venerable on account of the victim you offer; the second, because it is built with the victim itself; the first, because, while of stone, it is consecrated by the body of Christ that it receives; the second, because it is the body of Christ. But it is possible for you to contemplate it everywhere — in the streets and in the squares — and at any hour you can offer sacrifice at it" (*In II Cor,* hom. 20; *P.G.,* 61, 540).

> True God and true man, therefore, unique is Christ, rich in
> his riches, poor in our misery, receiving our offerings and
> distributing his gifts, sharing our mortal condition and
> giving life to the dead.[31]

Elsewhere, the same Doctor celebrates the marvelous condescen-
sion of Christ who, "in order that his presence might be available
to us, gave the mystery of his humility and his glory so that the
one we adore as King and Lord in the majesty of the Father, we
could nourish in his poor."[32] For Leo, the incarnation did not consist only of Christ's assuming a concrete human nature but of his
assuming that of all men sanctified by his grace, and so all men
are called to be sanctified: "It is beyond doubt, beloved, that the
Son of man assumed human nature in a union so intimate that not
only in this man who is the first-born of all creation (Col 1, 15),
but also in all his saints was there but one and the same Christ;
and just as the head could not be separated from the members,
likewise the members from the head."[33]

---

31. *Sermo* 91; *P.L.*, 54, 452-453. The meaning is clear: Christ is "rich in his
    richness," "distributes his gifts," "gives life to the dead" in virtue of
    his presence in the eucharist; he is "poor in our misery," "receives our
    gifts," "shares in our moral condition" in virtue of his presence in men
    and more especially in the poor, insofar as the latter constitute a per-
    manent calling.
32. *Sermo* 9; *P.L.*, 54, 163; ed. "Sources chrétiennes," no. 49, 18. See the fine
    formula of *Sermo* 48: "Generosity cannot lack means where it is Christ
    who nourishes and is nourished" ("ubi Christus pascit et pascitur"), *P.L.*,
    54, 301; ed. "Sources chrétiennes," no. 49, 79.
33. *Sermo* 63; *P.L.*, 54, 355; ed. "S.C.," no. 74, 80: "Non est dubium, dilectis-
    simi, naturam humanam in tantam connexionem a Filio Dei susceptam,
    ut non solum in illo homine, qui est primogenitus totius creaturae, sed etiam
    in omnibus sanctis suis, unus idemque sit Christus; et sicut a membris
    caput, ita a capite membra dividi non possint." It is well known with
    what great intensity the apostle of El Kbab in Morocco, Fr. Peyriguère,
    lived this mystery: "Contemplation is having the experience of the
    Presence. Here, in caring for children, I see him, touch him, have almost
    the physical impression of touching the body of Christ. It is an extra-
    ordinary grace .... The children on whom I put a shirt — it is the body
    of Christ I am dressing. By dint of living [this presence], my mass is
    renewed ...." Gravely ill, he nevertheless delayed his departure in order

V

Such is St. Paul's idea of the "perfect" Christian, one who, having reached adult age, has ceased being a "child." It is clear that this "perfection" is appropriate for all without exception. However elevated the ideal may be, all men are called to bring it to reality. St. Paul reproaches the neophytes of Corinth, who had just abandoned a very gross form of paganism (see I Cor 6, 9-11), not only for submitting their legal suits to pagan magistrates, which he considers a real crime of lese-majesty against Christian dignity (I Cor 6, 15), but also for conducting suits against each other. He explains that this presupposes, first, that "you yourselves do wrong and defraud your brethren" (v. 8), next, that the latter do not wish "to suffer wrong and be defrauded" (v. 7). If the latter condition is not a "crime," as the translation of the Vulgate *delictum* might suggest, it is at least a "failing" in the Christian ideal (v. 7: *hēttēma*). St. Paul, therefore, did not consider the formulas of the Sermon on the Mount as pious exaggerations (see Mt 5, 38-42; Lk 6, 29-30): when the rights of others are not in question, the "perfect" Christian abandons his own. Paul does not say that it is as serious "not to want to be defrauded" as it is "to commit injustice"; his language is very carefully phrased. But he reproaches the Corinthians for both conditions, a clear sign that he considers both contrary to an ideal to which every Christian is called.

Still, in the following chapter of the same Epistle, he foresees a clear distinction between two categories of Christians and his problematic is like the one that is familiar to us when we speak of "counsels" and "precepts." It is important to examine what he means by this, especially since the situation seems unique in his writings.

In the beginning of this chapter St. Paul proposes to answer questions that have been raised by the faithful of Corinth: "Now concerning the things whereof you wrote to me" (I Cor 7, 1). Since we do not know the exact tenor of these questions and the con-

---

to begin once more distributing some clothes. To the Little Sister who asks him why he did not go sooner to get healed in Casablanca, he simply answers: "But sister, I would not have had the joy of seeing Christ clothed once again!" (Georges Gorrée, *Le Père Peyriguère,* 54 and 70).

crete circumstances that provoked them, Paul's response does not always admit of an easy interpretation. For example, the initial formula of v. 1b: "It is good for man not to touch woman," could very well pertain to the question raised, the Apostle's response beginning only with v. 2.[34] At any rate, on certain essential points, which suffice for our discussion, his teaching leaves no doubt. The use of marriage is declared not only legitimate for the Christian but obligatory (vv. 2-4), except in the case of mutual consent, although such consent is not always advisable (v. 5). As to the married state, it too is legitimate, but it is not obligatory (v. 6); moreover, the celibate state, which Paul himself has chosen, is a good he desires everyone to possess (v. 7a), provided, however, that they are called to it by God, otherwise it is preferable they should marry (v. 9). The married state and the celibate state are both a gift (*charisma*) of God: "Each one has his own gift from God, one in this way, and another in that" (v. 7b).[35]

After having recalled the "Lord's commandment" regarding the indissolubility of marriage (vv. 10-11) and mentioned the so-called Pauline privilege (vv. 12-16),[36] he returns to the problem he had already touched on briefly: the superiority of virginity over marriage (vv. 25 ff.). As in v. 6, he again distinguishes between "commandment" and "counsel" (v. 25; see v. 40). He restates em-

---

34. This is the opinion, for example, of Fr. Léon-Dufour, "Mariage et virginité selon saint Paul," in *Christus. Cahiers spirituels*, no. 42 (1964), 181. This article (179-194) can be read with profit. It supplements another by the same author "Mariage et continence selon saint Paul," published in *A la rencontre de Dieu. Mélanges Albert Gelin*, 1961, 319-329.

35. But one can also understand when Fr. Léon-Dufour says: "Married people can have received charisms other than that of virginity" (*art. cit.*, 186). In this case, marriage would not be called by Paul a "charism"; but such is not the obvious meaning and the reason used is not compelling, namely, that "marriage in Paul's eyes is in no way charismatic, in the proper sense of the word." Certainly the married state does not consitute a charism in the precise sense in which the gifts of speaking many tongues, prophecy, etc., of which Paul will speak five chapters later on (12, 1), are charisms. But can we not say the same thing of virginity? Thus, most translators render here the Greek word as "spiritual gift."

36. The "Pauline privilege," also called "privilege of faith," is that whereby the married person who converts to Christianity can contract a new marriage if his partner refuses to become converted.

phatically the legitimacy of marriage (vv. 28, 38, 39), which some people in Corinth seem to doubt; perverted tendencies may have existed along with the lax tendencies mentioned in I Cor 5, 1ff. and especially 6, 12ff. The superiority of virginity is founded on what Paul calls "the present distress" (v. 26), that which characterizes the Messianic era inaugurated by Christ's resurrection and, therefore, the "Christian condition."[37] "If you have risen with Christ," as he will say to the Colossians, you Christians must live on this earth a resurrected life: "seek the things that are above," "mind the things that are above, not the things that are on earth" (Col 3, 1-2). What follows tells us what "the things of earth" are: "immorality, uncleanness, lust, evil desire, and covetousness (which is a form of idol-worship)," in short, egotism under its current forms (v. 5), while the "things that are above" are "a heart of mercy, kindness, humility, meekness, patience, and above all charity, which is the bond of perfection" (vv. 12-14).

In this world, the Christian must live a "celestial" life.[38] Like others, the Christian "weeps," "rejoices," "buys" (I Cor 7, 30), but he does not do so like others: for him, all these human activities cease to exist in themselves. Through them, he pursues an ideal which is not of this world; for him, they are means of living out

37. St. Paul does not base the superiority of the state of virginity on the imminence of the end of the world, as certain commentators claim, nor on the relative proximity of death which will affect each man; nor is he thinking of the "problems of married life." Indeed, here as elsewhere (e.g., Rom 13, 11-14), he "is relying on another order, expressed, moreover, with the help of inadequate categories taken from the Old Testament and the apocalyptic literature." The "present distress" designates the "eschatological" era, which the Bible often calls "the last days"; the latter, starting with the death and resurrection of Christ and coextensive with the period of the the Church Militant, differs essentially from the preceding period, so that the Christian is now freed from the darkness of Satan's reign to become a son of life and light in the reign of God (see the *Jerusalem Bible,* apropos of Rom 13, 11). See also X. Léon-Dufour, *art. cit.,* 187.

38. Thus, we understand in what sense the liturgy invites us to "scorn earthly things" and to "love heavenly things," under different formulas all of which seem to go back to this text from the Epistle to the Colossians and about which more will be said in the following chapter.

this celestial life, in other words, of loving. Christians "use this world [*chrōmenoi*] as though not using it [*katachrōmenoi*]" (v. 31), or "they do not use it for their own pleasure" (E. B. Allo). The same is true of the first of those human activities mentioned by Paul, conjugal life itself: "It remains that those who have wives be as if they had none" (v. 29). St. Paul is certainly not retracting what he had said at the beginning of the chapter, and after having not only permitted but advised, indeed ordered, Christian couples to make use of marriage, he is not now going to forbid it. But they will make use of it as Christians, already participants in the life of the resurrected Christ; there again everything will be oriented to the love of charity. Here he affirms implicitly what he will say explicitly in the Epistle to the Ephesians, when he will offer as a model for conjugal love the very love Christ has for the Church (Eph 5, 25).[39]

But instead of being a means of attaining a life completely inspired by the love of charity, the married state can also be an obstacle.[40] Indeed, the universality present in every love inspired by charity, by virtue of its own disinterest, runs counter to the obligation that binds the married couple together: "He who is unmarried is concerned about the things of the Lord, how he may please God. Whereas he who is married is concerned about the things of the world, how he may please his wife; and he is divided." And the same is true for "the unmarried woman, and the virgin," in contrast to "she who is married" (I Cor 7, 32-34). No doubt, Paul is stressing this aspect of the problem because the community at Corinth needed enlightenment on this point. But by giving the married state as well as the state of virginity the name *charisma* (v. 7) and, at any rate, by advising celibates to marry if God did not give them the gift of continence (v. 9), he shows clearly that the married state offers for certain people—those whom God does

---

39. See below, p. 226f.
40. See X. Léon-Dufour, *art. cit.*, 188-189: "Since God has taken on a human figure in Jesus Christ, any other figure tends to become an idol, a link, a source of deception . . . . The sign can become a screen . . . . The word can, in becoming simply a human word, turn men away from the Word of God."

not call to another state—a better way for living out this celestial life to which all men are called here on earth.

Neither virginity nor the married state, therefore, constitutes "perfection"; they are both means, which are appropriate, although not equally so, for promoting the life of charity, which the state of perfection consists of in the final analysis. The first condition is, of itself, more appropriate, provided, however, a person is called to it by the Lord, the master of man's gifts (v. 7).[41]

Thus the problem of conscience raised by the question of the Corinthians and which led the Apostle to distinguish between precept and counsel, confirms, rather than contradicts, the result of our inquiry on the vocation of the Christian—of every Christian—to perfection. The means adopted will vary according to the various callings of the Lord, but all men are invited to become "perfect," adult Christians, to live the life of the risen Christ, in short, to love with the very love by which Father and Son love one another and love us in the Holy Spirit.

---

41. On this greater "objective and subjective" aptitude, see the conclusions of the article already cited several times of Fr. Léon-Dufour, 192-194.

VIII

Perfection of the Christian "Led by the Spirit" and Action in the World, According to St. Paul*

Three passages from St. Paul's letters clarify in a particular way the problem of the perfection of the lay person, the "authentic" son of God led by the Spirit (Rom 8, 14), in the world where providence asks him to live. For what Christ says of his apostles in speaking to his Father, pertains even more to the lay person: "They are not of the world, even as I am not of the world," but "I do not pray that thou take them out of the world, but that thou keep them from evil"; indeed, "even as thou hast sent me into the world, so I also have sent them into the world" (Jn 17, 14-18).

I

The first passage is taken from I Cor 8, which, regarding the superiority of virginity, is the only passage in Paul that discusses *ex professo* the distinction between counsel and commandment.[1]

---

* The text of this chapter appeared in the volume entitled *Sainteté et Vie dans le siècle* (Collection "Laïcat et Sainteté," II), Herder, 1965, 13-38.
1. See above, p. 215f.

Actually, the Apostle refers this particular problem to a much more general one which concerns the Christian condition as such, that of the relationship between the Christian and the world. But the solution he offers shows quite clearly the novelty of Christianity on this important point, and namely with respect to Judaism. The Jew who wanted to be perfect, that is, to observe the law in all its rigor, had to cut himself off from the pagan world, not only by not practicing its vices—no requirement is stated more often by St. Paul to neophytes—but by renouncing all dealings with it. The law raised up between the Jew and the non-Jewish world a "hatred" intended to protect the follower of Yahweh, an insuperable barrier which St. Paul will mention (Eph 2, 14) and which is symbolized by the wall in the Temple of Jerusalem which separated the court-yard of the Jews from that of the Gentiles; everyone not circum-cized was forbidden to cross it under penalty of death.[2]

The New Testament gives us enough information about the requirements of the Jewish law in this area so that we can appre-ciate the revolution that Christianity brought. The centurion Cornelius was a "devout man" who gave much alms to the people and prayed to God continually (Ac 10, 2), "a just and God-fearing man, to whom the whole nation of the Jews bears witness" (v. 22). And yet, even after Pentecost, St. Peter needed a formal order from God, received in revelation, to respond to that pagan's call and enter his house. And no doubt in order to avoid the scandal of those who accompanied him, Peter explained his conduct: "You know it is not permissible for a Jew to associate with a foreigner or to visit him; but God has shown me that I should not call any

---

2. The interdiction is mentioned by the Jewish historian Josephus Flavius (e.g., *Antiquities*, XV, 11, 5). An inscription bearing the text in Greek and Latin and forbidding, under penalty of death, any unauthorized person from entering into the Holy of Holies, even if he be a Roman citizen, was found and published by Clermont-Ganneau in the *Revue archéologique*, 23 (1872), 224ff., 290ff. As is well known, the reason why the Jews assem-bled in a crowd in Jerusalem and called for Paul's arrest was precisely for his having brought into the Temple, beyond the courtyard of the Gentiles, an uncircumcised man, the Christian Trophimus (Acts 21, 27-29); only the intervention of the "tribunal of the cohort" saved Paul from the violence of the crowd who wanted to put him to death (vv. 30-36).

man common or unclean; therefore I came without hesitation when I was sent for" (Ac 10, 28-29). In the Epistle to the Galatians, St. Paul tells how later on the same Peter thought he should yield to the pressures of those of Jewish background, who were still attached to a past they had not thought changed, and would cease eating with the converts from paganism, influencing by his example all the Christians of Jewish origin, including Barnabas himself. So serious was the problem that St. Paul intervened and protested publicly against an inconsequential matter which endangered Christian freedom and the "truth of the Gospel" (Gal 2, 11-14).

In light of these facts, which could easily be multiplied, we understand better the importance of the principle stated three times by St. Paul in I Cor 7: "As God has called each, so let him walk" (v. 17). "Let every man remain in the calling in which he was called" (v. 20). "Brethren, in the state in which he was when called, let every man remain with God" (v. 24). Conversion to Judaism included not only a break with the customs of paganism; most often, if the proselyte to Judaism wanted to observe the law, and observe it to perfection, it demanded that he change his state in life. The "publican," for example, whose business forced him into those contacts with non-Jews forbidden by the law, was by definition a "sinner," and the two terms are equivalent in the Gospel. The Corinthians who were converted to a religion which in many ways resembled Judaism—whose Scriptures were in large part the same and whose moral requirements often coincided— could, indeed automatically tended to, think that their conversion implied a similar separation from the society in which they had previously lived.

To forestall such an error regarding the nature of the new religion, Paul, who was so concerned about reminding his followers of their obligation to renounce pagan practices (e.g., I Cor 5, 1ff.; 6, 9ff.), not only refrained from imposing on them anything that would imply a change in their state of life, but made it a rule that they should remain in the state in which they were when called to the faith, so long as this state did not endanger their faith or morals.

The most typical case was that of the slave, especially since he frequently had to go to the cosmopolitan city of Corinth, where slaves were very numerous and Christianity had recruited largely among the poor and the ordinary people (see I Cor 1, 26). In virtue of his very condition, the slave obviously could not observe Jewish law: how could he observe, for example, the very strict commandment of rest on the Sabbath or the many rules regulating the serving of meals, based on the distinction of pure and impure animals and the consumption of blood. As a result, the first duty of a slave who became a convert to Judaism was naturally to obtain his freedom. But in the case of slavery St. Paul does not hesitate to apply the general principle which he had just stated regarding those who were circumcised or not before their conversion: "Let every man remain in the calling in which he was called. Wast thou a slave when called? Let it not trouble thee. But if thou canst become free, make use of it rather" (vv. 20-21).

Paul's advice, as we know, was cause for scandal. More than one modern commentator has concluded that Christianity was uninterested in social progress.[3] In order to preclude such accusations, others, beginning with the sixteenth century, Protestants and Catholics alike, strove to give the words used by the Apostle another interpretation: while, faithful to the principle given, they stated that slavery is not completely incompatible with the profession of Christianity, they maintain that St. Paul would not go so far as to invite the Christian slave to remain a slave, "even if he had the opportunity to become free." This would be to attribute to Paul feelings that would run counter to the goodness of his soul and the saneness of his judgment.[4] On the contrary, Paul would advise such a slave not to lose the opportunity to emerge from his state, when such an opportunity presented itself. Noble intentions, no doubt, but perhaps they do not take sufficiently into account the problem that arose in the community of Corinth and to which St. Paul tries to give a solution. If indeed he does foresee this extreme case, it is not because the slave's condition seems to him to

---

3. Even a critic like F. Büchsel, who generally defends St. Paul's teaching, concedes here: "Of course, Paul did not conceive Christianity as a source of social progress, proof of which is seen in his attitude regarding the question of slavery (I Cor 7, 20-24)" *Theologische Blätter*, 1942, 121 and 127f.

4. This idea is expressed in one of the best commentaries on the Epistle, that of the Anglicans Robertson and Plummer, in the *International Critical Commentary*, 148.

be a good thing (still less a condition to be preferred over that of the free man) inasmuch as it would favor the development of certain virtues, such as humility.[5]

The New Testament never identifies the slave's condition with, for example, that of the poor man—he who does not have an abundance of material possessions—a condition which was deliberately chosen by Christ for himself and his family and which constitutes, in fact, a *conditio optima* for salvation and perfection, in itself better than riches.[6] The Apostle does not intend to forbid the Christian slave from accepting freedom, if this becomes possible; the context clearly shows that a counsel is involved here. The only motive that inspires this counsel is to make clear to those who are automatically convinced of the opposite how much the law of Christ is different from the Jewish law and to what extent the Christian can work for the perfection of Christianity while remaining part of society and retaining the place he occupied before.

5. Thus, among the older commentators, St. Thomas comments: "Maneas in servitute, quia causa est humilitatis. Et sicut ait Ambrosius: quanto quis despectior est in hoc saeculo propter Dominum, tanto magis exaltabitur in futuro." Likewise, among the moderns, Catholic and otherwise, e.g., Ph. Bachmann, cited and approved by Allo (166).

6. Poverty is often understood in the sense of "destitution," that is, the state of someone who lacks the basic necessities: in this case, far from wishing such "poverty," the Christian asks God to preserve him from it, according to the prayer which the priest says during the month of August: "Paupertatem et divitias ne dederis mihi sed tantum victui meo tribue necessaria" (Roman Breviary, first nocturn, citing Prov 30, 8). Thus, there are three states: that of the destitute person completely deprived of the necessities of life; that of the poor person deprived of some of the necessities; that of the rich person in possession of an overabundance of goods, which are given to him so that the first category might disappear as much as possible from the City of Man, according to the teaching of Acts 4, 34: "Nor was there anyone among them in want," and Dt 15, 4: 'There should be no one of you in need." [*Trans. note*: See the encyclical of Pope Paul VI, issued in 1967, *Populorum Progressio*, for it remarks on the distribution of the world's wealth and the obligation of the more fortunate among men to aid the less fortunate people of this world. For a penetrating discussion of the problem of "the rich and the poor," see the study of Michel Cépède, François Houtart, and Linus Grond, *Population and Food* (New York: Sheed and Ward, 1964)].

The consequences of such a rule are quite clear. The Christian slave, while remaining a slave, became in his own environment a living witness of Christ much more by his life than by his words; and so too in all the milieux, all the concrete situations that make up each and every day. The only exception envisaged is that of the husband or wife who would convert and whose spouse would refuse to live with him.[7] But when the spouses continue to live together, "the unbelieving husband is sanctified by the believing wife, and the unbelieving wife is sanctified by the believing husband" (v. 14).

Thus the Christian will continue to live in the state in which he was when he was a pagan; externally there will be no change, but internally his conduct will be radically transformed, and such conduct, completely new, will affect everything, without exception. For in the Apostle's mind a second, but no less important, principle governs the Christian's relationship with the world. It is expressed in this same chapter a little further on, and we have already made a brief reference to it.[8] In this world the customary activities of the Christian are identical with those of the pagan; but a new spirit penetrates all his efforts. It does not regulate only his dealings with God, or what could be called his "life of prayer"; it transforms even those of his efforts which others would consider secular. Like the pagan, he "weeps," he "rejoices," he "buys," in short, "uses this world." But he does so differently, which is what Paul means when he says he "weeps, as though not weeping," "rejoices, as though not rejoicing," "buys, as though not possessing," "uses this world, as though not using it." All these activities he engages in, not with less seriousness and sincerity than the pagan, but with more, for he is not motivated by self-love but by disinterested love, that very love with which God and Christ love us and which is given to him by his conversion to Christianity.

It is not by chance that the Apostle states this principle in regard to Christian virginity and applies it above all to the conjugal life of married Christians.[9] For there is perhaps no area that shows more

---

7. This is the question of the so-called Pauline Privilege. See above, n. 36 of Chapter 7.
8. Above, p. 216f.
9. Above, p. 217f.

clearly how the Christian "led by the Spirit" is both in the world
and yet not of the world, and how, while remaining in the world, he
can transform the realities of the world. Christ, who wanted to
communicate his own life—grace—to us, through the medium of
matter—the water of baptism, the oil of the sacrament of the sick,
etc.—did not hesitate to consecrate the union of married couples
and make of an apparently wholly carnal reality a sacrament, a
bearer of the Spirit, to such an extent that conjugal love becomes
the symbol of the most spiritual love imaginable, that of Christ for
his Church (Eph 5, 25). But in assimilating the most authentic
conjugal love to the strictly supernatural and divine, theological love
of *agapē*, celebrated by the Apostle in chapter 13 of the First
Epistle to the Corinthians, St. Paul was not playing on words, no
more than is the Church when she commands the spouses on the
day of their marriage, in the words of St. Paul: "Husbands, love
your wives, just as Christ also loved the Church" (Eph 5, 25).[10] As
proof, the lived experience of Christian couples is enough to demonstrate this. To take but two examples, chosen from among many.
The first comes from a Protestant, a victim of Hitler's persecution,
who was hanged at the age of thirty-eight in his prison at Berlin,
"for having dared," he said, "to discuss with some Protestant and
Catholic friends certain ethical and practical imperatives of Christianity." The person involved is Count Helmuth von Moltke, grand
nephew of Marshal von Moltke. During the days preceding his execution, he was able to write three letters to his wife, in which he
reveals the most intimate thoughts of his noble soul, which profoundly trusted in and was nourished on the Bible. He describes
in these letters his experience of conjugal love:

> And now I wish to speak of you. I have not yet mentioned
> you, for you occupy in my life a place far different from the
> others. You are not an instrument of God to make of me
> what I am. You are rather myself. For me you are chapter
> 13 of the First Epistle to the Corinthians, a chapter without
> which a man is not a man. Without you, I would have re-

---

10. This love is the "caritas conjugalis" of which the encyclical *Casti con-
nubii* speaks regarding Christian marriage.

ceived love, as I accepted it from my mother, with joy and
gratitude, as one is grateful to the sun for warmth. But
without you I would not have known love. . . . You ːe that
part of me that can only be lacking to myself. Toge her we
form one human being. That is true, exactly true. We are
. . . an idea of the Creator. Thus am I also certain that you
will not lose me on this earth, not even for a minute. And
this reality we may symbolize once more by our common
participation in Holy Communion, for me the last communion. . . . I hope that one day our children will understand
this letter.[11]

The second example, that of a "broken home," is perhaps no less
significant. We will reproduce it here, despite its length, according
to the text published after World War II in a collection containing
numerous examples of laymen's witness in the world.[12] It is entitled
"Witness of a Broken Home."

Feeling the ground give way under my feet, rolling at a
dizzying pace into an abyss—this was the sudden feeling I
had in regard to the catastrophe that was breaking up my
home. Then I was seized by an immense sadness, composed
of anguish, fear, disillusion, and humiliation, regret, abandonment, and solitude. Thereafter came the determination to
fight with my own means, which proved to be ineffective:
that is, maintaining a permanent state of legitimate defense,
attacks corresponding to those that came from the intruder,
attempts at awkward moralizing with respect to the deserter,
sadness or simulated indifference, falling back on myself,
finally lassitude ending in bleak resignation.

At that moment, tired of fighting alone and overwhelmed
by this interior drama and the problems of daily life, the
Christian that was within me came alive. With all my

11. "Lettres de la prison de Tagel" by Helmuth von Moltke, in *Esprit et
Vie* (ed. Maredsous), August 1949, 358-359. An English translation of
the German original appeared under the title *A German of the Resistance,*
Oxford.
12. "Parmi les hommes," a special issue of the A.C.I., Easter, 1946, 39.

strength I called out to God. Many years before, when fortune smiled on me, unsatisfied, however, and looking for something, I had asked God to help me love him more than anything else, but instead I gave preference to the many goods that surrounded me.

After months of struggling against the temptation to rebel, months of prayer and reflection, the Spirit dictated to me a line of conduct and gave me the strength to hold fast over the course of long years. Despite his failing, my husband remained my husband before God. It was necessary to love him, not with the affection and love that drew me to him at the start of our marriage, but with the completely disinterested charity which had to be the fruit of the sacrament that still united us. It was necessary to continue to live with my husband; and although his mistress passed me by every day, it was necessary to live as if all that did not exist. And again I showed gentleness and sincere kindness in an attempt to make our house-hold pleasant, even though he spent a very small part of his time there.

At that moment I really understood what was meant by "He who loses his life finds it" . . .

— Exterior peace, my attitude disarming necessarily "the enemy";

— Interior peace, above all, consciously obeying the suggestions of the Spirit.

But what I did not imagine, was that in the meantime there was taking place within me a complete stripping of self that would draw me to the God whom I had prayed to in vain when fortune smiled on me. Detached from my bitterness and egotism, I was then, and only then, free enough to love God with an immense love and in it all those whom he had put on the road of my life. I was overwhelmed with joy. And little by little, in the opinion of several friends, serenity displaced the pitiful shrinking up of my features. I felt lighthearted, borne on wings. I have since found out that my husband, although he was caught in a web from which he could not free himself, respected and admired me. But it was not in God's plans that our household should be restored.

But this stripping of self aroused in me an ardent desire to allow others to profit from the experience of my life and the graces that had been given me.

Such examples of witness amply show how the Christian's state of perfection, far from separating one from the world, enables one to become part of it and to transform it.

II

This is also the message of a second passage from the Epistles,[13] where St. Paul treats of Christian hope. He too was often misunderstood and subjected to the classic accusations brought against a religion which, it is claimed, in turning the Christian's gaze toward the heaven yet to come, deters him from his present duty regarding the world below. Actually, St. Paul does invite Christians, "risen with Christ," to "seek the things that are above, where Christ is seated at the right hand of God," to "mind the things that are above, not the things that are on earth" (Col 3, 1-2).

At first sight, the Apostle would seem to favor that "scorn for secular things," the *terrena despicere et amare caelestia* that is found in so many prayers of the Missal and which is derived, in fact, directly from this Pauline text, as if the liturgy and St. Paul were urging us to forget this world of misery and suffering, injustice and sin, to live beforehand in a dreamlike paradise, somewhat like the child who tries to alleviate the burdens of school work by already experiencing some of the joys of his next vacation.[14]

---

13. This was mentioned in passing, above, p. 216.

14. The danger is not an artificial one; it would be easy to cite a number of formulas that at least suggest such an interpretation. Msgr. Zoa, for example, stated: "The average African who believes in Catholicism has, as it were, a complete lack of interest in secular reality. The expressions used in our language to express *interest in heaven* and *interest in the things of the earth* are so contradictory that the Christian, to be a true Christian, must become uninterested in everything terrestrial.... The constant repetition of this idea has created among Catholics and Christians in Africa a lack of interest as regards mastery of the world." See the entire discourse in *Documentation catholique* of July 7, 1963; the passage cited is found in col. 873.

Thus understood, the "thought of heaven" would indeed constitute a true "alienation," and the religion where it occupies a central position would merit the charge of "opium of the people."[15] To this, a Jew like J. Klausner would in vain offer the sage realism of Jewish morality, where "the Kingdom of heaven" consists of "an improvement of the world, as was announced by the prophets."[16]

But all this is caricature. To understand the real meaning of the Pauline statements, we should place them in their context, which is limpidly clear. The Apostle is careful in specifying what he means by "the things that are above" which the Christian must seek and "the things that are on earth" which he must avoid. Repeating, deliberately, in v. 5 the formula expressed in v. 2, he explains: "Therefore mortify your members, which are on earth: immorality, uncleanness, lust, evil desire, and covetousness which is a form of idol-worship," adding, as is his habit, to sins of sex, a vice, *pleonexia,* which he considers very serious, identifying it with idolatry, and which consists, according to the very etymology of the word, of wishing always to have more (*echein pleon*), naturally in disregard of the rights of others, the exact antithesis of *agapē.*[17] Verse 8 adds: "anger, wrath, malice, abusive language, and foul-mouthed utterances," and v. 9 says: "Do not lie to one another," with Paul reserving for the Epistle to the Ephesians the precise motive

15. Such is the meaning of Lenin's remark in his work *On Religion:* "Soothing with the promise of a heavenly reward [which, for Lenin, is a completely false one] the person who labors in misery all during his life, religion teaches him patience and resignation .... Religion is the opium of the people."

16. Joseph Klausner, *Histoire du second Temple* (Jerusalem, 1950-1951). See J. Bonsirven, in *Biblica,* 34 (1953), 109. In his *Conceptions messianiques juives* (Jerusalem, 1951), the same author contrasts the Jewish Messias and the Christian Messias, the first a national and terrestrial figure, the second, a man sent from heaven and uninterested in this world for the sake of an all-spiritual Kingdom of God. To this, Fr. Bonsirven responds: "Is this not reversing the true sense of reality? Jewish Messianism inaugurates a static period, while Christ opens up the Kingdom of God which will transform the world, a period of intense dynamism in which must be formed the new humanity" (*ibid.,* 110).

17. See above, p. 200f. and n. 5 in Chapter 7. For the Greek Fathers, the sin of *pleoneksia* is, so to speak, the sin par excellence, origin of all social disorders.

for this: "because we are members of one another" (Eph 4, 25).

If the Apostle does not leave any doubt as to what he means by those "things that are on earth" which the Christian must not "seek after" (*zētein*), "think about" (*phronein*), "taste," or "enjoy," as the Vulgate translates it (*sapite*), those *terrena* which the liturgy tells him sometimes even to "despise," he expresses himself no less clearly as to what he means by those "things that are above," that are "heavenly," which the Christian must on the contrary seek out, taste, enjoy. Such things concern everything that belongs to "the new man," which the Christian "has put on," after getting rid of the old man, once and for all at baptism, but which needs to be "renewed according to the image of his Creator" (v. 10). St. Paul hastens to urge his readers toward that unceasing renewal based on the image of God, the definition of which is love:

> Put on therefore, as God's chosen ones, holy and beloved, a heart of mercy, kindness, humility, meekness, patience. Bear with one another and forgive one another, if anyone has a grievance against any other; even as the Lord has forgiven you, so also do you forgive. But above all these things have charity, which is the bond of perfection (vv. 12-14).

Thus St. Paul is far from exhorting the Christian to evade the world in which God placed him. Citizen, no doubt, of the other world in which lies his true fatherland (Phil 3, 20), already participating in the life of the risen Christ, a life "hidden with Christ in God" (Col 3, 3), the Christian must live a heaven-like existence. But he will live it in this world, in the midst of the earthly city, with troubles and sorrows—for as long as he lives in a "mortal body" (Rom 6, 12), the flesh continues to fight against the spirit (Gal 5, 17ff.; Rom 8, 5ff.)—"by the Spirit putting to death the deeds of the flesh" (Rom 8, 13). True son of God and led by the Spirit (Rom 8, 14), he deserts the earthly city so little that he "edifies" it, for only "charity edifies" (I Cor 8. 1).[18] Such a city is subject to the

---

18. We may recall St. Augustine's beautiful commentary apropos of the dedication of a Church: "If this wood and these stones, cut from the forest

demands of the nature of man who is created in the image and likeness of the God of love and who is made for love, a city where men love each other and where one is happy in proportion as one loves himself, a foretaste of the heavenly city, where "at last one can love without limitation or the possibility of betrayal, the two greatest causes of suffering in our state of exile."[19]

St. Paul invited the Colossians, and all Christians, to seek out and enjoy the things from above, from the moment when their life was "hidden with Christ in God" (Col 3, 3).

Far from being uninterested in the world, Christians must mix in it the leaven which consists of those "things that are from above," and thus make the earthly city somewhat more conformed to God's plan, described by the prophets and even more so by Christ and the apostles.

It is also true that St. Paul declared: "This world as we see it is passing away" (I Cor 7, 31), and that, therefore, "the improvement of a world destined to perish" can appear as a rather vain task. But the same Paul also says, in the same Epistle, that "charity abides" (I Cor 13, 13). But such charity belongs par excellence to the "things on high," "heavenly things," which the Christian must seek out in his earthly activity. By such things "is built on earth the body of Christ who already reigns in heaven."

> Everything that helps to construct that body is, therefore, inscribed in the eternal, not only as something of merit, a title to glory, but as an imperishable achievement in itself.

and taken from quarries, did not fit together, if they did not cling to each other harmoniously, if they did not connect with each other as through a mutual love, no one would come near here; for to enter into a building with confidence, without fear of a catastrophe, it must be certain that beams and pillars hold together. Thus, our Lord Jesus Christ, wishing to enter into and live with us, first begins to build: I give you a new commandment .... Do you want to get out of your present state of distress? Love one another. And note, brothers, that throughout the universe, as it was predicted and promised, people are building up this house .... This new canticle(sung by the Jews when they rebuilt the temple of God) is the new commandment of Christ ..." (*Sermo* 336).

19. Pierre, Lyonnet, *Ecrits spirituels*, Paris, 1951, 145.

Charity abides. Every authentic love, every social link made in charity will, therefore, survive at the *parousia*. The heavenly Jerusalem will be nothing else but the communion of saints, now become conscious. It will come from heaven (Apoc 21, 2), because in heaven are gathered all those who have died in Christ and because in heaven already living mystically are those who have been reborn in baptism (Col 3, 1-4; Eph 2, 6). But it is on earth that the bond of love which gives it its consistency will have been sealed. The beatific city will not be a substitute for the fraternal city which charity succeeds in sketching, invisibly, here below; it will complete it in the light.[20]

The same truth is stated at the end of the same article:

The Christian, therefore, will live out the paradox of committing himself wholeheartedly in every task, however temporal, that tends to fulfill on earth some part of the Kingdom of God—knowing that its complete realization is impossible and even partial success problematic. He will commit himself because the tiniest, most ephemeral achievement of real human fraternity—achieved through a scientific, economic, cultural, or social effort—inscribes itself in the eternal and *is a joy forever*. He will commit himself without hesitation, precisely because the precariousness of the results will prevent him from becoming complacent. . . . He will commit himself without sadness, because the failure that threatens him will add to the effectiveness of the action the greater merit of the sacrifice, at least provided that striving with all his might to succeed, he will cease struggling only at the end of the battle, before certain failure.[21]

III

A third passage from the Epistles of St. Paul, taken from the

20. *Ibid.*, 7.
21. *Ibid., art. cit.*, 13-14.

Epistle to the Romans, will open up still greater horizons by showing us that "the search for the things from above" will also teach
the Christian to see even in the material universe, apparently
"destined to perish," an important element of eternity that he would
never have dared to imagine.

For if "charity abides," the universe at least would not seem
made to last for ever. It is invaluable, of course, since it is the
necessary framework in which man does his work and thereby
acquires the perfection to which God calls him. For this fact alone,
the Christian, more than anyone else, can neither scorn it nor be
uninterested in it. But when an instrument, no matter how precious,
is no longer of use, it is laid aside, and no doubt, many a Christian
is not far from thinking in this way, feeling that the only thing
that counts is the salvation of his soul, for which a person must
sacrifice everything. Of course, his soul is what must be saved, but
Christianity teaches him that individual salvation is part of a larger
whole. It includes, first, the resurrection of our body and, next, a
mysterious transformation of the material universe itself, to which
the human body belongs. So true is this that St. Paul does not
hesitate to speak of a longing of the "cosmos," particularly in the
passage from the Epistle to the Romans on which we are commenting.

The Apostle not only declares that the Christian looks forward
to "the redemption of his body": he believes that all of creation
will one day share in the freedom of the sons of God:

> For the eager longing of creation awaits the revelation of
> the sons of God. For creation was made subject to vanity—
> not by its own will but by reason of him who made it sub-
> ject[22]—in hope, because creation itself also will be delivered

22. The reference is to the sin of the first man according to the account in
Genesis. But Paul does not say that man's sin brought creation to "corruption," as if it had previously been of a different nature, incorruptible,
not subject to change; it was only "subject to vanity." It is true that here
the Fathers often identified "vanity" and "corruption" and, owing to a
literalist interpretation of the account of Genesis, thought that as a result
of Adam's sin the universe had become "corruptible" (Chrysostom), subject to mutability and change, or as a Gregory of Nyssa or even a Theodoret presuppose, that it had from the beginning been created by God in

from its slavery to corruption into the freedom of the glory of the sons of God. For we know that all creation groans and travails in pain until now. And not only it, but we ourselves also who have the first-fruits of the Spirit—we ourselves groan within ourselves, waiting for the adoption as sons, the redemption of our body (Rom 8, 19-23).

We see here the emphasis given to the resurrection of the body: Paul has just said in v. 11 that the Spirit is the bearer of life who "will bring to life your mortal bodies"; in v. 17, he says that we will one day be "glorified with Christ," evidently like him, in our body as well as our soul. Finally, in v. 18, the same "glory" that has been revealed in Christ—body and soul—on the day of Easter must

the present state of corruptibility in anticipation of man's sin. But in biblical terminology "vanity" is a quality of the moral, and not the physical, order, that of something deprived of its authentic value and meaning. Man's sin did not change the nature of the universe, but the latter ceased to exercise its providential role: instead of leading man toward his end, it deters him from it; the creature becomes "idol," precisely "vanity" in biblical language.

Such was also the opinion of St. Thomas, who does not hesitate to oppose explicitly on this point other Doctors such as Alcuin, whom he names, or even Venerable Bede: "Spinas et tribulos terra germinasset si homo non peccasset.... Quamvis Alcuinus dicat quod ante peccatum terra omnino spinas et tribulos non germinasset" (*Summa theol.* II-II, q. 164, a. 2 ad 1). "Quidam dicunt quod animalia quae nunc sunt ferocia et occidunt alia animalia, in statu illo fuissent mansueta, non solum circa hominem sed etiam circa alia animalia. Sed hoc est omnino irrationabile. *Non enim per peccatum hominis natura animalium est mutata,* ut quibus nunc naturale est comedere aliorum animalium carnes, tunc vixissent de herbis, sicut leones et falcones" (*Summa theol.*, I, q. 96, a. 1 ad 2). But such an opinion is precisely that expressed by Bede, e.g., *Hexameron,* I: "Dixitque Deus: Ecce dedi vobis omnem herbam ... (Gen 1, 30). Iam hic patet quod ante reatum hominis nihil noxium terra protulit, nulla herbam venenatam, nullum arborem sterilem: cum manifeste dictum sit, quod omnis herba et universa ligna data sint hominibus ac volatilibus, terrae quoque animantibus cunctis in escam, patet quia nec ipsae aves raptu infirmorum alitum vivebant, nec lupus insidias explorabat ovilia circum, nec serpenti pulvis panis eius erat, sed universa concorditer herbis virentibus ac fructibus vescebantur arborum" (*P.L.,* 91, 32).

For the interpretation of Rom 8, 19ff, the reader may consult the article "La redemption de l'univers," in *Lumière et Vie,* no. 48 (1960), 43-62.

"also be revealed in us." This is what he calls, in v. 23, the "redemption of our body." It is true that for a Greek, a disciple of Plato—and perhaps even today for many a Christian—salvation consists essentially of being freed from the body which holds the soul captive as if in a prison. With great yearning, Paul longs for his body, as well as his soul, to be freed from its carnal condition and to share in the spiritual condition of the risen body of Christ. If the Christian "by the spirit must put to death the deeds of the flesh," as was just stated in v. 13, it is not only so that the body may remain servant of the soul; it is also so that, because the body will have fulfilled that function for which God created it, it may in turn be saved. Thus the body is not only the instrument of salvation, it is also the object of salvation. Actually, the Christian will never have to sacrifice the body to the soul; he will try to deliver both from the servitude of sin and thus prepare for the glorification of each.

But the body itself is part of the universe. In the thought of St. Paul, which is also that of the whole Christian tradition, the universe is called in turn to participate in that condition of "freedom" proper to "the glory of the sons of God." On the day of the *parousia*, the dead will arise when Christ "will have destroyed the last of his enemies, Death" (I Cor 15, 26) and "all things will be subject to him . . . that God may be all in all" (v. 28). At this triumph of redeemed humanity, the material universe will not stand aside, as if it had fulfilled its role; it will take part. It will not be "annihilated," "destroyed," as was supposed by many in the time of Paul, but transformed and, like the human body, in its own way, "glorified." Like the body of man, the universe is not only an instrument of redemption for man, but an object of redemption.

Paul is, of course, content to state the fact; he says nothing about the "how" of that transformation, nor does he enable us to imagine what that future state will be. Obviously, the universe can participate in that freedom of the sons of God only in its own way, which is a very mysterious one, like the condition of the glorified body. This teaching is of a religious rather than scientific nature; like the resurrection of the body, the "new heaven" and "new earth" are objects of faith, not of science. By reason of its nature, the universe, like the human body, is destined for death; but faith teaches us that God made nothing for death, and, after sin, in virtue of the redemption effected by Christ, unless man puts an obstacle in the way by refusing to cooperate, everything is oriented toward life. By faith we know that in spite of appearances the body, which may already show the effects of illness and which will one day be decomposed and fall into dust, is nevertheless given the promise of sharing in the glory of the risen Christ. But that same faith teaches us that this is not the privilege of the human body alone; this will also be true of the universe, to a proportionate degree.

This teaching of the Epistle to the Romans will be repeated in the Epistles to the Colossians and Ephesians. The Apostle declares that all of creation, and not only humanity, "has been created through and unto him [Christ]" and "in him all things hold together" (Col 1, 15). Fr. Huby states:

> All things have been created in him as in the very principle of their existence, the supreme center of unity, harmony, cohesion, which gives the world its meaning, its importance, and thus its reality, or, to use another metaphor, as in a house, the meeting-point [Lightfoot] where are bound together and coordinated all the wires, all the generators of the universe.[23]

For the Apostle, who is, moreover, faithful in this regard to the teaching of the Old Testament which is so sensitive to the unity of the creative and redemptive design,[24] "the universe," as Fr.

---

23. J. Huby, *Epitres de la captivité,* 40. See 166, apropos of Eph 1, 10: "Christ, the Son of God, is the universal Link, the one whose presence and influence to reach to the final element of things, the one by which everything is held together in the world and in the mind that thinks of the world . . . . The Church as continuation of Christ here below has as its mission to sanctify all human experience, to unify it in faith and love, and thereby to sanctify and unify that universe that enters into man's consciousness, where it acquires its meaning and value."

24. Thus Ps 135 (Heb. 136), which sings of God's love in the history of salvation, begins with the creation of the heavens, the sun, and the moon (vv. 4-9), and without any transition continues with the deeds of God in favor of Israel (vv. 10-24). Likewise, Ps 8, the "cosmic psalm," which celebrates the domination of the "son of man" over the universe, and which is examined very movingly from this point of view in *Israël*

Huby remarks in commenting on Rom 8, 19ff., is not a simple pedestal, with man as statue; one may compare it to an immense stalk of which humanity is the flower. As long as the latter will not flourish in the glory of the sons of God, creation will suffer in travail. It will be in agony and will groan, not like a sick man who is dying, but like a woman about to give birth. He continues:

> This passage of St. Paul's, where the relationship of the universe to the destinies of man is stated so clearly, is one of the most remarkable in the Pauline doctrine for fullness and depth of its views. It is also one of those that often surprise, and even disconcert, readers, even Christian readers. The grandeur of the Pauline view overwhelms them because they are not sufficiently conscious of the insertion of humanity in the whole of creation and because they imagine the human world as being closed in upon itself, whereas each man is a transmitter and receiver, connected by numerous waves to the rest of the entire universe. Such people thus tend to think of Christ as having a relationship only with humanity, the savior and redeemer of souls exclusively, or the one who resuscitates bodies, which are cut off from all solidarity with the rest of creation. Conceiving Christ's work in that way means reducing the scope of the Pauline doctrine: the Apostle envisaged clearly the repercussions of the incarnation and the redemption not only for the history of humanity but for the universe. For St Paul, Christ did not assume an abstract human nature, cut off from the relations that bind man to the whole of creation. His redemptive work extends to everything; he has marked everything with the seal of his cross. The Epistles of captivity, Colossians and Ephesians, will show rather clearly that this is not for the Apostle a fleeting, soon-to-be-forgotten, imaginary idea, but an essential part of his doctrine.[25]

regarde son Dieu, Paris, 1964, 252-262, by Evode Beaucamp and Jean-Pascal de Relles, O.F.M.

25. J. Huby, *Epître aux Romains,* 297-298.

In stating that "Christ has marked everything with the seal of his cross," Fr. Huby evoked the hymn of Lauds during the time of the Passion: *Terra, pontus, astra, mundus, Quo lavantur flumine!*, which he had also recalled when he commented upon Col 1, 20.[26] But there is no doctrine that is more familiar to the Fathers of the Church. In particular, when they explain the passage we have taken from the Epistle to the Romans, all, both Latin and Greek, stress the profound unity of all creation, which is both victim of man's sin and destined to share in his glorified state. Let it be enough for us to cite the famous expression of St. Ambrose read in the Roman Breviary: in the presence of the risen Christ, as "firstfruits" (I Cor 15, 25), it is not only all of redeemed humanity that the bishop of Milan contemplates "risen in him," but the whole universe, heaven and earth: "In him the world is risen, in him heaven is risen, in him the earth is risen. There will be a new heaven and a new earth."[27]

Thus a Christian cannot "despise" a world destined for "glory." Just as the Church, in virtue of the dogma of the resurrection of bodies, surrounds the human body, even when reduced to the state of a cadaver, with a respect that sometimes astonishes us, so the material universe, which is to share in its own way in the

---

26. *Idem., Epîtres de la captivité*, 46.
27. "Resurrexit in eo mundus, resurrexit in eo caelum, resurrexit in eo terra. Erit enim caelum novum et terra nova" (*De fide resurrectionis; P.L.,* 16, 1403). The passage is read in the Roman Breviary, second nocturn of the fifth Sunday after Easter. See also the last chapter of the *Summa contra Gentiles* which summarizes the facts of tradition and invokes in particular Rom 8, 19ff.: "Quia omnia corporalia sunt quodammodo propter hominem [such is, in effect, the foundation of all doctrine], tunc etiam totius creaturae corporeae conveniens est, ut status immutetur ut congruat statui hominum, qui tunc erunt. Et quia tunc homines incorruptibiles erunt, a tota creatura corporea tolletur generationis et corruptionis status. Et hoc est quod dicit Apostolus, Rom 8, 21ff. Quia igitur creatura corporalis finaliter disponetur per congruentiam ad hominis statum, homines autem non solum a corruptione liberabuntur sed etiam gloria induentur, oportebit quod etiam creatura corporalis quamdam claritatis gloriam suo modo consequatur. Et hinc est quod dicitur Apoc 21, 1: Vidi caelum novum . . . , et Is 65, 17: Ego creabo caelos novos et terram novam, et non erunt in memoria priora et non ascendunt super cor; sed gaudebitis et exsultabitis usque in sempiternum. Amen."

destiny of the human body, acquires thereby a unique dignity and, as it were, a consecration.

Likewise, human work, man's efforts to master that universe, discover its secrets, civilize it, put it more and more at the service of mankind, and thereby enable it to attain its end, the one for which God created it—which already means, in a certain way, "spiritualizing" it—all this acquires a genuine importance for all eternity.

Of course, work is also for man the means of developing his own personality and, more prosaically, of "earning his living." Not by itself but by the difficulty which, as a result of sin, is inherent to it, work is also a means of expiation and purification, the means par excellence, willed by God: "In the sweat of your brow you shall eat bread" (Gen 3, 19). But it is also, even *first* in God's plan, a way for man to contribute his part toward the fulfillment of creation and thus complete the very work of God. Consequently, every new form of mastery over the universe by man, every new conquest, even though sinful man may use it for evil ends, enters nevertheless into the divine plan. And if it is true that every successful effort of the mind to gain control over the human body, thus making the body more docile to the soul, prepares in a real, though enigmatic, way for the future resurrection of the body, should we not say that every effort tending to put the universe at the service of men prepares in a no less mysterious way for that "new heaven" and "new earth" of which St. Ambrose spoke, under the inspiration of the Bible?

This explains why one day in August, 1962, on the balcony of the palace of Castelgandolfo, not without causing some surprise and perhaps even scandal, John XXIII did not hesitate to praise the-as-yet-unheard-of mission of the Soviet astronauts who had set out that very morning on their first voyage into space. And yet, before the diplomatic assembly gathered together for Christmas greetings, he made it a point to reemphasize a principle of Catholic doctrine and to celebrate once again the efforts of those who

> devote themselves not only to the great economic and social tasks which impose themselves, but also to the exploration of the cosmos and to the most advanced achievements of modern technology. Whether it is the investigations of the scholar, the labor of the technician, the daringness of the

performer, the Church applauds man's increasing control over the forces of nature. It rejoices in every advance, present and future, that enables man to gain a better understanding of the infinite grandeur of the Creator and to render him, with increasing admiration and humility, the adoration and thanksgiving that are due him.[28]

The teaching of faith regarding the future of the universe does not offer any new contribution to the sciences of nature; still, it is not a matter of indifference to the scientist of Christian faith to know that the universe entrusted to him is also destined, not to be destroyed forever by some sort of cataclysm, but to be associated for all time to the destiny of man's body.

Thus the future of the universe is closely allied with the future of man. Here again, we note the parallelism with the resurrection of the body. Just as every so-called ascetic attempt to submit the body to the soul without striving at the same time to save that soul, can only end in the destruction of both, so every conquest of the universe that is not oriented toward saving man—or in other words, toward inaugurating in him the reign of charity rather than reinforcing the tyranny of egotism— can only lead to the destruction of both man and the universe itself.

Nothing explains more clearly why the Christian, citizen of heaven, is not asked to flee from the world. Indeed, because he is a citizen of heaven, he sees that he is assigned a task in a world which he has become capable of bringing to its destiny.

The Greek placed man's perfection in his imitation of God, assimilation to God, and for this reason he tried to flee from the sensible world, the world of matter: in the act of intelligence, he aimed to participate in some way in the immateriality of "pure Act." For the Christian too, every authentic act of perfection can only be an imitation of God.[29] And yet, the God of the Christians is not the God of the Greek philosophers. While, for Aristotle, God's very perfection prevents him from knowing the world and being interested in it, the God of St. Paul and of the Bible is a God whose

28. *L'Osservatore Romano* of December 24-25, 1962.
29. Above, p. 168f.

definition is love and who so loved the world that he became man and died for men. Thus, in both religions, the same "imitation of God" will have a radically different meaning.

The contact between men and the world, which was for the Greek the main, if not the only, obstacle to "divinization," since it prevented him from giving himself completely to the act of his intellect, which was supposed to unite him with God, becomes for the Christian the very condition of a life completely dedicated to "doing good" and of thus entering into the great salvific plan of God for humanity and for the world that began at the creation of the universe (Gen 1, 1) and will reach its completion at the *parousia* (Apoc 22, 20): "When he has put all his enemies under his feet, the last of whom is Death, he will deliver the kingdom to the Father, so that God may be all in all" (I Cor 15, 24-28).

IX

The Fundamental Law of the Apostolate as Formulated and Lived by St. Paul (II Cor 12, 9)[*]

The circumstances under which St. Paul wrote the impassioned prose of the Second Epistle to the Corinthians[1] led him to discourse at length upon what the authentic apostolate was. The Pauline expressions pertain in particular to those whom the Lord sends personally into his vineyard, but they also apply to every Christian who, by the gift of the Spirit received in baptism and confirmation, which conditions him to be a "witness of Christ" (Ac 1, 8), is given the responsibility of working for the expansion of God's Kingdom. But among the many passages where the question of the apostolate is under consideration, there is one that seems to reveal the secret of the Apostle's own spirituality and to express in an incisive way what could be called the *Magna Charta* of the apostolate.

After a brief commentary on the verses in question, we shall see how the Apostle's statements become clear in light of what we know of his life and how they are part of a biblical spirituality.

---

[*] The substance of this chapter (without notes) appeared in Italian in *Parole di Vita*, of February 1962.

1. They were written in the midst of the Corinthian crisis. See below, p. 261.

I

The year is 57 or 58.[2] Paul has just spoken of graces of a mystical order, "visions and revelations of the Lord," received "fourteen years ago," thus around the years 43-44. This is when Paul begins his apostolic ministry, when St. Barnabas went to find him at Tarsus to bring him to Antioch where the vast number of conversions required many missionaries (c. 43). If at that very time Paul "was caught up to the third heaven" and "heard secret words that man may not repeat" (vv. 3-4), it is probable that those graces were intended by God to prepare him for a mission soon to be entrusted to him.

At any rate, to this first bit of self-revelation Paul adds a second, a revelation of another kind, which was closely related to the previous ones[3] and, for him, of no less importance: "And lest the greatness of the revelations should puff me up, there was given me a thorn for the flesh, a messenger of Satan, to buffet me!" (v. 7).[4]

There has been a long debate as to what Paul was alluding to by the strange expression "thorn for the flesh." Because of the defective translation of the Vulgate, which speaks of a "thorn of the flesh," using a genitive *carnis* instead of the dative used in the Greek, and in view of the specific meaning the term "flesh" had assumed in theological and ascetical terminology, many Latin commentators thought that Paul was referring to temptations against chastity, permitted by the Lord to humiliate his apostle. Such an

---

2. Practically all commentators agree on the date, at least the approximate one of 57-58, especially for the section that includes chapters 10-13. See, for example, the leading opinions in A. Robert and A. Feuillet, *Introduction à la Bible*, II, 437-444.

3. G. Delling dated it as of the same period as the "visions and revelations" mentioned in 12, 2 (*Theol. Wört. z. N.T.*, VII, 414). Likewise, Ph. Bachmann, *Commentary of Zahn*, 398, etc.

4. Opinions differ considerably on the reading of the text, especially verses 6b and 7a. See J. Cambier, "Une lecture de 2 Cor 12, 6-7a. Essai d'interprétation nouvelle," in *Studiorum paulinorum congressus internationalis*, I, 475-485; supplemented by: "Le critère paulinien de l'apostolat en 2 Cor 12, 6f.," in *Biblica* 43 (1962), 481-518. But the different readings do not modify the meaning of the passage as regards the problem that concerns us here.

interpretation, unknown, by the way, to the Greeks, is not at all a likely one and is today no longer proposed by any exegete.[5] And yet, another one suggested by many is no less probable. Such people observe correctly that the "thorn for the flesh" is specified in the following verse as a "weakness" (*astheneia*) and that, in the Epistle to the Galatians, the same term seems to designate a "sickness." The latter, by immobilizing St. Paul in areas where he did not at first expect to stay, would be the opportunity for him to establish churches in the "Galatian region" (Gal 4, 13). Such commentators conclude, somewhat hastily, that the word has the same meaning in II Cor 12, 8 and, consequently, that Paul must have suffered from a severe illness, such as malaria or the like.[6]

The precise nature of the "thorn for the flesh" is less important than its contextual meaning, and, before going on to a passage which in no way proves to be parallel, it is better to find out first if the immediate context may not furnish some light. Verse 7 actually contains a very important element: Paul sees in that "thorn for the flesh" a "messenger of Satan" (literally, an "angel of Satan"), that is, of him who is, for St. Paul and for the Bible, essentially "the adversary of God's kingdom," that "enemy of the human race," envious after his original happiness (Wis 2, 24), the one, for example, who prevents the Apostle from coming to Thessalonica (I Thess 2, 18) or who "blinds unbelieving minds, that they should not see the light of the gospel of the glory of Christ" (II Cor 4, 4),

---

5. Such an interpretation certainly does not deserve to be considered as "the traditional Catholic exegesis" (K. L. Schmidt, in *Theol. Wörterb. z. N.T.*, III, 820). Not only is it exclusively Latin, but it is not even supported by all the Latins' much less as, the sole exegesis. Pseudo-Primasius seems to have been the first one to mention it, and does so to reject it; St. Thomas points it out as only being in second place, etc. See R. Cornely, apropos of II Cor 12, 8; E. B. Allo, *Seconde épître aux Corinthiens*, 313.

6. See the long discourse of Fr. Allo, *op. cit.*, 313-323; in his opinion, "the explanation of the thorn and the attacks of Satan through a sickness is today [1937] almost universal; there seems to be no other plausible one" (313). Since that time, exegetes have been more reserved: see, among recent studies, those of H. Clavier, "*La santé de l'Apôtre Paul*," and especially of Ph. Menoud, "*L'écharde et l'ange satanique*," both published in *Studia paulina in honorem Johannis de Zwaan*, Haarlem, 1953, 66ff. and 163ff.; finally, the article of F. G. Delling on *skolops* in *Theol. Wört. z. N.T.*, VII (1964), 413-414.

the one who St. Luke says "comes and takes away the word from men's hearts, that they may not believe and be saved" (Lk 8, 12). Whatever its precise nature, it is a test which St. Paul considers an obstacle to his apostolate.[7]

This is completely confirmed by vv. 9 and 10 which generalize and speak of "infirmities," in the plural (*en astheneiais*), and add, as if Paul wanted to explain what he meant: "insults, hardships, persecutions, distresses"; in short, what are, for St. Paul, the habitual trials of the apostolic life, which he had already enumerated at least twice in the preceding chapters (4, 8-10 and 6, 4) and which are expressly said to be "endured for Christ's sake" (12, 10).

Such an explanation agrees perfectly with the Pauline use of the "vocabulary of infirmity": while in the rest of the New Testament either the noun *astheneia* or the verb *asthenein* or the adjective *asthenēs* signify almost always a corporal infirmity, an illness, in Paul they almost always have a "religious" meaning and signify an infirmity of the spiritual order, namely, "carnal infirmity," "the limitation of man who needs the help of the Spirit."[8] Presupposing

7. Such is also the conclusion of J. Héring, *La seconde épître de saint Paul aux Corinthiens* (Commentary on the New Testament), Neuchatel-Paris, 1958, 96: "What seems certain is that the 'slaps of the angel' were a serious handicap for the Apostle's missionary efforts. That is the main reason why Paul asked the Lord three times to free him from them." Likewise, Allo, 312: "Paul saw [in this persecution of the angel of Satan, which for Allo is a chronic illness] such an obstacle to his ministry that he immediately asked the Lord three times . . . to send his persecutor away."

8. See in particular J. Cambier, *Biblica*, 1962, 489-490. The following table speaks for itself; the first number indicates the number of examples outside of Paul; the second, the number in the Pauline letters and the epistle to the Hebrews:

Physical infirmity:
   astheneia 8 and 2 (I Tim 5, 23; Gal 4, 13a)
   asthenein 16b and 3 (II Tim 4, 20; Phil 2, 26f.)
   asthenēs 5 and 1 (I Cor 11, 30)

Spiritual weakness:
   astheneia 0 and 15c
   asthenein 0 and 14
   asthenēs 2 and 14d

that Paul is thinking of an illness, it is in virtue of the state of the infirmity or lack of strength it causes him that he mentions it here and that it constitutes for him a "thorn for the flesh."

Paul says that he asked the Lord three times to free him from this obstacle (v. 8). The emphatic tone of the prayer, like that of Christ in the garden of Gethsemane, shows how strongly Paul felt about being set free. But the Lord responds with a refusal: "And he has said to me, 'My grace is sufficient for thee'" (v. 9), which is in line with what Paul had said in I Cor 15, 10: "But by the grace of God I am what I am, and his grace in me has not been fruitless—in fact I have labored more than any of them, yet not I, but the grace of God with me."

Although his aid is invoked, the Lord seems to reject his Apostle's prayer. In reality, he could not answer it more completely. Paul asked him to take away that "thorn for the flesh," because he thought it was an obstacle that limited the scope of his mission; the Lord, on the contrary, will point out to him that it was a condition that would enable him to fulfill it completely: "For strength it made perfect in weakness" (v. 9b). God's power, which acts in and through his Apostle, attains its "fulfillment," its "consummation," according to the meaning of the Greek verb used, *teleitai,* in the weakness of the apostolic instrument; it seems, as it were, to need such weakness to exercise all its potentialities, to demonstrate all its power, in a word, "to go to the very end."[9]

a) In Gal 4, 13, the meaning of "illness" is generally granted by modern commentators; but the ancient Greek and Latin commentators are of another opinion, likewise modern commentators like Schlatter, Häuser; see H. Schlier, *Der Brief an die Galater,* 1951, 148, n. 3.

b) Including Acts 20, 35, where the term seems to designate the "sick" or the "infirm," those whom their physical condition prevented from earning their living by manual work and who are thus poor. See above, p. 203, n. 7.

c) With the sole example of *asthenēma* in Rom 15, 1.

d) Including I Thess 5, 14, as is shown in the context where "weak" is juxtaposed with "fearful"; likewise, the sole use of this vocabulary in I Pet (3,7).

9. In the sense in which St. John, at the beginning of his account of the passion (Jn 13, 1) says that Christ "loved his own to the end" and

Thus, what used to be a reason for doubting becomes a basis for confidence. We understand, therefore, why Paul should continue: "Gladly therefore I will glory in my infirmities, that the strength of Christ may dwell in me" (v. 9c).

"I will glory in . . ." is indeed the meaning of the Greek verb *kauchasthai,* so dear to St. Paul, which does not connote braggadocio or boasting as much as satisfaction. If, for example, the "Jew" sought his justification in the fulfillment of a law, the Pauline notion of justification by faith excludes such boasting (Rom 3, 27).[10] In order to be saved, man must rely only "on the Lord" (I Cor 1, 30) or, to put it another way, on what constitutes his own weakness.[11]

"That the strength of Christ may dwell in me": the verb chosen by Paul is the very one which expressed in the Old Testament the presence of Yahweh's glory over the Ark of the Covenant, called for that reason the "Dwelling-place" par excellence; then over the Temple of Jerusalem, the only place where God lived on earth;[12] finally, in the New Testament, the incarnate presence of God's word, as is expressed in the prologue of St. John (1, 14): "The Word was made flesh and dwelt among us" [*eskēnōsen en hēmin*]. To the extent that the Apostle becomes conscious of his weakness, he becomes, as it were, an incarnation of the very power of Christ.

The conclusion follows naturally, as Paul expresses it in v. 10:

"went to the ends of his love" (C. Spicq, *Agapè,* III, 148). See above, p. 207, n. 16.

10. In the act of faith, man attests explicitly, more than in any other act, his fundamental inadequacy; he sees the truth of his statement in a light that seems to his conscience to come from Another; he does not affirm in virtue of evidence, but "on the authority of God who reveals"; see above, p. 210f. J. Cambier notes that the doctrine concerning *astheneia* "goes back to the Pauline idea of faith, according to which God's strength works in the man who recognizes his nothingness before God" (*Biblica,* 1962, 490).

11. Thus "the cross of Christ" (Gal 6, 14), expression of defeat, supreme absurdity for pagans and scandal for Jews (I Cor 1, 18ff.), or the "tribulations" (Rom 5, 3). On the concept of "gloriatio," the reader may consult: *Quaestiones in epistulam ad Romanos,* I, 2d ed., 104-106.

12. See Ex 40, 34-35; Num 9, 18 and 22; II Chron 5, 7 - 6, 2.

"Wherefore [*dio*] I am satisfied, for Christ's sake, with infirmities, with insults, with hardships, with persecutions, with distresses. For when I am weak, then I am strong."

Such is the general meaning of the passage. But to penetrate its full meaning, it will be helpful to place it in the context of St. Paul's life. This, as we shall see, will clarify the passage even more.

II

If Paul expressed this law of the apostolate in such a forceful way, perhaps it is because it was revealed to him through his own apostolic experience. Before learning it from the lips of the Lord, he himself had lived it. And if he makes it known in a letter addressed to the Corinthians, perhaps it is because he had lived it out in a special way when he had founded their Church.

To understand Paul's state of soul at that time, it is necessary to recall what he was doing and, in particular, the series of failures that preceded the founding of the Corinthian Church.

The latter took place in the course of the second "missionary journey," around the year 50. Coming from Asia Minor to respond to the invitation of the mysterious Macedonian seen in a dream at Troas, Paul sets foot for the first time on European soil. He preaches at Philippi, where he cures a slave "possessed by a divining spirit" and who "brought her masters much profit by soothsaying" (Ac 16, 16). The latter, "seeing that their hope of profit was gone, seized Paul and Silas and dragged them into the market place to the rulers." Miraculously freed from prison, they had to flee from the city (16, 40). Having reached Thessalonica, "where there was a synagogue of the Jews" (17, 1), they at first met with some success, notably with some proselytes, pagans who had not accepted Jewish beliefs, and a few "women of rank" (17, 4). "But the Jews, moved with jealousy, took certain base loafers, and forming a mob, set the city in an uproar"; unable to lay a hand on Paul and Silas, the mob took hold of their host Jason and certain brethren, whom they dragged before the magistrates of the city" (17, 7).

Anxious not to create any new disturbances among the Christians of Thessalonica, Paul and Silas took advantage of the night to steal away, and arrived at the nearby city of Beroea, where "the Jews were of a nobler character than those of Thessalonica" (17, II). The Jews of Beroea "received the word with great eagerness" and "many of them became believers, and so did no small number of prominent Gentiles, women and men" (17, 12). But learning of Paul's success, the Jews of Thessalonica came to Beroea "to stir up and excite the multitude" (v. 13). From Corinth, writing to the community at Thessalonica, Paul will speak of those people "who both killed the Lord Jesus and the prophets, and have persecuted us. They are displeasing to God, and are hostile to all men, because they hinder us from speaking to the Gentiles, that they may be saved" (I Thess 2, 15-16). Nonetheless, out of respect for the brethren, Paul considers it best not to press his point: again he sets off, this time for Athens.

To win the intellectual capital of the ancient world to the message of Christ was too important an undertaking for Paul not to make use of all the resources of his genius. The discourse at the Areopagus is, in fact, a model of adaptation: never does Paul seem to have taken such great pains to elicit the goodwill of a most difficult audience. Everything is seen in a most favorable way: the Athenians, who erected so many votive steles in honor of numerous gods, are "in every respect extremely religious" (17, 22). In constructing an altar "to the Unknown God," they were already, without knowing so, paying adoration to the one Paul has come to talk about (v. 23). For once, the Apostle puts aside his favorite authors, those of the Bible, and calls upon a Greek poet, Epaminondas of Cnossus, reinforced by a citation from Aratos (vv. 28-29). The citation of Tit 1, 12, from the same Epaminondas, is unique in Paul's writing. But all of these efforts are practically in vain. Proof of Paul's complete lack of success is the fact that in spite of the few conversions mentioned in the Acts—"Dionysius the Areopagite and a women named Damaris, and others with them" (v. 34)—St. Paul decides to leave the city, without feeling in the least way constrained to do so. No doubt, he feels there is nothing more to do. For an apostle, open resistance is less demoralizing than indifference.

With pleasure, therefore, "he departs from Athens" (18, 1). He follows the "sacred road" that goes by Eleusis, where he naturally does not stop, and soon reaches Corinth. The reputation of that cosmopolitan city, enriched by commerce, is well known in the ancient world: "to live like a Corinthian" (*korinthiazein*) had become a proverb to signify a dissolute life, and the picture of pagan customs sketched in the Epistle to the Romans, which Paul wrote from Corinth, must have corresponded rather closely to what he observed with his own eyes. The few allusions he makes here and there in I Cor to the past life of the faithful are no less flattering.[13] The Apostle takes up quarters in the Jewish community, which had jealously avoided corrupting contacts. He has the good fortune of coming upon a Christian household,[14] that of Aquila and Priscilla, who had been ordered out of Rome by an edict of the emperor Claudius, about 49 or 50 (18, 2). "As he was of the same trade, he stayed with them and he set to work," using the Sabbath days to preach in the synagogue to the Jews and the proselytes who came there (vv. 2-3). The arrival of Silas and Timothy, returning from Macedonia with many alms, allowed him to "occupy himself wholly with the word, emphatically assuring the Jews that Jesus is the Christ" (v. 5).

But a stronger opposition than elsewhere develops. The repeated lack of success is strongly felt. The text of the Acts is explicit: "But as they contradicted him and blasphemed, he shook his garments in protest and said to them, 'Your blood be upon your own heads; I am innocent of it. Henceforth I will go to the Gentiles'" (v. 6). No doubt, Paul had done likewise in a similar situation at Antioch (Ac 13, 5); he will do the same at Ephesus (Ac 20, 26). But in no other place does St. Luke put on Paul's lips the imprecation then used. When we think of what the incredulity of Israel was for him, of "the great sadness and continuous sorrow in my heart. For I could wish to be anathema myself from Christ for the sake of my brethren who are my kinsmen according to the flesh" (Rom 9, 2-3), we can imagine what such a statement means and what intense pain it presupposes in the Apostle's soul. If the

---

13. See I Cor 5, 9-11, and especially 6, 9-11.
14. That it is a question of Jews already converted to Christianity can be deduced rather certainly from the fact that Paul does not mention them among those whom he himself converted (I Cor 1, 14-16) and from the fact that the title of "first-fruits of Achaia" is bestowed on "the house of Stephan" (I Cor 16, 15).

Jews refused to believe in Christ, what reasonable hope was there
that a pagan population, so little prepared to receive the evangelical
message, would prove to be more docile? Paul seems determined
to give up the struggle. The Acts speak here of a "vision of the
Lord," clearly intended to restore his courage, at that very moment:[15] "And one night the Lord said to Paul in a vision, 'Do not
fear, but speak and do not keep silence; because I am with thee,
and no one shall attack thee or injure thee, for I have many people
in this city'" (vv. 9-10).

Then Paul, bereft of all human hope, fully conscious of his weakness and placing his trust in God alone, pays heed to the Lord's
voice. And Corinth became probably one of the most flourishing
communities founded by St. Paul. The Lord had not deceived him:
"I have many people in this city" (v. 10).

The state of the Apostle's soul when he confronted the pagan
environment of Corinth, the one which in fact provided the young
Church with the majority of its members, is revealed in a remark
Paul makes to these same Corinthians. In the first letter he wrote
to them, he describes, in effect, the feelings that moved him at that
very moment:

> And I, brethren, when I came to you, did not come with
> pretentious speech or wisdom,[16] announcing unto you the
> witness to Christ. For I determined not to know anything
> among you, except Jesus Christ and him crucified.[17] And

15. Previously Luke affirms that "many of the Corinthians who heard Paul
    embraced the faith and were baptized" (v 8). But this is one of the
    "summaries" dear to Luke; here he intends to indicate in a general way
    the conversions that took place in the course of Paul's residence in Corinth.
16. We think automatically of the speech at the Areopagus in Athens, which
    seems to indicate an effort of this kind and ends in the failure we have
    noted. Likewise, the expressions of v. 4.
17. See I Cor 1, 18-25. The "scandal of the Jews" is due especially to the
    fact that the crucified one passed before their eyes, in the name of
    Scripture, as an "accursed man of God," according to Dt 21, 23, defiling
    by his presence alone on the cross the sacred land of Israel. That "scandal-
    ous" aspect is underscored by Paul (Gal 3, 13) and John (19, 31) and
    stated by the early catechism (Acts 5, 30; 10, 39; 13, 29; see I Pet 2,
    24). That is the essential objection against which the Jew Tryphon

I was with you in weakness and in fear and in much trembling.[18] And my speech and my preaching were not in the persuasive words of wisdom, but in the demonstration of the Spirit and of power, that your faith might rest, not on the wisdom of men, but on the power of God (I Cor 2, 1-5).

Here, St. Paul seems to be commenting upon the affirmations of II Cor 12, 9: "... Strength is made perfect in weakness. Gladly therefore I will glory in my infirmities, that the strength of Christ may dwell in me."

III

But this general law of the apostolate is verified not only in a single episode from St. Paul's life. It has affected the whole "history of salvation" and all of the great servants of God have experienced it, all those whom God has wished "to use" to accomplish his salvific plan.

The story of Gideon in the book of "Judges," those "liberators" raised up by God to save his people, offers a very instructive example. The Bible is not satisfied with recounting the episode; it draws from it a theological teaching.

The people of God have finally reached the Promised Land. But they find it occupied by other people. They must seize it in a fierce battle. But the first victories won seem to have them more

argued, even after having admitted that the Scriptures speak of a suffering Messiah: "We know that he must suffer and that *he will be led like a lamb to the slaughter*" (Is 53, 7); but that he must be crucified, that he must die in that degree of shame and dishonor of a man accursed under the law, prove this to us for we cannot even conceive of it" (St. Justin, *Dialogue with Tryphon*, c. 90, 1).

18. Literally: "in weakness" (*en astheneiāi*) and in "much fear and trembling" (*en phobōi kai tromōi pollōi*). If the formula "with fear and trembling" is a "stereotyped biblical expression" (*Jerusalem Bible*), here it is preceded by "in weakness" and specified by "much" (*pollōi*), which is not the case with the other examples cited (II Cor 7, 15; Eph 6, 5; Phil 2, 12).

surely at the mercy of their enemies. Actually, in punishment for their sins, "the Lord delivered them into the power of Midian for seven years," so that to avoid Midian, they had to hide in "the mountains and the caves" (Jg 6, 1-2). The situation seems desperate and, "reduced to misery, the Israelites cried out to the Lord" (v. 6). At first, the latter sent a prophet who reminded the people of the marvelous works once performed by God in their favor and exhorted them to belief (vv. 7-10). Then the angel of Yahweh appeared to Gideon, while he was in the process of "beating out wheat in the winepress to save it from the Midianites" (v. 11).

The conversation begins:

> "The Lord is with you, O Champion!" "My lord," Gideon said to him, "if the Lord is with us, why has all this happened to us? Where are his wonderous deeds of which our fathers told us when they said, 'Did not the Lord bring us up from Egypt?' For now the Lord has abandoned us and has delivered us into the power of Midian." The Lord turned to him and said, "Go with the strength you have and save Israel from the power of Midian. It is I who send you." But he answered him, "Please, my lord, how can I save Israel? My family is the meanest in Manasse, and I am the most insignificant in my father's house." "I shall be with you," the Lord said to him, "and you will cut down Midian to the last man" (Jg 6, 12-16).

Strengthened by Yahweh's promise, which is comfirmed by a sign asked for and given, Gideon goes about collecting as many men as he can, in order to meet the enemy head on. A great number answer his call: thirty-two thousand men! Truly God is with him. Is not so great an army already a guarantee of victory? "Early the next morning Gideon encamped by En-Harad, with all his soldiers. The camp of Midian was in the valley north of Gabaath-Hammore" (7, 1). Then Yahweh intervenes once again: "You have too many soldiers with you for me to deliver Midian into their power" (v. 2a). The very power of the army, which Gideon thought was his greatest asset, was, in fact, for God an irremediable obstacle. And Yahweh gives the reason: "Israel might vaunt itself against me and say, 'My own power brought me the victory!'" (v. 2b).

To achieve his salvific plan, God wants "to have need of men," but such men are only instruments in God's hand, and all—themselves and everyone else—must realize it. As St. Paul will explain, the apostolate is a completely divine work: therefore, "we carry this treasure in vessels of clay, to show that the abundance of the power is God's and not ours" (II Cor 4, 7).

Gideon uses various means to reduce the number of the combatants, but to little avail: "Now proclaim to all the soldiers, 'If anyone is afraid or fearful, let him leave!'... Twenty-two thousand of the soldiers left, but ten thousand remained." The Lord said to Gideon, "There are still too many soldiers..." (vv. 3-4). And then, down to the ridiculous figure of three hundred. Then the Lord said to Gideon, "By means of the three hundred I will save you and will deliver Midian into your power" (v. 7). The power of the instrument was an obstacle for God; its weakness enables him to deploy all his strength.

Gideon's case is typical, but in no way rare; it comes up on almost every page of the Bible and especially at critical moments. Without mentioning Abraham who set out for a distant country without a family and without any hope of having any, relying solely on God's word, then obeying that same God who orders him to immolate the sole depositary of divine promises, such is, no doubt, the lesson of the whole episode of David and Goliath. David, moreover, expresses it in very explicit terms:

> Thou comest to me with a sword, and with a spear, and with a shield; but I come to thee in the name of the Lord of hosts, the God of the armies of Israel, which thou hast defied this day; and the Lord will deliver thee into my hand.... All the earth will know that there is a God in Israel. And all this assembly shall know that the Lord saveth not with sword and spear, for it is his battle, and he will deliver you into our hands (I Sam 17, 45-47).

This same law presides over the birth of Moses and, thus, at the event that dominates the whole history of Israel. The "liberator" is a child condemned to death even before his birth (Ex 1, 22), abandoned in a papyrus basket along the waters of the Nile: "Noticing the basket among the reeds, Pharaoh's daughter sent her handmaid to fetch it. On opening it, she looked, and lo, there was a baby boy crying!" (Ex 2, 5-6). Why be surprised that this same law presides over the birth of the second "liberator," of whom the first one is only a type, and that the sign given to the shepherds by the angels is on the same order: "You will find an infant wrapped in swaddling clothes and lying in a manger" (Lk 2, 12)? And then, later on, there is Calvary, where supreme weakness will take hold over supreme power (see I Cor 1, 18-25).

Thus it was natural for Christ to recall that same law when he made the fishermen of Galilee "fishers of men." He wanted a night of complete failure to precede the "miraculous catch." This invaluable experience will enable the apostles to become in God's hands instruments capable of working miracles, without being in the least tempted to believe themselves the authors: "'Master, the whole night through we have toiled and have taken nothing; but at thy word I will lower the net.' And when they had done so, they enclosed a great number of fishes, but their net was breaking. . . . —'Depart from me, for I am a sinful man, O Lord!'—'Do not be afraid; henceforth thou shalt catch men.' And when they had brought their boats to land, they left all and followed him" (Lk 5, 5-11).

IV

If today we try to discover how this fundamental law of the apostolate (according to which, "the power of God is deployed in weakness") may be applied practically in our own daily life, we will realize that St. Paul sees a first application of it in the choice Christ makes of his apostles, namely, in the Christian vocation itself. To the community at Corinth, dazzled by the abundance of the spiritual gifts with which they had been blessed,[19] Paul recalls that "the doctrine of the cross is foolishness"—absurd, meaningless—"to those who perish, but to those who are saved, to us, it is the power of God" (I Cor 1, 18). And to convince them of this, he invites them to look at themselves:

19. See I Cor 1, 5; 4, 8; 12-14.

For consider your own call, brethren; that there were not
many wise according to the flesh, not many mighty, not many
noble. But the foolish things of the world has God chosen
to put to shame the "wise," and the weak things of the world
has God chosen to put to shame the strong, and the base
things of the world and the despised has God chosen, and
the things that are not, to bring to naught the things that
are; lest any flesh should pride itself before him (I Cor
1, 26-29).

This was the case with Gideon, "of the meanest family in
Manasseh," and who was "the most insignificant in my father's
house" (Jg 6, 15); or with David, the youngest of the sons of
Jesse, whom no one had thought of, neither Jesse nor Samuel
(I Sam 16, 6-12). This was also the case with the Twelve Apostles, as
the Fathers of the Church love to point out in commenting upon
these Pauline verses. Let us imagine the state of soul of those un-
educated, Galilean fishermen, when they heard themselves called
to evangelize the pagan world: "Go therefore, and make disciples
of all nations..." (Mt 28, 19). For such a mission, they were
in no way prepared—added to which was the fact that they belonged to the Jewish race, which was scorned by pagans! Thus
they did not immediately understand things, and so it took several
successive visions to persuade St. Peter to enter into the house of
a pagan, the centurion Cornelius, and catechize his family (Ac
10, 28). The latter, however, "was devout and God-fearing, giving
much alms to the people and praying to God continually" (Ac 10,
2), "to whom the whole nation of the Jews bears witness" (v. 22).
And only the visible descent of the Holy Spirit on those "uncircumcised" compelled Peter to give them baptism (vv. 44-48).

But it may be objected that this was certainly not the case with
St. Paul, Apostle par excellence! For it seems difficult to find an
instrument better prepared, on the human level, for the task that
was entrusted to him: to unusual natural gifts was added a culture,
both Jewish and Greek, thanks to the education received in Tarsus
and Jerusalem.[20]

---

20. See Gal 1, 13-14; Acts 26, 4-5.

Many human qualities did indeed make of St. Paul a "born apostle" to the pagan world. However, we will recall that personally he did not feel prepared to convert pagans, but rather the Jews, his compatriots. He tells us this himself. No doubt, he was aware that his conversion was at the same time a call to the apostolate and to the apostolate of the pagans;[21] but he did not become conscious of God's special plan for him until later on, after an attempt at preaching to the Jews of Jerusalem: "And it came to pass that, when I had returned to Jerusalem and was praying in the temple, I was in an ecstasy and saw him as he said to me, 'Make haste and go quickly out of Jerusaelm, for they will not receive thy testimony concerning me'" (Ac 22, 17-18). To Paul, it seemed, on the contrary, that his reputation as a persecutor of Christians should give that testimony a unique value:

> "'Lord, they themselves know that I used to imprison and beat in one synagogue after another those who believed in thee; and when the blood of Stephen, thy witness, was shed, I was standing by and approved it and took charge of the garments of those who killed him.' And he said to me, 'Go, for to the Gentiles far away I will send thee'" (Ac 22, 19-21).

And so, St. Paul was not the apostle of those for whose conversion he seemed in every way prepared.

But by a clear, divine disposition, the human qualities of Paul were constantly, as it were, thwarted by that thorn buried in his flesh, those "distresses, persecutions, anguish," about which he spoke to the Corinthians. In large part, it is through them that he experienced his fundamental "weakness" and thus his "strength," that "poverty" of the instrument, so rich in other ways, which God needs in order to get "a full return" from it. The chapter immediately preceding touches on those "tribulations" inherent to the apostolic life: physical tests, no doubt: "labors, prisons, lashes, shipwreck, labor and hardships, many sleepless nights, hunger and thirst, fastings often, cold and nakedness." But even more so, moral

---

21. See Gal 1, 16; Rom 1, 5.

tests, among which he points out expressly hostility "on the part of the Jews, his compatriots," who frustrate his preaching to the pagans, who[22] plot many times against his life,[23] and succeed in having him arrested in Jerusalem (Ac 21, 33); hostility "on the part of pagans," such as the procurator Felix, who keeps him a prisoner for two years in Caesarea, in the hope that "money would be given him by Paul, and for this reason he would send for him often and talk with him" (Ac 24, 26); hostility also and above all —because that was, of course, the most painful test—on the part of those whom he calls "false brethren," "friends," who normally should have helped him since they were all working toward the same goal: "Jewish-oriented" Christians, who fail to renounce Moses and accuse Paul of infidelity to Scripture.

Indeed, during Paul's life, from the beginning of his ministry to the second Roman captivity inclusively, God permitted St. Paul to encounter such adversaries on his way. At Antioch, in Syria, they forced him to go up to Jerusalem with Barnabus to defend himself before the apostles (Ac 15, 1-4; Gal 2, 1-2). Paul is successful, although not without great difficulty, and the principle of Christian freedom is won, at least for the converts from paganism;[24] but the adversaries are not put off. They appear again in the communities of Galatia, where they almost succeed in separating the converts from their Apostle (Gal 1, 6; 4, 16-20; 5, 4). To this end, they did not hesitate to denigrate his person, to present him as an apostle of second rank, who did not know Christ and thus is ignorant of his true teaching, who "seeks the favor of men," and who, in order to be seen in a good light, multiplies conversions at the expense of the Gospel truth (Gal 1, 10; 2, 6; etc.).

At Corinth, about the same time, they accused him of fickleness and compromise (II Cor 1, 17), of pride and arrogance (II Cor 1, 24; 3, 1), and so successful are their efforts—at least Paul thinks so —that he does not dare return to the Church he had established, out

---

22. See above, p. 251f.
23. See Acts 9, 23; 20, 3; 21, 31; 23, 12-31.
24. See Acts 15, 5-30. The long sentence, filled with parentheses, repetitions, anacoluthons, which recounts the event in Gal 2, 3-10, expresses in its own way the complexity of a situation which will work out — but with great difficulty — to Paul's advantage.

of fear of not being received there, and at first sends Titus to get
an idea of the situation (II Cor 7, 5-7). At Philippi, the existence
of many undoubtedly influential Judaizers is attested to by the incisive allusions in the letter addressed to that community (Phil
3, 2 and very probably vv. 18-19). At Jerusalem, in the mother
Church, where they are at home, their presence intimidates Paul
to such an extent that he wonders if the alms he brings will be
refused: those gifts of the Churches gathered with all the more
care since they were for him the symbol of the Church's unity and
since a rejection would signify a rupture that could reduce his
entire apostolate[25] to nothing. Thus he implores the community of
Rome to "help me by your prayers to God for me, that I may be
delivered from the unbelievers in Judea, and that the offering of my
service may be acceptable to the saints in Jerusalem" (Rom 15, 31).
The accounts of the Acts show that Paul's fears were not without
foundation: having just arrived, he hears his attitude toward the
Law criticized and must give assurances of his devotion to Moses.[26]

25. Paul is conscious of the fact that, without such unity, he runs the risk
    "of running or having run in vain" (Gal 2, 2). Thus the importance he
    attaches to this collection for the poor of Jerusalem and the considerable
    place it has in his efforts: Gal 2, 10; I Cor 16, 1-4; II Cor 8-9; Rom 15,
    25-31.
26. See Acts 21, 20: "Thou seest, brother, how many thousands of be-
    lievers there are among the Jews, all of them zealous upholders of the
    Law. Now, they have heard about thee that thou dost teach the Jews
    who live among the Gentiles to depart from Moses, telling them they
    should not circumcise their children nor observe the customs." In fact,
    Paul did not teach the Christians of Jewish origin not to circumcise their
    children, but only those who came from paganism; he even had cir-
    cumcised Timothy, whose mother was a Jew (Acts 16, 1), and to the
    Corinthians he gave as a rule of conduct: "Let every man remain in the
    calling in which he was called to Christianity" (I Cor 7, 18). However,
    one must admit that if Paul acted thus, it was because he considered
    circumcision to be without value, a matter of indifference: "Circumcision
    does not matter, and uncircumcision does not matter" (I Cor 7, 19).
    Such was not the thought of the Judaeo-Christians of Jerusalem! The
    Council of Jerusalem had decreed only for the Christians of pagan origin;
    as to the others, "One feels that James still held them as obliged to the
    Mosaic law." See Fr. Renié in *La Sainte Bible*, ed. First--Clamer, XI,
    291).
    It is true that from Paul's teaching one could deduce that rightfully, if

Finally, at Rome, where he is a prisoner for the first time—
if the Epistle to the Philippians is written from that city, as is generally believed[27]—we learn that "the greater number of the brethren
in the Lord, gaining courage from my chains, have dared to speak
the word of God more freely and without fear" (Phil 1, 14). But he
adds this surprising bit of information: "Some indeed preach Christ
even out of envy and contentiousness. . . . Some proclaim Christ . . .
out of contentiousness, not sincerely, thinking to stir up affliction
for me in my chains" (vv. 15 and 17). And what we know of Paul's
second captivity in that same city seems to show rather clearly that
there too his adversaries had not labored in vain.[28] It is enough for
us to read the moving letter which he dictated from his prison, a
short time before his martyrdom, for Timothy, his "beloved son,"
and which has justly been called his "spiritual testament." If he
thanks Onesiphorus explicitly for having "often comforted me," not
having "been ashamed of my chains"; if he congratulates him for
the "active efforts" he had made, as soon as he had arrived in Rome,
to "find out" the place where Paul was imprisoned (II Tim 1, 16-
17), is it illogical to conclude that the Christian community of
Rome had not been concerned about the one it will later venerate
as its "founder"?[29]

---

not in fact, the law no longer held for Judaeo-Christians, provided, however, that one showed that the Christian in fact accomplished — superabundantly, "in its fullness" — the Mosaic law itself just as St. Paul tries
to do, for example, in Rom 13, 8-10 (and already in Rom 3, 31; 8, 4).
See *Quaestiones in epistulam ad Romanos*, I, 2d ed., 48-50.

27. Ancient commentators always placed the composition of Phil. in Rome,
during the first captivity of the Apostle, with Col, Eph, and Phm. But
many modern-day commentators tend to place it at Ephesus, even though
the Acts do not mention any imprisonment of Paul in the latter city. See
L. Cerfaux, in A. Robert and A. Feuillet, *Introduction à la Bible*, II, 485-
486, which remains "faithful to the Roman captivity." Besides, if Phil
is written from Ephesus, the information retains all its value: it holds
true only for Ephesus and no longer for Rome.

28. This is what A. Penna points out in "Le due prigione romane di S.
Paolo," in *Rivista biblica*, 9 (1961), 193-208, especially 204. See also
O. Cullmann, *Saint Pierre*, 93-96. St. Clement of Rome, the first suc-
cessor of St. Peter, attributes the martyrdom of the two apostles to
"jealousy" and "envy" (*ad Cor* 5, 2).

Moreover, Paul does not only deplore the defection of his own disciples: "This thou knowest that all in the province of Asia have turned away from me, among them, Phigelus and Hermogenes" (1, 15). ". . . Demas has deserted me, loving this world. . . . Alexander, the coppersmith, has done me much harm. . . . Do thou also avoid him for he has vehemently opposed our words" (4, 14-15).[30] The complaint that follows concerns an event that has just taken place in Rome itself: "At my first defense no one came to my support, but all forsook me, may it not be laid to their charge!" (v. 16). Indeed, a strange example of desertion, and one for which the Apostle feels the need to implore the Lord's pardon.[31]

Never had he felt so alone, so powerless. But at the very moment when all abandoned him, the Lord gives him the unhoped-for occasion—at that pagan tribunal where, when a trial of a Roman citizen took place, the highest ranked people, including sometimes the emperor himself, were frequently spectators[32]—of offering to

29. Fr. Spicq notes: "The relations between Paul and the Christian community seem to have been impossible; perhaps they even did not know where he was imprisoned; and yet, Onesiphor managed to *find* him and reach him. This might have been due to the complicity of the guards . . . . What a contrast between that long and clever search of Onesiphor and the abandonment by everyone else!" (*Les epîtres pastorales*, 338).

30. Perhaps this is the same person mentioned in I Tim 1, 20, whom Paul "delivered up to Satan" with Hymeneus, "that they may learn not to blaspheme." At any rate, according to Fr. Spicq, that Alexander "must have played a role in the arrest of Paul in Troas or in Ephesus," and "he may have followed him to Rome as an accuser" (*ibid.*, 394).

31. Presumably it is a question of the *actio prima* of the last trial of St. Paul. Fr. Spicq notes: "Even those who were there and on whom he could count, lacked courage and abandoned him, just like the disciples of the Lord a long time ago (see Jn 16, 32), and in that moment of solitude the Apostle completed his identification with Christ" (*ibid.*, 394).

32. See C. Spicq, *ibid.*, 395: "If Paul appeared before the criminal jurisdiction of the imperial court, he took his place in the vast enclosure, shaped like a basilica, in the midst of a huge crowd . . . . In the trial of Isidore and Lampon, two Greek instigators of the pogroms of Alexandria, Claudius sits in the presence of 25 senators, 16 consuls, the empress and her ladies in waiting (see Juster, *Les Juifs dans l'empire romain*, I, 125)." See also the discourse XVIII, 398-402: "Paul probably appeared before the personal tribunal of Nero . . . . His defense lasted several hours."

Christ a more solemn example of witness than ever. He hastens to add: "But the Lord stood by me and strengthened me, that through me the preaching of the Gospel might be completed, and that all the Gentiles might hear . . ." (v. 17).

One last time, at the end of his life, Paul was to experience how far "God's power is deployed in weakness." Or rather, the next to last time. For the last will take place a few weeks or months later, when the executioner's sword, which he had evoked in his letter to the Romans as one of the signs of Christ's love for us (Rom 8, 35),[33] will reunite him forever with his Master and will, by his martyrdom, make of him along with Peter, "founder" of the Church of Rome.[34]

---

33. The "tribulations," of whatever kind they are, far from causing us to doubt Christ's love for us, are irrefutable proofs of it, by reason of the strength that is communicated to us "by him who loved us" and who leads us to victory (*hupernikōmen*, Rom 8, 37). In this sense, "the trials are not occasions of victory but, as it were, sacraments of conquest," and "the faithful are not only victorious *in* the trials, but *triumphant* by them" (C. Spicq, *Agapè*, I, 255).

34. Peter and Paul, generally mentioned together, are the "founders of the Church of Rome" in virtue of their martyrdom more than by their preaching: thus St. Irenaeus around the year 180, or the inscription of the priest Caius around the year 200. See *Quaestiones in epistulam ad Romanos*, I, 2 ed., 28-29.

Appendix:
The Origin and Basic Meaning of the Word "Lay" *

For several years there has been a very strong movement to give back to the lay state of life its complete significance in the Church. One talks of "the age of the layman," and theologians try to work out a "theology of the laity." One of the essential points of such a theology should be to define, at the start, the exact meaning of the word "lay." Several authors have made such attempts.[1] Nevertheless, it is surprising that no study has yet appeared which thoroughly examines the derivation of the word and its original meaning. *An amusement for specialists!* one will perhaps say. Not at all. For the doctrine on the laity which is emerging in several places is related by several authors to the basic meaning of the

---

* The text of this article first appeared in *Nouv. Rev. Théol.*, 80 (1958), 840-853. We have revised it in certain places.

1. The following are studies which we have used: F. X. Arnold, "Bleibt der Laie eine Stiefkind der Kirche?" in *Hochland*, 46 (1954), 401-412, 524-533; *Idem.*, "Kirche und Laientum," in *Theol. Quartlschr.*, 134 (1954), 263-289; S. H. Box, *The Principles of the Canon Law*, Oxford, 1949; Y. Congar, O.P., "Qu'est-ce qu'un laic?" in *Suppl. Vie spir.*, 15 (November, 1950), 363-392; *Idem.*, *Jalons pour une théologie du laïcat* ("Unam Sanctam," 23), Paris, 1953; E. Magnin, *L'Eglise enseignée. La discipline du clergé et des fidèles* ("Bibl. cath. des sc. rel."), Paris, 1928; K. McNamara, "Aspects of the Layman's Role in the Mystical Body," in *Ir. Theol. Quart.*, 25 (1958), 124-143; G. Philips, *Le rôle du laïcat dans l'Eglise* ("Cah. de l'act. relig."), Casterman, 1954; *Idem.*, "La vocation apostolique du laïc," in *Rev. eccl. de Liège*, November 1957, 321-340; R. P. Spiazzi, O.P., *La missione dei laici*, Ediz. di Presenza, 1952; A. Sustar, "Ded Laie in der Kirche," in *Fragen der Theologie Heute* (ed. J. Feiner, etc), Einsiedeln, 1957, 519-548; S. Tromp, S.J., *De laicorum apostolatus fundamento, indole, formis*, Rome, 1956 (pro manuscr.); G. W. William, "The Role of the Layman in the Ancient Church," in *The Ecumenical Review*, 10 (1958), 225-248.

word "lay." However, a brief survey reveals that on the fundamental meaning of the term and, therefore, on its theological import, there are many gratuitous statements or at least statements which rest on a certain equivocation.

Some seem to think that the term *laikos,* at the beginning of the Christian era, was not in use in the pagan world; some point out in passing that it is found in Greek translations of the Bible done by Jews in the second century (Aquila, Symmachus, and Theodotion), but they do not give to this fact the importance it deserves. The first text usually concentrated on is that of Clement of Rome, and the statement is made that "lay" is an ecclesiastical term. Most of the time, since one must state that the word *laikos* is not biblical, commentators try to compensate for this lacuna by saying that "lay" is derived from the substantive *laos,* people, which occurs frequently in Scripture where it usually indicates the people of God in contrast to the pagan nations; and automatically one gives to the adjective *laikos* all the theological meaning of the noun *laos* understood in this sense: etymologically, a "lay person" would thus be a member of the *laos,* the people consecrated to God. In such a case, the word originally would have been a synonym of "sacred," and it would be necessary to conclude that "the lay state, if only by its name, is the bearer of a vocation." If, later on, "lay" has become almost synonymous with "secular," this would be by deformation and a complete reversal of the original meaning.

Unfortunately, such an interpretation rests on a confusion of two things. First, it is supposed that the adjective was formed in the early Christian communities or in contemporary Judaism, whereas it is noted as early as the third century B.C. in the Greek papyri. Second, one always refers *laikos* to the noun *laos* taken in its general meaning, which for Christians is that of "people of God" (con-

The reader may find a good bibliography on the subject in R. Tucci, S.J., "Recenti pubblicazioni sui 'laici' nella Chiesa," in *Civ. Catt.,* 109 (1958/II), 178-190.

Let us add here: J. B. Bauer, "Die Wortgeschichte von 'Laicus,'" in *Zeistschr. für kath. Theol.,* 81 (1959), 224-228; and two issues of *Lumière et Vie,* devoted to the theme *Laïcs et mission dans l'Eglise,* n. 63 (May-July 1963) and n. 65 (November-December 1963); see in particular the study of M. Jourjon, "Les premiers emplois du mot laïc dans la littérature patristique," n. 65, 37-42.

sidered as a whole). But this noun, in the Bible as well as in secular works, has another, special meaning: the inferior "people," as distinguished from their leaders. It is from this restricted usage that the adjective *laïkos* was formed, before the Christian era. The sole purpose of the following pages is to prove this by a number of passages, in order to help clarify an idea which is of great importance in present-day ecclesiology.

FORMATION OF THE WORD LAIKOS

The suffix -*ikos* makes its appearance at the end of the fifth century B.C. P. Chantraine, who has studied this question in depth,[2] describes its function: "The adjectives ending in -*ikos* expressed the idea of belonging to a group" (105); further on, he states: "belonging to a category, in a specific way" (121). Such adjectives, therefore, express clearly "a categorizing value" (*ibid.*); "expressing a belongingness, the suffix lent itself to classifying things" (116). Let us restrict ourselves to but one example: *asteios*, derived from *astu* (city), means: cultivated, elegant, clever, which can be said of city people as well as of country people; *astikos*, on the contrary, has a specialized meaning: urban, city, in contrast to rural.

The importance of all this for our present study is clear: it leads us to think that *laïkos* will refer to someone who belongs to the *laos;* but if this noun has a specific meaning—and we shall see that this is so—the suffix -*ikos* will probably give the adjective this specialized meaning, and indicate, within a people, one category as opposed to another. This is what we shall learn in various texts.

PAPYRI AND INSCRIPTIONS

In classical literature, the noun *laos* designates not only the people in general, but also and above all the *mass* of the population (especially the mass of soldiers) in contrast to their leaders.[3] In the

---

2. P. Chantraine, *Etudes sur le vocabulaire grec*, Paris, 1956, part 3: "Le suffixe grec-*ikos*" (97-171).
3. See the article *laos* in Kittel, *Theol. Wört, zum N.T.*, IV, 29-39. For

Egyptian papyri, it occurs regularly to indicate the inhabitants of
the glebe, the mass of peasants, called today "fellahs,"[4] for example,
in this papyrus of the third century B.C.: "The peasant population
(*ho laos*) comes to the city to have their gourds cooked."[5] In the
religious context of the service of temples or mysteries, the word
laos sometimes designates the "lay people," the people who come
to attend the ceremonies of the cult.[6]
As for the adjective *laïkos*, it is nowhere seen in the literary
texts. We find it only in the papyri, to indicate what concerns the
laos, in the specialized sense we just spoke about.[7] The oldest text
in which the word is found seems to be a papyrus of Lille (third
century B.C.), which unfortunately at this point is fragmentary; in
a kind of enumeration, we read the words *laika tethrammena, which*
the editor himself admits not understanding.[8] But we can grasp the

Homer, this restricted meaning is described as follows: "die *untergegebene*
Bevölkerung gegenüber dem Herrscher" (30); see 31, lines 29-35. The
use of *laos* to designate the *whole* of the people is seen for the first time
in Pindar; see *ibid.*, 31, line 10.

4. This is the definition given by F. Preisigke, in his dictionaries of papyri,
   to the word *laos*: "die eingeborenen Agypter (heute Fellahs) .... Sie
   bilden die breite Masse des kleinen Landvolkes," *Fachwörter des offent-*
   lichen Verwaltungsdienstes Agyptens in den griechischen Papyrusurkunden,
   Gottingen, 1915, 116; "der eingeborene, den tieferen Volksschichten
   angehörige Ägypter (im Gegensatz zu den herrschenden und höherste-
   henden Kreisen)," *Wört. der griech. Papyrusurkunden*, II, col. 6.
5. *Papiri Greic e Latini* (Pubbl. della Società Italiana), 280, 5 (cited in
   Preisigke, *Wört.*, II, 6): *ho laos* (Bauernvolk) *en tēi polei tas kolukun-*
   thas optōsin. Let us also cite a very illuminating text from the inscription
   of Rosetta, of Ptolemy V (beginning of the 2nd century B.C.): *ho te*
   laos kai hoi alloi pantes (line 12); see C. and T. Müller, *Fragm. hist.*
   graec., Paris, Didot, 1853, (1)-(42). This expression was thus commented
   upon by Letronne, (16)-(17): "... remarkable contrast. I believe that
   ho laos designated *the people*, the *working* and *artisan* classes, and *hoi*
   alloi pantes everything that was not the people, such as the *military*,
   civil servants and *priests.*"
6. See the examples in Kittel, *Th. Wört.*, IV, 31, 1; 33-37 and n. 7.
7. F. Preisigke, *Wört.*, II, col. 2, defines *laïkos* in the papyrus as follows:
   "den ägyptischen Zivilisten betreffend (in Gegensatz zum königlichen
   Beamten, Lehensträger, Staatspächter, usw.)"
8. P. Jouguet, *Papyrus grecs de Lille*, Paris, 1928, I, 10, 1, 4 and 7.

meaning of this expression, thanks to a papyrus of Strasbourg (120 B.C.) where the same expression reoccurs.[9] An official of the state writes to a subordinate about speeding up the delivery of wheat to the loading docks of the Nile; to this end he gives the following order: "Henceforth put at the disposition of the foragers all the beasts of burden of the *people* of your district: *panta ta en tois kata se topois laika (tethrammena).*" Here "lay" means: what belongs to the *people of the countryside,* as distinguished from the official administration. A much more important text (262-260 B.C.) is found in a royal edict of the Rainer collection (Inv. 24552),[10] which describes the collection of taxes to be paid on the purchase of slaves in Syria and Phoenicia; the word *laïkos* occurs twice here in the expression *soma laikon eleutheron,* which the editor translates: "a free *native*"; similarly, *gunaixi laïkais* would signify "*native* women"; the adjective *laïkos* would seem then to apply to those who belong to the *laos,* the *local population;* but the context suggests rather clearly that this "lay" (= native) population must be understood as being in contrast to the garrison soldiers or all those who are part of the civil administration.[11] The same meaning appears also in the expression *laïkē boēheia*:[12] a debtor is obliged by contract not to have recourse to "the aid of *the people*" to protect himself against the legitimate demands of his creditor. Finally, let us point out a formula which assumed a technical character in Roman times: *laïkē suntaxis,* and which signifies the "capitation," the per capita tax, which had to be paid by each member of the population to the civil administration.[13]

9. F. Preisigke, *Griech. Papyrus zu Strassburg,* 93, 4.
10. Published in Preisigke-Bilabel-Kiessling, *Sammelbuch griechischer Urkunden aus Ägypten,* V (Wiesbaden, 1955), 8008, 11, 33, 52, 54; see especially the first edition and the commentary on this papyrus by H. Liebesny, in *Aegyptus,* 16 (1936), 257-291, and the report of Cl. Préaux, in *Chronique d'Egypte,* 24 (1937), 275-278.
11. See J. B. Bauer, *art. cit.,* 226.
12. For this expression, we modify the interpretation we had given in *N. R. Th.,* 1958, 843, n. 11, and support the one proposed by J. B. Bauer (*art. cit.,* 226), following F. von Woess and H. Lewald.
13. This expression is found several times in the papyri of Tebtunis in the collection of the *Michigan Papyri*: II (= *P. Tebt.,* I), 121, recto, II, 8, 2 and III, 3, 2; V (= *P. Tebt.,* II), 241, 31 and 35; 355, 6. It is synony-

These different texts indicate that, in the papyri, *laos* has a specific and limited meaning: to repeat the expression of P. Chantraine, the word has a classifying value, a categorizing sense. Thus, it is not used to designate the people considered as a whole, as one ethnic group distinguished from another, but rather, within this group, *the mass of inhabitants,* the populace, inasmuch as it is distinguished from those who govern it.

GREEK TRANSLATIONS OF THE BIBLE

Of more interest to us are the texts of the Greek Bible, for very probably they constitute the immediate preparation for Christian usage, since *laïkos* is always employed here in a religious context. In the Septuagint, if *laos* most often indicates the people of Israel considered as a whole, in contrast to the pagan nations (*ethnē*), it is also applied to the mass of the people, in contrast to their leaders, especially the priests or all those who exercise a religious function (prophets, Levites). On Sinai, Yahweh gives this order to Moses: "But the priests and the people (*hoi hiereis kai ho laos*) must not break through to come up to the Lord" (Ex 19, 24). After the speech of Jeremiah against the Temple, it is said: "Now the priests, the prophets, and all the people [*hoi hiereis kai hoi pseudoprophētai kai pas ho laos*] heard Jeremiah speak these words in the house of the Lord" (Jer 26, 7).[14]

It is from this special usage of *laos* in the context of worship that the use of *laïkos* in the Jewish and Christian tradition is derived. But the word is not found in the Septuagint. It is all the more significant that the Jewish translators of the second century, Aquila, Symmachus, and Theodotion, unsatisfied with what they found in

mous with the much more frequent term *laographia*, which designates the tax to be paid for inscribing the population in the records of the civil state. See J. A. S. Evans, "The Poll-Tax in Egypt," in *Aegyptus,* 37 (1957), 259-265.

14. Other examples: Neh 7, 73; Is 24, 2; Jer 23, 34; 26, 11, 29, 1; 36, 9; Os 4, 9.

this regard in the Greek Bible, felt the need to introduce the Hellenistic term *laïkos* into their translations and even developed an entirely new term, *laïkoō* as we will show later on.

In the rest of these late Greek translations,[15] the adjective *laïkos* is found in only three places: in I Sam 21, 5 (and 6) among the three translators, Aquila (vs. 120-140), Symmachus and Theodotion (at the end of the second century); in Ezek 48, 15, among the second and third; lastly, in Ezek 22, 26, in Symmachus only.

Let us begin with the text of I Sam 21, 5-6. This concerns the well-known incident in which David arrives in the sanctuary of Nobe and asks for five loaves of bread from Achimelech the priest. The latter says to the fleeing man: "I have no common bread at hand, but only *holy* bread." The Hebrew word translated here as "common" is *hol*, profane; the translation of the Septuagint was correct: *artoi bebēloi*, profane bread, that is, bread that can be used for everyday usage. Later translators, however, substituted *laïkos* (lay); but the idea remains the same: it is a question of bread that is not reserved for religious purposes, and which therefore anyone can use. In the following verse, the word appears again in the text of Symmachus. We are still in the context of religious worship: the priest is willing to give David and his men consecrated bread, provided they are clean according to rite (literally, "holy"), that is, that they have had no relationship with women. David reassures him: they are in a state of cleanness, even though the journey they are making at that moment is only a "profane journey" (LXX: *hodos bebēlos*). The translation of Symmachus says here: *hodos laikē*, likewise the *Questiones in I Reg.* of the Pseudo-Jerome: "*Via haec laica est*" (*P. L.*, 23, 1342 C). This "lay journey" is therefore an expedition in which the law of sanctity, the ritual law of continency, was not in force. Throughout this passage the contrast is always the same: "holy" or "consecrated" (*hagios*, in the ritual sense) is in opposition to "profane" or "lay."

The two other texts occur in the book of Ezekiel (22, 26; 48, 15). One should recall that this prophet was a priest, that his

---

15. The fragments that remain have been published by F. Field, *Origenis Hexaplorum quae supersunt . . .* , 2 vol., Oxford, 1875.

theology was especially focused on the law of sanctity, the worship
of the Temple and the liturgy. In the holy city of the future, the
priests will fulfill their duties faithfully in the Temple (44, 15-31);
in particular, says Yahweh to the prophet, "they shall teach my people to distinguish between the sacred and the profane (LXX: *ana
meson hagiou kai bebēlou*) and make known to them the difference
between the clean and the unclean" (44, 23). The same expressions
were already present in 22, 26, but as an indictment against the
priesthood, whose members had until then neglected their duties.
Here the opposition between "sacred" and "profane" of the Septuagint has become in Symmachus the opposition between "sacred"
and "lay"; but the meaning remains the same.

In the description of the city of the future at the end of the
book, this distinction between sacred and profane is strongly emphasized. Our passage (48, 15) belongs to that series of symbolic
visions which show the future restoration of Palestine, the division
of the country into tribes, and the new Temple. In the center of
the country, between the territories of Judah and Benjamin, will be
found the square tract of land reserved for Yahweh; it will consist
of three parallel tracts running from east to west: in the center, the
section for the priests with the Temple; in the north, the section for
the Levites; in the south, that of the whole house of Israel (45, 1-6;
48, 9-22). The inner area of the Temple will serve "to separate the
sacred from the profane" (42, 20). We must recall this typically
sacerdotal doctrine in order to understand our verse. It describes
the role, within the reserved area, that is set out for the city; it is
clearly distinct from that reserved for the priests and the Levites:
"The remaining five thousand cubits along the twenty-five-thousand-
cubit line are profane (*hol*) land, assigned to the City for dwellings
and pasture" (Ezek 48, 15). Here as in 42, 20 (cited above), the
Septuagint translated *hol* by *proteichisma*, the territory which extends "before the wall"; they very likely read *hel* or *heil* (rampart,
embankment) instead of *hol*. For this word Aquila gave the exact
translation: *bebēlos*, profane; but Symmachus and Theodotion replaced this with the term *laïkos*: "a *lay* territory." We see then the
significance the word had for these two translators: it indicates
that part of the tract of land that is outside the section intended

for the priests and Levites, and to which *everyone* (*laos*, "the people," in the restricted sense) had access.[16]
We see, therefore, that in I Sam 21, 5-6 as well as in Ezek 22, 26, and 48, 15, *laïkos* is always used in a religious sense: "lay" is in opposition to "sacred" (*qodes, hagios*) and characterizes what can be employed by everybody for profane usage;[17] we note also that in these biblical texts the term is not yet used for persons, as an later

16. It is interesting to note that these different terms, in their etymological and fundamental meaning, express practically the same thing: the Hebrew *hol* (it is related to the Arab *halla*) means that which each one can use, there where everybody can come, in short, what is not reserved for one thing or another; the Greek *bebēlos* of the LXX (root *ba-*, see *baino*) = where one can *walk*, where *access* is not forbidden, thence, profane; the Latin "profanus" (= quod "pro fano") is that which is outside the sacred sanctuary; finally, the new work *laïkos* = that which concerns the people, in certain circumstances, the mass of the population that is not affected by the worship of the religion. All these terms express the same idea; they designate something which does not belong to the area reserved for the sacred.
One may wonder what led later translators to introduce the Hellenistic word *laïkos* into the sections we have examined. In Ezek 48, 15, they probably thought that the word *proteichisma* of the LXX was a faulty translation. Aquila reintroduced the ordinary term *bebēlos*, to render the Hebrew *hol*. Symmachus and Theodotion substituted *laïkos*. If the word *bebēlos* seems to have been avoided by the last two translators (in as much as one can judge from literature that is left us), we think it is because the term had taken on a new connotation in Hellenistic Judaism. In the LXX, this word, the normal translation of *hol*, simply designated profane, non-consecrated things, within the Jewish people (see Lev 10, 10; I Sam 21, 4-5; Ezek 22, 26; 44, 23); but in the second and third book of Maccabees it has a clearly pejorative meaning and is used to describe the *impious*, especially pagans who desecrate sacred objects (II Mac 5, 16; III Mac 2, 2, 14; 4, 16; 7, 15; see Ezek 21, 25, 30). To say that a thing was not profane, soiled, but simply "secular," i.e., non-sacred, another word was desirable. Let us note that in Philon and in the New Testament also *bebēlos* is always used in the pejorative sense. The word *laïkos* was, therefore, a good substitute for it.

17. Thus we understand the meaning that must be given to the very rarely used verb *laïkoō*, which, to our knowledge, is found nowhere else at any time except in the translators of the second century, in three places, Dt 20, 6; 28, 30, Ezek 7, 22 (and in some manuscripts of the LXX for

Christian usage, but only for inanimate *things* (loaves of bread, a trip, a territory). One must grant to current opinion that the word could not have been chosen to characterize pagans, non ˙˙ws: it always designates realities which are part of the people of G d; but what the word "lay" designates formally was not belongingness itself, but within the people, things that were not consecrated to God.

EARLIEST CHRISTIAN TEXTS

Let us begin by emphasizing this rather surprising fact: *laïkos* is a very rare word in the early Church before the third century. For the Greek texts, the tabulation is quickly made: a single passage from Clement of Rome, three from Clement of Alexandria, and a single one from Origen.[18] We will not find the term elsewhere in

Ruth 1, 12). The two passages from Deuteronomy refer to a religious prescription of Leviticus (19, 23-25): whoever planted a vineyard should for three years consider its fruit as impure, the fourth year should dedicate it to Yahweh, and only in the fifth year could begin to gather fruit for himself. The first of the two texts says: "Is there anyone who has planted a vineyard and never yet enjoyed its fruits?" The verb *halal,* which the last few words translate, signifies most often "to soil, desecrate," but here and in Dt 28, 30 its meaning is less strong: "to begin to treat as common (or profane)" something which was previously reserved for God. The LXX (*kai ouk euphranthē ex autou*) did not give this meaning. But the three other translators (and Aquila alone for Dt 28, 30) expressed it perfectly by a new verb: (*kai ouk*) *elaïkōsen* (*auton*). Likewise, St. Jerome in the Vulgate: "Quis est homo qui plantavit vineam et *necdum fecit eam esse communem* et de qua vesci omnibus liceat?" This translation — or rather this paraphrase — expresses very well the subtle meaning of the verb *laïkoō* (which was probably invented by Aquila): not "to profane" but "to introduce into common use what was previously dedicated to God." (One would be tempted to say "to reduce to the lay state," except that this expression is reserved for a very special situation in canon law). In Ezek 7, 22, on the contrary, there is hardly any difference between *laïkōsousin* of Aquila and *bebēlōsousin* of the LXX; perhaps Aquila chose this translation for the simple literary reason of avoiding the repetition of the same word, since *bebēlōsousin* was already used at the end of the preceding verse.

18. Let us add the text of the epistle of Clement to James (5, 5), in *Pseudo-Clementine.*

the Apostolic Fathers, nor in the Apologists nor in Irenaeus. This means that by itself it ought not to express a particularly important theological idea.

Many indications lead us to believe that this word was borrowed directly from Hellenistic Judaism: the first author who uses it, Clement of Rome, was probably of Jewish descent; we find the expression in Pseudo-Clementines, a leading work of heterodox Judaic-Christianity; and the context in which Clement of Rome uses it, in his Epistle to the Corinthians, is related to the worship of the old Temple, exactly as in the Jewish translators of the second century.

The text of Clement is as follows. The "lay people" are opposed to the high priest, the priests, and the Levites: "To the high priest, priests, and Levites, special functions have been given; to the priests have been given particular places; to the Levites are assigned certain duties; the lay people [*ho laïkos anthrōpos*] are bound by precepts familiar to lay people" (40, 6). What strikes us here at once is the clear distinction between priests, Levites, and lay people. This is what we had already observed for Ezek 48, 15, in the translations of Symmachus and Theodotion; the description of the territory reserved for Yahweh in the ideal Palestine distinguished three sections: that of the priests, with the Temple in the middle; in the north, that of the Levites; in the south, the "lay" area, intended for the city and its inhabitants. The difference from the text of Clement is that in this description of Ezekiel, as in most of the non-Christian texts cited up to now, *laïkos* was used for things; Clement now applies it to persons (*ho laïkos anthrōpos*), and this usage will become predominant in the Church.

With Clement of Alexandria, the transposition from the Jewish context to the properly Christian one is completed, but the same triple division is maintained: the series "priests, Levites, lay people," which we have seen so far, is now followed by this one: "priests, deacons, lay people," which will occur constantly later on. Clement writes: "He [St. Paul] admits of marriage between a man and only one woman, whether for priest, deacon, lay person."[19] Another passage from the *Stromata* shows once more that the term

19. *Strom.*, III, 12, 90, 1 (*G.C.S.*, *Klemens*, II, 237, 21; *P.G.*, 8, 1189 C).

"lay" came from Jewish terminology; it recalls the text of Ezekiel commented on earlier. In the description it gives of the Temple of Jerusalem in order to bring out the allegorical significance, it distinguishes the place where only the high priest may enter (the Holy of Holies), the one that is reserved for the priests (the Holy), and the square open to all the Jews; the Holy was separated from the square by a curtain (*kalumma,* see Ezek 27, 16). Playing on words, Clement points out the use of this curtain in worship: *to men oun kalumma kōluma laïkēs apistias;*[20] the words are to be taken metonymically in the sense of *laos apistos:* "The curtain kept at a distance the unfaithful people" (literally: lay infidelity). This example shows very clearly how "lay" is used to designate the people as distinct from the priests in charge of the worship, and even separate from them; here, the context gives the term a frankly pejorative connotation.[21]

In the only passage of Origen in which *laïkos*[22] is found, this word is used in contrast to *cleric, priest,* and *deacon.* The word *klēros* is new in this context; but apart from that, we continue in the line of interpretation begun by Clement of Rome, and found again in Clement of Alexandria. It may be said that this terminology will become indeed traditional.[23]

Let us now examine the earliest Latin texts. Were men in the Western Church going to adopt the word "lay" directly from the Greek, or would they try to translate it by an authentically Latin

20. *Strom.,* V, 6, 33, 3 (*G.C.S., ibid.,* 347, 33; *P.G.,* 9, 57 A).
21. A nuance which is even stronger in *Paedag.,* III, 10, 83, 2 (*G.C.S.,* 1, 213, 16): *lagneia keklētai to laïkon kai dēmōdes kai (to) anagnon* (the text of Migne, *P.G.,* 8, 508 B, instead of *laïkon* contains *lagnikon*); here "lay" signifies "what is characteristic of the people, vulgar, gross," and serves to explain *lagneia,* libertinage. It is difficult not to see in this esoteric and aristocratic concept of opposition to *laos* (the "people," in the pejorative sense) the influence of Clement's Greek education.
22. *In Jerem,* hom. XI, 3 (*G.C.S., Orig.,* III, 80, 19 and 81, 6; *P.G.,* 13, 369 C-D).
23. See, for example, Eusebius, *Hist. Eccl.,* V, 28, 21; VI, 19, 17; 43, 6, 10, 13; *Pseudo-Clementine, Hom., Ep Clem.* 5, 5: here, the lay are referred to as *discentes* or as those who are involved in the affairs of everyday life (*en tais biotikais rehiais*), while the bishop, on the other hand, concentrates his efforts on the Church and on the preaching of the word of truth.

word? One of the most interesting texts in this regard is the very
old Latin version of the Epistle of Clement of Rome: we observe
here, so to speak, an attempt at transposition of our word from the
Greek to the Latin context. Discovered by Dom G.

Morin at the
major seminary of Namur and published by him in 1894,[24] this version is probably the oldest Christian text in Latin that we possessed
at that time: it dates from the second century, perhaps even from
the first half of the century.[25] Our passage (*ho laïkos anthrōpos tois
laïkois prostagmasin dedetai*, 40, 6) is given an important translation: "*Plebeius homo laicis praeceptis datus est.*"[26] We have here
the first evidence of the word *laicus* in Christian Latin. But, as one
may observe, of the two examples of *laïkos* in the Greek, only the
second is rendered by *laicus:laicis praeceptis* for *tois laïkois prostagmasin*, but *plebeius homo* for *ho laïkos anthrōpos;* the borrowed
word, "laicus," is thus used only for the inanimate *thing* (*praeceptis*), not for "homo." However, we have just seen above that
this was the usage in the Jewish texts and in most of the pagan
texts; the difference in translation in the two cases is therefore a
sign of archaism.[27]

What meaning did the translator give to *plebeius homo?* At first

24. *Anecdota Maredsolana,* II, Maredsolii, 1894.
25. Chr. Mohrmann, "Les origines de la latinité chrétienne à Rome," in
Vig. christ., 3 (1949), 67-106, 163-183 (see 86-92); see also R. Braun,
"Deus christianorum" *Recherches sur le vocabulaire doctrinal de Tertullien,*
Paris, 1962, 17, n. 3.
26. The manuscript contained "plebs eius" which does not make any sense;
Dom Morin corrects it to *plebeius.* As to the words *datus est,* they presuppose the incorrect reading of *dedotai* attested to by certain manuscripts (instead of *dedetai*).
27. Chr. Mohrmann (*art. cit.,* 102) sees here a purism: choice of the
authentically Latin word (*plebeius*) alongside the borrowed word *laicus.*
But why was *laicus* retained after two more words? The translator saw
a difference between the two uses of *laïkos* in the Greek. According to
Mohrmann he was very sensitive to the different nuances of his text.
It seems more probable to us that this translator, still used to seeing
laïkos used only for things, must have found Clement's formula *ho
laïkos anthrōpos* very strange; he preferred to translate it by a Latin
word. Thus it seems that the word "lay," to designate a group of *men*
within the Church — clearly attested to,. starting with Tertullian — was
not yet customary in the early Christian Latin.

sight one would be tempted to understand: that which is of the "plebs," that is, the Christian community. For, as Father Congar writes: "*Plebs* has this meaning constantly in Tertullian and in St. Cyprian, and long after."[28] However, this term is used much more often in the restricted sense; it then designates "the faithful, the people (in contrast to the clergy), the lay."[29] One must therefore avoid, for the Latin, the same confusion as the one we observed earlier for the Greek. As for the adjective *plebeius* itself which is used here, it is never found in a general sense to designate a member of the Christian community. Among the Romans, it was used to indicate those who did not belong to the patrician class. In Christian terminology, we find it only in the sense of "layman" as opposed to "priest," for example, in the *Vita Cypriani*, where the martyrdom of the catechumens and the simple faithful (*"plebeiis* et *catecumenis* martyrium consecutis"*) is contrasted to that of the bishop Cyprian ("Cypriani tanti *sacerdotis* et tanti martyris passio," n. 1); or again, when it is said of Cyprian: "Presbyterium vel sacerdotium statim accepit . . . multa sunt quae jam *plebeius,* multa quae jam *presbyter* fecerit" (n. 3).[30] Rather soon, in addition to *plebeius,* which continued, however, to designate lay people up to the Middle Ages,[31] the borrowed word *laicus,* which would become the ordinary term, was introduced. It would be used henceforth almost exclusively to designate persons, and for that reason, would be considered above all as a substantive. The old translation of *laïkos anthrōpos* by *plebeius homo* is therefore very interesting since it shows us how "lay" was understood in our first Latin texts, in the second century.

Starting with Tertullian, the meaning of the word *laicus* seems to be established. Among the *Montanists,* he says, "alius hodie episcopus, cras alius; hodie diaconus, qui cras lector; nam et laicis sacerdotalia munera injungunt" (*De Praescr.,* 41, 8; *Corp. chr.,* I,

---

28. *Jalons pour une theologie du laïcat,* 20, n. 4.
29. See A. Blaise, *Dict. lat-fr. des auteurs chrétiens,* Strasbourg, 1954, 629, which gives many examples.
30. Ed. Hartel (*C.S.E.L.,* III, p. xc, 12-13; p. xciii, 12-20). See also Rufin, *Orig., hom. in Num.,* II, 1 (*P.G.,* 12, 590 D).
31. See Ducange, *Glossarium mediae et infirmae latinitatis,* VI, 363, which, for *plebeius* (and its synonym *plebeges*), cites as examples conciliar texts of 817 and 908. He defines: "laicus, nullum in clero ordinem adeptus."

222). After embracing *Montanism*, he will write: "Vani erimus, si putaverimus, quod sacerdotibus non liceat laicis licere. Nonne et laici sacerdotes sumus?" (*De exh. cast.*, 7, 2, 3; *ibid.*, II, 1024).[32] In St. Cyprian the same contrast appears again: "clero et plebi" (*Ep.* 45, 2; *C.S.E.L.*, II, 602, 1); he speaks thus of the apostasy of a bishop: "Evaristum de episcopo jam nec laicum remansisse, cathedrae et plebis extorrem et de ecclesia Christi exulem" (*Ep.*, 52, 1; *C.S.E.L.*, II, 616, 15).[33] As we can see, the same distinction is found everywhere: "lay" designates a Christian who is neither bishop nor priest nor deacon, in short, one who does not belong to the clergy.

We have reserved for the end a text of St. Jerome in the Vulgate (I Kings 21, 4), where the word *laicus* seems to have a special meaning; the dictionaries that point out this meaning mention only this one passage as an example.[34] One should not conclude that Jerome has a special vocabulary: elsewhere he uses the term exactly in the same sense as the authors of the third century whom we have examined.[35] But the Vulgate was from a Latin translation. There we read in the section indicated (it is the response of Achimelech to David in the sanctuary of Nobe, see above, p. 272): "Non habeo *laicos panes* ad manum, sed tantum panem sanctum." The expression of the Septuagint, *artoi bebēloi*, was rendered correctly in the old Latin by *panes profani*. Why then did Jerome change this expression to *laicos panes?* The answer is without doubt: he simply took over the word *laïkos* from the translation of Aquila.

Actually we know that in doing his Vulgate Jerome was greatly inspired by Jewish translators of the second century, and in a very special way by Aquila; however, in the fragments that remain, I Kings 21, 4 is precisely the only passage in which this translator

---

32. See also, for the first period, *De Bapt.*, 17, 2 (*Corp. chr.* I, 291 [bis]); for the Montanist period: *De Fuga*, 11, 1 (*ibid.*, II, 1148); *De Monog.*, 11, 4 (*bidi.*, II, 1244).

33. See also *Ep.*, 67, 6 (*C.S.E.L.*, II, 740, 17).

34. Forcellini, *Totius latinitatis lexicon*, III, 682: "ad populum pertinens, communis, vulgaris"; A. Blaise, *Dict. lat.-fr. des auteurs chrét.*, 484: "common, for the people, non-consecrated: *panis l* (*aicus*): 1 Kg 21, 4." Let us note that this text is the only passage in the whole Vulgate that contains the word *laicus*.

35. See St. Jerome, *Dial. contra Lucif.*, 4 (*P.L.*, 23, 157 D — 158 B).

used the adjective *laïkos*.[36] Jerome then borrowed it from him, thus giving to this word a nuance different from what was current in his time: in the Christian world, we recall, the term was applied most of the time to a class of *people* in the Church; in I Kings 21, 4 of the Vulgate, it again designates a *thing,* bread. It is an archaic expression. But it is from this usage of Hellenistic Judaism—of which Jerome's Latin translation has preserved for us this important vestige—that the properly Christian usage of the word "lay" draws its origin.

It is an opinion widely held that in the early Church "the lay people" indicated "the members of the laos, the people of God," as Dom Gregory Dix has remarked.[37] He adds that the word *laïkos* retained this meaning until the fourth century, but that around 450 it was used largely to mean *profane,* in contrast to *sacred.*[38]

The different texts, as we have observed, say nothing of the sort. Several authors state that in the early Church the meaning of the word "lay" was very different from what it is today in expressions like *lay laws, lay school,* etc., in which the term has become practically synonymous with "neutral" (from the religious viewpoint), or even "anti-Christian," "atheistic." It is clear that this meaning was as nonexistent in early Christian texts as it was in the non-Christian texts that introduced it. But it does not at all follow that "lay" at that time meant "sacred." That would be an extreme example of semantic evolution, since in the two terms of this evolution there would be an exactly contradictory meaning. On the contrary, the very fact that "lay" can now mean "atheistic" makes it more probable that its fundamental and primitive meaning did not include the idea of "sacred." This is precisely what we have observed. A parallel

36. At first sight, it may seem surprising, since the Hebrew word *ḥol* is elsewhere rendered several times in Jerome's translation by *profanus* (Lev 10, 10; Ezek 22, 26; 48, 15); elsewhere, he prefers *pollutus* (I Kg 21, 5; Ezek 44, 23).

37. G. Dix, *Le ministère dans l'Eglise ancienne* ("Bibl. Théol."), Neuchatel, 1955, 59. Likewise, E. H. Schillebeeckx, O.P., *De Christusontmoeting als sacrament van de Godsontmoeting,* Anvers, 1958, 146-148, and note 16.

38. *Op. cit.,* 134; see also his work *The Shape of the Liturgy,* Westminster, 1945, 480.

case that can shed much light here is that of *bebēlos* (profane): in the ancient biblical texts, this term meant simply: profane, non-sacred; later, in Judaism and early Christianity, the word was used most often in the pejorative sense of: impious, unclean. It is for this reason, we said, that later Jewish translators introduced the word *laïkos* to designate things which, without being defiled or unclean, were simply profane. But in our society, product of the French Revolution, the word *laïc* itself has undergone a similar evolution in a clearly pejorative sense.

At present, efforts are being made to reevaluate it. It is perfectly true that *laïkos* derives from *laos*. However, *none* of the Jewish or Christian texts that we have examined make this connection between the noun and the adjective, on which some people are insisting today so eagerly. The reason is that *laïkos* was not created in these contexts, but had had for a long time an autonomous existence. Moreover, the meaning of *laos* from which *laïkos* is derived is not its general meaning (*people*, in contrast to another people), but its restricted, "categorizing" meaning: "a certain part of the people." None of the texts examined considered the "lay people" as the community of the people of God, in contrast to secular people. The contrast we find in the texts is always the same: that of two categories, within the people of God.[39] In the Jewish context, "lay" was everything that was non-consecrated, non-reserved to the priests and Levites for religious worship; the word was synonymous with "profane." Similarly, in the Christian texts, "lay" was opposed to "priest," "deacon," or "cleric"; the word thus still meant a special consecration for the service of God. Undoubtedly, the duties and responsibilities of lay people may have been more important in the Church of yesterday than today. But from a semantic point of view, we may discern no trace of evolution in the meaning of the word "lay" itself.[40]

39. On the other hand, if the word "lay" signified the members of the people of God taken as a whole, it would be hard to understand why priests would not also be "lay," since they too are Christians. On the contrary, the texts always contrast the latter with the former. This is proof that "lay" is a specific term, one that clarifies a certain segment of the Christian people.

40. There is, however, this difference between Jewish and Christian usage: the former used the word for *things*, the latter almost exclusively

For it is important to distinguish carefully the study of terminology and of theology, however related they may be. Everything we have said so far may give the impression that the role of lay people was conceived in a very negative way: "laymen" are those who are not clerics. This is not so. The complete meaning of a function in the Church can not be drawn from an analysis of the term that designates it. The effort to give emphasis to the lay state should not include giving to the word "lay" a meaning it does not have; rather, one should point out the role of the function itself. Theologically speaking, it remains entirely true that lay people are members of the people of God.[41] We have simply wished to show that this teaching is not part of the formal meaning of the word "lay." Let us point out further, in conclusion, that if in current language the word has sometimes taken a new, frankly pejorative meaning (lay = atheistic), this is not so in the canonical terminology of the Church: there "lay" still designates what it meant in the third century. A similar stability in terminology is not so frequent a phenomenon that it does not deserve careful study.

for *people*; furthermore, the Jewish texts brought closer and closer together "lay" and "secular," which did not happen in the Christian texts. But the formal aspect remained the same in both milieus: the category of the "non-sacred," within the people of God.

41. The early Church was very conscious of that. The general use of *laos*, "the people of God," was more frequent than the more particular meaning, more frequent also than *laikos,* derived from that particular meaning. And to illustrate this conviction of the ancient Church that the lay people were truly members of the people of God, let us cite the magnificent text of the *Didascalia* (verse 225): "Audite ergo etiam vos, laici, electa Dei ecclesia. Nam et prior populus ecclesia vocabatur; vos autem catholica sacrosancta ecclesia, regale sacerdotium, multitudo sancta, plebs adoptata, ecclesia magna, sponsa exornata Domino Deo" (II, 26, 1; ed. Funk, 102). On the other hand, from one end to the other of the *Didascalia* we note the traditional opposition between lay people and bishops (or other members of the clergy).